THE PROSECUTOR

Books in this series:

Volume 11. Sage Criminal Justice System Annuals

THE PROSECUTOR

WILLIAM F. McDONALD, *Editor*

Foreword by **THOMAS F. EAGLETON**

 **SAGE Publications** *Beverly Hills* • *London*

WITHDRAWN

For information address:

SAGE PUBLICATIONS, INC.
275 South Beverly Drive
Beverly Hills, California 90212

SAGE PUBLICATIONS LTD
28 Banner Street
London ECIY 8QE

Printed in the United States of America

Library of Congress Cataloging in Publication Data

Main entry under title:

The prosecutor.

(Sage criminal justice system annuals; v. 11)
Includes bibliographical references.
1. Public prosecutors—United States—Addresses, essays, lectures.
I. McDonald, William F. 1943-   II. Series.
KF9640.A75P76   345'.73'01   79-14388
ISBN 0-8039-0815-6
ISBN 0-8039-0816-4 pbk.

FIRST PRINTING

CONTENTS

800504

For Lisa Latini and Irene Angela

FOREWORD

The administration of criminal justice is constantly before the American public. Our newspapers give it daily coverage, and our television features it in many of our most popular shows. Perry Mason is a household name in America. Because of this familiarity, we think we know how criminal justice is administered and we do not hesitate to offer our criticisms and suggestions for change. But, despite all the attention, there is good reason to believe that we do not really know our system of justice as well as we think.

The images of justice with which most Americans are familiar are ones which have been filtered through two powerful shapers of public opinion: the news media and the televised entertainment medium. Both media select those aspects of the administration of justice which meet their purposes and limitations.

Perry Mason is always at trial and almost always involved in a murder case. But, statistically speaking, both trials and murders are comparatively infrequent events in the administration of justice. For every murder case there are thousands of other cases; and for every trial there are thousands of cases dropped or plea bargained. For every sensational case that gets the maximum exposure in the press, there are thousands of cases that grind through the machinery of justice. These latter cases will be handled in a routine manner that is usually not possible under the bright lights of publicity.

The images of justice conveyed by the news and the entertainment media convey disjointed, partial, and frequently atypical glimpses of the workings of justice. It is noteworthy, for instance, that while there have been numerous television series based on police work and defense work, few have featured the prosecutor in the heroic role. Little wonder that a recent national survey found that a third of the American public was under the impression that the prosecutor is the attorney for the defendant.

It is not just the man on the street who is not sure what the office of the public prosecutor is all about. A half century ago the first systematic studies of the actual administration of justice showed (much to the surprise of criminal justice scholars) that the prosecutor is the central decision maker in the system. His office determines the disposition of more cases than any other component in the system. The implications of this finding have been clear ever since. If we are to understand and improve the administration of justice, we must understand the crucially important office of prosecutor.

Unfortunately, until recently only limited efforts have been made in this direction. The little body of scholarship that was produced came almost exclusively from lawyers—who quite understandably wrote from a legal perspective. Certainly this is a necessary perspective, but it is not the only one from which we should scrutinize this important topic.

This volume of original essays on the prosecutor is a long-needed and welcome addition to the literature. It addresses the kinds of questions that we need to answer. Who is the prosecutor? From what strata of society does he come? Whose values does he represent? How does the prosecutor do his job? What factors influence his decisions? What is the optimal way of organizing his office? What impact do his policies have on the administration of justice?

Those of us concerned with the administration of justice cannot afford to operate solely on the basis of Hollywood stereotypes. Neither can we allow ourselves to adopt the lawyer's view of legislation and standard setting as the solution to all problems. A volume such as this offers a broader and needed perspective; even those of us who have been or still are prosecutors can learn a great deal from such a book. As William Wessel says in his chapter, prosecutors' offices have gone from cracker barrel to supermarket operations. This book documents the change and lays the groundwork for a more thorough understanding of our system of justice.

—Thomas F. Eagleton
United States Senate

PREFACE

In introducing an earlier volume in this series (McDonald, 1976), I noted that the victim of crime was the most under-researched topic in the field of criminology and criminal justice. I might have added that second place honors go to the prosecutor. Although the role of the prosecutor has not been as thoroughly neglected as that of the victim, it has not received anywhere near the attention given other components of the criminal justice system. A brief sampling of some of the text books and readers in the field bear this out. Typically these works divide the criminal justice system into three parts: the police, the courts, and corrections. If there is any discussion of the prosecutor at all, it usually constitutes a small subdivision of the section of the courts (e.g., Sutherland and Cressey, 1978; Prassel, 1975; Duffee, et. al., 1978; Cohn, 1976; Pursley, 1977). A few books devote an entire chapter to the prosecutor (e.g., Chambliss and Seidman, 1971; Felkenes, 1973; Kalamanoff, 1976; Cole, 1975). Some are organized so that there is no separate discussion of the prosecutor *per se*; rather, certain processes in which the prosecutor may or may not play a role such as charging or plea bargaining are described (e.g., Kratcoski and Walker, 1978; Johnston and Savitz, 1978; Newman, 1975).

Despite these organizational differences, almost all the published works have one thing in common: the prosecutor and his functions get far less attention than other components of the justice system. For instance, in their classic textbook, Sutherland and Cressey (1978) give the police, pretrial release, the criminal courts, and the juvenile courts each one full chapter or more; and sentencing, corrections, and penal philosophy an additional ten chapters. The prosecutor receives three and a half pages of the thirty-one-page chapter on the criminal court. Johnston and Savitz (1978) include twelve articles on police, two on bail, one on defense attorneys, three on juries, one on plea bargaining and forty-five on corrections, deterrence, and penal philosophy. The second half of Reid's (1976) introductory criminology text is devoted to the administration of justice. An entire chapter is on the police. A chapter entitled "The Role of Lawyers and Judges" consists of fifty-six pages, of which three are devoted to the prosecutor. Chambliss and Seidman (1971) devote four long chapters to the police and one to the prosecutor. Some texts whose titles suggest they are introducing the reader to the criminal justice system manage to make no mention at all of the prosecutor or his key functions (see, e.g., Blanchard, 1975; Galliher and McCartney, 1977; and Reckless, 1973).

This ratio, 4 to 40, of space devoted to the prosecutor and to the police and corrections is as good an approximation as any of the differences in the amount of research and scholarly attention paid to the prosecutor and that paid to other aspects of the administration of criminal justice. There is an irony in such disproportions. The fact is that there is general agreement in the field that the prosecutor is an extremely important actor in the system if not the key actor. The American Bar Association Project on Standards for Criminal Justice (1970:76) refers to the prosecutor as "the chief law enforcement official of this jurisdiction." The textbook writers usually describe the prosecutor either as the most important official in the criminal justice system or as an official of equal importance to any other official. Sutherland and Cressey (1966:432) describe him as "the most important person in the judicial system under present conditions;" notwithstanding this opinion, however, they devote only three and a half of thirty-one pages of one chapter on the courts to a discussion of his role. Prassel (1975:124) states that "the prosecutor occupies a position of significance fully comparable to those of the police and judges." However, Prassel devotes four chapters to the police, three to the courts and only a half of one to the prosecutor. Wright and Lewis (1978:134) declare that "the prosecutor, as chief law enforcement officer in any jurisdiction, is the most important person in our system of criminal justice." They devote two pages of a twenty-two page chapter entitled "The Administration of Justice" to the prosecutor. In contrast they devote an entire chapter to the police, one to the bail system, and even one to the grand jury.

Another indicator of the lack of interest in the prosecutor comes from the field of survey research. In 1972 the Bureau of Social Science Research (Biderman et al., 1972) compiled an inventory of all major public opinion surveys taken in the preceding five years which dealt with crime justice and related topics. Numerous surveys had been conducted, but they focused on the usual three parts of the system: the police, the courts, and corrections. Nowhere in BSSR's system of classification and subclassification of the surveys is there a category devoted to the prosecutor. More recently there has been a national survey (Auerback and Kiernan, 1978:A2) which while devoted primarily to the public opinion of the courts did include one question on the prosecutor. It found that one-third of the public thought that the job of the district attorney was to defend people who are accused of crime but cannot afford their own lawyer.

This litany of neglect is not meant to suggest that no scholarship or research has been done on the office of the prosecutor. We are only suggesting that the relative proportions are unaccountably and grossly out of whack. A decade of massive federal funding of criminal justice research, evaluation, and scholarship has just ended. Criminal justice grantees and grantors have been trying to keep from replowing old furrows. Yet, for all that, the prosecutor is a relative unknown. For instance, the history of the American police, American corrections, and American juvenile courts has been documented in great detail many times over (see, e.g., Richardson, 1970; Lane, 1971; Platt, 1969); but the history of the American public prosecutor remains a sketchy mixture of a few facts and some conflicting speculations (Kress, 1976).

There has long since been textbooks and collections of readings devoted exclusivily to the management of and activities of police, corrections, probation and parole, and the courts. There has yet to be one on the office of the prosecutor. This volume of essays on the prosecutor is the first of its kind. It is intended to help offset the tradition of scholarly neglect of this important actor in the criminal justice process. We agree with the frequent refrain of the scholars that in today's criminal justice system the prosecutor is the most important component in the process. But rather than simply mouthing that claim like church dogma, our purpose is to contribute to the much needed work of documenting that statement and demonstrating its many ramifications. The essays assembled here examine the prosecutor from several angles. What are the functions of the public prosecutor? How did the office evolve? How have those functions been performed in other times and in other places? How different from our own is the German system with its requirement of compulsory prosecution. What differences are there in the ways prosecutors perform their functions? What accounts for these differences, and what are their consequences? Who are the prosecutors? From what strata of society are they recruited, and what implications does this have? To what extent can prosecutorial discretion be controlled, and what differences would it make?

The scholarly and research community's long inattention to the office of the public prosecutor cannot be remedied by one volume of essays. But with this work we hope to provide a stimulus and groundwork for the additional work that is so clearly needed.

The production of this volume received several kinds of support from different sources for which I would like to express my thanks. The book springs from my participation in the research program of the Institute of Criminal Law and Procedure of Georgetown University. I am grateful to the Institute's Director, Sam Dash, for his encouragement for this type of work; to the Ford Foundation and Georgetown University for their financial support; and to Mary Ann DeRosa for her superior and tireless typing effort on this work. In addition, special thanks go to the Law Enforcement Assistance Administration, which supported the research upon which several chapters—including the ones I wrote—are based. I would also like to thank the many prosecutors and other criminal justice officials who have given me the benefit of their experiences and insights into the function of the public prosecutor. Of course, the views and opinions expressed in this volume are those of their respective authors and are not necessarily endorsed by any of the people or organizations mentioned above.

—W.F.M.

Washington, D.C.

REFERENCES

American Bar Association (1970). Standards Relating to the Prosecution Function and the Defense Function. Chicago: ABA.

AUERBACK, S. and L. A. KIERNAN (1978). "Public wants court reform: Poll says." Washington Post (March 19):A2.

BIDERMAN, A., S. S. OLDHAM, S. K. WARD, and M. A. EBY (1972). An Inventory of surveys of the Public on Crime, Justice and Related Topics. Washington, D.C.: U.S. Government Printing Office.

BLANCHARD, R. E. (1975). Introduction to the Administration of Justice. New York: John Wiley.

CHAMBLISS, W. J. and R. D. SEIDMAN (1971). Law, Order, and Power. Reading, Mass.: Addison-Wesley.

COHN, A. W. (1976). Crime and Justice Administration. Philadelphia: J. B. Lippincott.

COLE, G. F. (1975). the American System of Criminal Justice. Belmont, Calif.: Wadsworth.

DUFFEE, D., F. HUSSEY, and J. CRAMER (1978). Criminal Justice: Organization, Structure, and Analysis. Englewood Cliffs, N.J.: Prentice-Hall.

FELKENES, G. T. (1973). The Criminal Justice System. Englewood Cliffs, N.J.: Prentice-Hall.

GALLIHER, J. S. and J. L. McCARTNEY (1977). Criminology. Homewood, Ill.: Dorsey.

JOHNSTON, N. and L. D. SAVITZ (1978). Justice and Corrections. New York: John
    Wiley.
KALMANOFF, A. (1976). Criminal Justice. Boston: Little, Brown.
KRATCOSKI, P. C. and D. B. WALKER (1978). Criminal Justice in America.
    Glenview, Ill.: Scott, Foresman.
KRESS, J. M. (1976) "Progress and prosecution." Annals 423 (January):99-116.
LANE, R. (1971) Policing the city: Boston, 1822-1885. New York: Atheneum.
McDONALD, W. F. (1976). "Criminal justice and the victim: An introduction." Pp. 17-
    55 in W. F. McDonald (ed.), Criminal Justice and the Victim. Beverly Hills: Sage.
NEWMAN, D. J. (1975). Introduction to Criminal Justice. Philadelphia: J. B. Lippincott.
PLATT, A. (1969). The Child Savers. Chicago: University of Chicago Press.
PRASSEL, F. R. (1975). Introduction to American Criminal Justice. New York: Harper
    & Row.
PURSLEY, R. D. (1977). Introduction to Criminal Justice. Encino, Calif.: Glencoe.
RECKLESS, W. C. (1973). The Crime Problem. Englewood Cliffs, N. J.: Prentice-Hall.
REID, S. T. (1976). Crime and Criminology. Hinsdale, Ill.: Dryden.
RICHARDSON, J. F. (1970) The New York Police: Colonial Times to 1901. New York:
    Oxford University Press.
SUTHERLAND, E. H. and D. R. CRESSEY (1966). Principles of Criminology.
    Philadelphia: J. B. Lippincott.
———(1978). Criminology. Philadelphia. J. B. Lippincott.
WRIGHT, J. and P. W. LEWIS (1978). Modern Criminal Justice. New York: McGraw-
    Hill.

Chapter 1

THE PROSECUTOR'S DOMAIN

WILLIAM F. McDONALD

An important part of the difficulty involved in the prosecution of crime lies in the inconsistent definition of the prosecutor's role [Tappan, 1960:342].

The prosecutor has a multifaceted role . . . trial advocate . . . executive officer who administers an agency . . . chief law enforcement officer of the jurisdiction . . . [who] must attempt to coordinate the prosecutor's office with the police department and other agencies . . . [but also] be sensitive to the community's preference for law enforcement [Kalmanoff, 1976:217].

The office of prosecutor is an agency of the executive branch of government which is charged with the duty to see that the laws are faithfully executed and enforced. . . . [He] is both an administrator of justice and an advocate; [his] duty . . . .is to seek justice, not merely to convict. [American Bar Association Project on Standards for Criminal Justice, 1970:43].

No good results can come from having the prosecutor's office overlap the functions of the police at one end and those of the magistrates on the other [National Commission on Law Observance and Enforcement, 1931:18].

The purpose of this chapter is to provide a framework for understanding the role of the prosecutor[1] in the administration of justice.

AUTHOR'S NOTE: This chapter is a product of the research program of the Institute of Criminal Law and Procedure of Georgetown University.

Reproduction of Figure 1 is permitted for any purpose of the Law Enforcement Assistance Administration of the U.S. Department of Justice, or any other agency of the U.S. government.

Instead of the concept of role we will use the concept of domain. We will show that domain is not something that is fixed and final. Rather, it has evolved historically and is continuing to undergo change. It differs considerably among various jurisdictions. We will identify some of the factors that have influenced its development and show how changes in the prosecutor's domain have accompanied changes in the respective domains of other components of the criminal justice system. Finally, we will illustrate some of the conflicts involved in such changes.

THE CONCEPT OF DOMAIN

The concept of domain is used here as it has been developed in the literature on organizational behavior (see, e.g., Thompson, 1967:26). The criminal justice system can be characterized as an "industry" with a "long-linked" technology. That is, it consists of a sequence of serially interdependent organizations whose combined efforts result in various products. As studies of other industries have shown, each organization in an industry must establish some niche, some boundaries around that total effort for which that organization takes initiative. For instance, in their study of relationships among health agencies in a community, Levine and White (1961) reported that among health agencies domain consisted of claims which respective organizations staked out for themselves in terms of the diseases covered, the population served, and the services rendered.

In the criminal justice industry the domains of the component organizations appear at first glance to be clearly defined and well established. Police do the policing; the prosecutors do the prosecuting;

The research upon which it is based was supported in part by Grant Nos. 75-NI-99-0129, 78-NI-AX-0025, and 77-NI-99-0049 awarded the Institute by the Law Enforcement Assistance Administration, U.S. Department of Justice, under the Omnibus Crime Control and Safe Streets Act of 1968. It was also supported by a grant to the Institute of Criminal Law and Procedure from the Ford Foundation, as well as by the Georgetown University Law Center. Special thanks go to Jim Cramer for his enthusiasm and good comments on several of the key concepts developed here; to Mary Ann DeRosa for her unstinting typing efforts; and to my fellow participants in the Special National Workshop in Plea Bargaining, French Lick, Indiana, June 1978, for the stimulus and insight that meeting provided. Points of view and opinions stated in this document are my own and do not necessarily represent the official position or policies of the U.S. Department of Justice, Georgetown University, the Ford Foundation, or any others acknowledged above.

and the judges do the judging. But appearances can be deceptive. This image represents only the formal division of labor, the textbook description of how the system works. It is quite misleading. It exaggerates the extent to which these various functions can be and are in fact divided among different components of the system. It wrongly suggests that various roles in the system are hard, fast, and final. An alternative view is to see these roles as blurred, shared, evolving, and always open to negotiation. Typically, the answer to the question "What is the role of the prosecutor (or any other official) in the criminal justice system?" has been in terms of what that official usually does in some particular jurisdiction or in terms of some ideal of what he is supposed to do. However, a few field trips to some jurisdictions will show the discrepancies between both of these answers and what actually happens. In some places prosecutors control the charging decision. In others they do not. In some of those jurisdictions where prosecutors formally control the initial charging decision, the actual decision is made informally by the police and only rubber-stamped by the prosecutor. The variety of things which one can find prosecutors doing in at least some jurisdictions is amazing. Some prosecutors control the court calendar; some appoint defense counsel in indigent cases; some dominate the sentencing decision through plea bargaining; some do extensive investigative and police work; some operate special services for victims and witnesses; some play active roles in parole decisions; and some actively lobby at the state legislature.

One conceptual solution to dealing with these differences is to try to reduce them to a basic core. A distinction can then be made between this core role and all of the peripheral things which may or may not be added to the role. This approach was taken by Bitner (1970) in his treatise on the function of the police in modern society, wherein he identifies the core of the police role to be the capacity to use force. While this approach does generate some light, it is also prone to generating some heat. One man's core may be another man's periphery. With regard to the prosecutor, for instance, we note that in revising its *Standards Relating to the Prosecution Function* the American Bar Association Commission on Criminal Justice Standards is considering dropping the description of the prosecutor as "the chief law enforcement officer in a jurisdiction." The ABA never claimed that this was the core of the prosecutor's role, but this characterization drew criticism in any event. Chiefs of police were antagonized by this description of the prosecutor, and other members of the ABA committee felt that it did not capture what the prosecutor actually did. One senses that any attempt to define the central role of the prosecutor would be subject to similar crossfire. Thus, it is not our purpose to attempt such a definition.[2]

A less subjective and hence less controversial approach to the study of roles in organizations is to focus on domains. Prosecutors' offices are prosecutors' offices, but the range of their domains varies considerably. Some have laid claims to substantial parts of the total effort that goes into the criminal justice process. Others have made more modest claims. All differ to some extent in regard to the particular parts of the process that they claim. These differences pose interesting questions of fact and of policy. What is the full range of differences in the domains of prosecutors? What significance, if any, do these differences have for the efficiency, effectiveness, and fairness of the administration of justice? What accounts for the differences among the domains of various prosecutors? What common ground is generally claimed by prosecutors today? Has that changed over time and why? When prosecutors do attempt to expand or contract the boundaries of their niches, what happens?

The policy question is, of course, "What should the prosecutor's domain be?" Ideally that should be answered only after answering the preceding questions. But, in historical reality that question has frequently been answered either by default or by operational necessity, or by pontification based upon formal legal theory. In any event, it is a question that needs to be repeatedly addressed. Its answer is always relative to the nature of the criminal justice system existing at a particular time, the problems that system is attempting to solve; and the priority among the various goals which that system is expected to achieve. As these things change, so will the appropriateness of alternative demarcations of the prosecutor's domain.

It is our purpose not to address this policy question directly but rather to provide a basis for future discussion of it by answering some of the factual questions we have posed above. We begin by sketching in rough outline the changes in the criminal justice process over time and the accompanying changes in the prosecutor's domain. We then attempt to identify some of the factors which account for these changes. We will report some case studies illustrating the dynamics of organizational competition over domain.[3] Finally, we attempt to predict the future changes in the prosecutor's domain.

Our overall thesis is that the role of the prosecutor has historically evolved from one virtually nonexistent role in the criminal justice process to one where the prosecutor claims substantial domain. Furthermore, the domain claimed is of such a strategic position in the criminal justice process that the prosecutor's overall influence in that process extends far beyond the particular boundaries of his domain. However, while this is the overall trend, there are substantial differences among jurisdictions in the extent to which it has been realized. Increases in the prosecutor's domain have come in two ways. On the one hand, the criminal justice process itself has become more complicated over time. As that process has become more elaborate, there has been more territory for organizations participating in the process to lay claim to. On the other hand, another major source of the increment in the prosecutor's domain has been at the expense of one or more other organizations participating in the process. As the prosecutor's domain has expanded, the domains of the police, the judiciary, the defense bar, and even the correctional system have been correspondingly diminished. This has led to conflict between agencies and to some blurring of roles.

The expansion of the prosecutor's domain has occurred over the last two centuries as a result of increasing urbanization with its associated increases in crime and the simultaneous transformation of the Anglo-American criminal justice system from a small scale, rurally based system of privately initiated criminal prosecutions with minimal formality operated largely by amateurs or part-timers to a sprawling, large-scale, urban bureaucracy in which criminal prosecutions are initiated on behalf of the state by full-time, publicly paid professionals who must dispose of large caseloads within the restrictions of an extensive legal procedure. Formerly, the criminal justice process was a trial-based procedure in which virtually all cases that entered the system were disposed of by jury trials. Today, the jury trial is a rarity. Most justice is dispensed administratively by the actions of the prosecutor who either terminates the prosecution or negotiates a guilty plea through plea bargaining. The gross outlines of this transformation had taken shape by the turn of the last century and were well documented by the crime commissions of the 1920s. But only recently have prosecutors begun to recognize and fully implement their potentially central role in the administration of justice. In jurisdictions where this realization has occurred, there have been significant further refinements upon this new system of justice through and by the public prosecutor.[4] These recent changes are the direction of the future.

HISTORICAL EVOLUTION OF PROSECUTOR'S DOMAIN

Today prosecutors have an extensive domain and are regarded as potentially, if not in reality, the key actor in the criminal justice system. But this is a comparatively recent development. In the older big cities it is less than 100 years old. But in a far greater number of jurisdictions, namely, those new cities, suburban areas, and other places that have experienced rapid population growth in the last few decades, this development either has only just occurred or is about to occur.[5]

A full history of the development of the office of the prosecutor has yet to be written. We make no attempt to do so here. But enough is known to allow us to sketch some broad outlines and to detect some major trends. We have tried to convey those trends graphically in Figure 1. The three major components of this sketch are: the time periods chosen; the changes in the size of the criminal justice process itself; and the changes in the scope of the prosecutor's domain relative to the domains of the other organizations[6] that participate in the criminal justice process. While our sketch of these components is empirically grounded in the available literature, it is not drawn to precise scale. The state of our knowledge will not permit such accuracy at this time. We offer the sketch for its heuristic value.

Criminal Justice in Colonial Times

The origins of the office of the public prosecutor are the subject of some controversy. Langbein (1973) argues that the office has its origins in the early English magistracy. He reports that the justices of the peace became the ordinary prosecutors in cases of serious crime. The Wickersham Commission (National Commission on Law Observance and Enforcement, 1931) speculated that the American office of the public prosecutor was the result of an anti-English backlash after the American Revolution which led to the modeling of that office of government after the French office of public prosecutor.

Several other scholars (Van Alstyne, 1952; Kress, 1976; and Reiss, 1975) argue that the American public prosecutor is a product of the Dutch influence in colonial America. Van Alsytne points out that from the very beginning the Dutch colony of New Netherlands had the services of a schout. Historians have translated "schout" into English as "sheriff" and have regarded this office as the forerunner of the police (see, e.g., Richardson, 1970). But this translation incorrectly portrays the powers and duties of the office. Reiss (1975) reports that the schout's duties were in fact transferred to the office of the sheriff in the transition from Dutch to English rule. But those duties were not limited merely to the apprehension of criminals. They included the responsibility for prosecuting criminal matters. Thus, after 1665, in New York, in parts of Delaware and New Jersey, and in Philadelphia, the sheriff acted as public prosecutor. In other places, however, the powers to prosecute were given to either the King's Attorney or to a special office of public prosecutor. In May 1704 the first office of public prosecutor was established at law in Connecticut, where the assembly required that the "attorney" for the Queen should "prosecute and implead in the law all criminal offenders, and do all things necessary or convenient as an attorney to suppress vice and immorallities" (Reiss, 1975:7).

Colonial Times

Late Nineteenth Century

Contemporary Times

Figure 1: Evolution of the Criminal Justice Process and the Public Prosecutor's Domain.

It seems that the American office of public prosecutor did not have a thoroughbred pedigree. It was neither of pure Dutch origin nor of pure English origin. In fact, Reiss notes in the original colonies there was considerable variability in the system of prosecution in criminal matters, with the English system of private and police prosecution appearing side by side with the Dutch system of public prosecution in the same colonies.[7]

Although public prosecutions did occur in some parts of some of the original colonies, it appears that before the American Revolution the administration of criminal law in most cases in England and America was largely a system of private prosecution. The apprehension and prosecution of criminals were left up to the initiative of the individual victims of crime. Police departments, as we think of them today, did not come into existence until 1829 in London and a few years later in America. A system of sheriffs and watchmen did exist but did not constitute a law enforcement system with full-time responsibility for preventing crime and apprehending criminals. Sheriff's services had to be purchased by victims (Lane 1967). Similarly, victims had to pay lawyers to prosecute their cases. In addition to these cases initiated by individual victims, other cases were brought to the criminal justice system by the actions of the grand jury and by a special class of "victims," namely, professional complainants. The latter were people who made a living by prosecuting law violations and collecting the rewards for successful prosecution (Hibbert, 1963). The role of the public prosecutor in routine criminal matters was either nonexistent or minimal. The front end of the criminal justice process was dominated by the individual victim.

The tail end of the criminal justice system was dominated by the judge and the jury. Once the decisions as to guilt and sentence were rendered, there was little left to do. There was no correctional system as such. The convicted criminal was hanged, banished, lashed, or given in servitude to the victim until he made good his debt.

The criminal justice process in this era was unencumbered by legal procedures. It was compact and swift. In his study of the administration of criminal justice at the Old Bailey in London between 1675 and 1735 Langbein (1978) found that ordinary criminal trials (as opposed to the famous state trials upon which much of our ideas about the origins of our legal history are based) took place with incredible rapidity. In one two-day court session in December 1678, thirty-two cases were processed to verdict in the courtroom at the Old Bailey. Throughout the next several decades an average of twelve to twenty cases per sessions-day went to jury trial. These were full jury trials, not pleas of guilty. Typically in the ordinary felony trial at the Old Bailey, there were no lawyers for either the prosecution or the defense. Neither the government nor the private prosecutor (who was anyone whom the J. P. bound over to prosecute, usually the victim or his kin) bothered to hire the assistance of counsel. Langbein (1978:283) writes that "what we think of as the lawyers' role was to some extent filled by the other participants in the trial, especially the judge. But a lot of what lawyers now do was left undone, which naturally shortened the proceeding."

Late Ninteenth-Century Criminal Justice

In the pre-Revolutionary administration of criminal justice, defendants who entered the system were not allowed to plead guilty. Whether or not this means that there was no "plea bargaining" depends on one's definition of plea bargaining and the inferences one is inclined to draw from the available records.[8] But whatever one's conclusions on this score are, it is clear that the pre-Revolutionary criminal justice system was not one in which cases were disposed of by guilty pleas (Nelson, 1974). After the Revolution, society began to change and so did the criminal justice process. There had been cities in colonial America, but they had been able to govern themselves as if they were big towns. By the early 1800s, however, a critical mass in the size of these cities was reached and a need for new institutions of government became apparent. By 1822 the system of policing by private individuals had greatly declined. There continued to be many crimes for which private informers could collect fines for prosecuting them. But in Boston for several years no such money was given out at all (Lane, 1971:37). On several occasions the city offered special rewards for the detection of certain types of serious offenses, but the only applicants were watchmen and constables. Private citizens were no longer much involved in the administration of the police. The time had arrived for the professionalization of the criminal justice system. By the end of a half century after the Revolution the basic outlines of the new system of criminal justice were in place. The major changes were a greater role for the public prosecutors, the establishment of a full-time professional police department, and the establishment of a professional correctional system.

By the end of the American Revolution all states had enacted legislation establishing the office of public prosecutor. These prosecutors began assuming a greater responsibility for the prosecution of crimes, particularly victimless crimes and threats to public order (Nelson, 1974). In 1787 the Philadelphia Society for Alleviating the Miseries of Public Prisons changed the Philadelphia Walnut Street Jail into the first American penitentiary (Johnson, 1974:404). Within a few years all of the states had built masive prison systems. In 1829 a full-time, publicly paid police force was established in London and quickly copied in

America. As a result of these two developments, the domain of the victim of crime in the criminal justice process was greatly reduced. He no longer played a correctional role; and his role in the investigation and apprehension of criminals was minimized. The criminal justice system was placed in the hands of professionals who theoretically would have both the motivation and the expertise to do the job right. Even the grand jury system came under attack as an institution of amateurs. Bentham and other reformers proposed that the grand jury should be abolished because the job could be done better by a competent prosecutor (Felkenes, 1973:234). This view was adopted in many American states as evidenced by the fact that their constitutions either did not provide for a grand jury system or provided for one but also allowed for the option of proceeding by way of information filed by the prosecutor. The expansion of the prosecutor's domain had begun.

Another important change affected the arrest powers of the police. Traditionally, the law of arrest provided that peace officers could make warrantless arrests when a felony had been committed if there were reasonable grounds for believing a crime had been committed and the arrestee had committed it; but if the officer were mistaken, he was subject to civil action for false arrest (Hall, 1936). In misdemeanor cases an officer could not make a warrantless arrest unless the crime was committed in his presence. In 1827 an English court decision insulated the new police forces from civil actions for false arrests in felony cases where the police had been mistaken about whether a felony had been committed (Hall, 1936). Similar protection was not extended to citizens. This had the dual effect of encouraging victims to rely on police to apprehend criminals and enabling the new police forces to pursue criminals with less fear of danger to themselves. It also contributed to the reshaping of the front end of the criminal justice process in another way. The role of the judiciary in the felony arrest decision was being curtailed, and the groundwork was laid for our modern system of justice in which most felony arrests are warrantless. Formerly, the "gatehouse" to the mansion of justice was watched over by judicial officers who sitting in the comparative calm of the mansion's chambers could coolly review the available evidence and decide whether a warrant should be issued. In the new system of criminal justice, the felony arrest decision would be made more frequently by police officers with little, if any, education, legal or otherwise, in the context of rapidly unfolding events on the street. This meant that two kinds errors were likely to happen with some regularity. Officers might arrest when probable cause did not exist, or they might arrest in cases where the crime turned out to be a misdemeanor rather than a felony. Given the archaic and confusing state of the law of arrest, the possibility of both of these errors was strong.

Most states had provided checks against errors in arrest by requiring some kind of post-arrest review of the arrest decision by some official, usually by a judicial officer in the form of a preliminary hearing but in a few places by the prosecutor in the form of a requirement that all cases must proceed on a warrant issued by the prosecutor.[9] This provision for the second-guessing of the arrest decision set the stage for what has eventually become the initial screening decision of the prosecutor. However, as we shall show later, the prosecutor's efforts a century later to gain control over the charging decision and partially over the arrest decision have frequently been accompanied by conflict with the police

Increasing police authority to make warrantless arrests not only helped expand their control of the arrest decision that had historically belonged to the judiciary, but also gave them an important influence over the charging decision. In many jurisdictions their arrest charges stayed with the case through the preliminary hearing and even through the grand jury. This happened simply because prosecutors' offices were either not adequately staffed or not legally structured to permit them to review police charges shortly after arrest and prior to the case's being processed any further. This review was supposed to be done by the lower judiciary. (Even today this is true in many jurisdictions.) In those places where the county prosecutors were legally in control of the charging process and were able to staff the initial charging process, they generally deferred to the police judgments.

Police domination of the front end of the criminal justice process was enhanced in some jurisdictions by the institution of a system of police prosecution.[10] Typically these prosecutors were municipal-level prosecution offices completely separate from the county prosecutor. Sometimes these police prosecutors were attorneys employed by the police department, but sometimes the police themselves performed the function. Usually these prosecutors had authority to prosecute minor violations of the law. But in some places their jurisdiction covered the full range of crimes (i.e., felonies, misdemeanors, other minor crimes, traffic violations, and juvenile matters.). Even in jurisdictions where the police prosecutor did not try felony cases, however, he would handle their processing from the initial charging to their being held for the action of the grand jury.

Part of the police interest in and control over the initial charging decision sprang from their quick appreciation of its value both for personal gain and effective police work. Almost as soon as formal police departments were established the police began what can be described as a form of plea bargaining. By 1840 bargaining between the police and criminals over whether charges would be filed, or, if filed, whether they would be dropped, had come to be recognized as an "essential" tool in detective work (Lane, 1971:57). The compounding of felonies through arrangements between police officers and thieves became standard police procedure. One infamous case in 1841 involved a $10,000 robbery of Davis and Palmer jewelers. The case was solved when one of the two robbers was arrested on an unrelated charge and the police struck a deal in which the money was returned in exchange for release. When compromising felonies was called into question, police officials defended it in uncompromising terms. In 1867 in Boston (Lane, 1971:152) the chief of police defended the practice in essentially the same terms as his predecessor had used seventeen years earlier (Lane, 1971:152). " 'A betting with rogues' and the compounding of felony were the very essence of the detective business." What made the practice of compounding felonies by the police in those days particularly unseemly was the fact that the police usually stood to gain large financial benefits as a result of these compromises. Large rewards and the payment of per diem expenses were given for the successful return of stolen goods. Thus, in the 1841 jewelry robbery the constable who arranged the plea bargain received part of the $2,000 reward. It was this aspect of plea bargaining by the police that brought the practice into question and disrepute. Detectives had begun arranging with criminals in advance of the commission of crimes to secure their release and to split rewards. Eventually, the taking of rewards by the police came to be regarded as improper police work, but bargaining with defendants did not.

The way the county prosecutor exercised his screening function in the late nineteenth century was primarily through an extensive use of their power of *nolle prosequi* (Emery, 1913; National Commission on Law Observance and Enforcement, 1931). This role for the prosecutor, however, was not accepted without question. In 1913 former Chief Justice Emery wrote an article (at the request of several lawyers and laypersons) to clarify the legal basis for the prosecutor's performance of this function. His article is interesting not only because it defends this function for the prosecutor but also because it exemplifies the traditional, formalistic legal approach defining the division of labor among criminal justice actors. In his argument Justice Emery (1913:201) cites Article III of the Maine Constitution which provides that:

> Section 1. The powers of this government shall be divided into three distinct departments: the Legislative, Executive and Judicial.

> Section 2. No person or persons belonging to one of these departments shall exercise any of the powers properly belonging to either of the others except in the cases herein expressly directed or permitted.

He argues that this language unambiguously indicates that Maine judges have no authouity to exercise anything other than a judicial function, which is to decide questions of law or fact. The question of whether a criminal prosecution shall be pressed to final adjudication or dropped is "clearly not a judicial question, but purely one of propriety or expediency, to be determined by some office of that department charged with the duty of taking 'care that laws be faithfully executed,' viz. the executive department." Continuing, he quotes approvingly (1913:201) from State v. Tufts, 56 N.H. 137: "For obvious reasons the functions of the court and the prosecuting officer are entirely distinct. The court cannot usurp the duties of his office and say which cases shall and what shall not be prosecuted."

The legal basis for the prosecutor's role as gatekeeper was clear. What remained was for prosecutors to exercise that function in its most rational form, which meant moving their filtering work to the earliest point in the criminal justice process, namely, the initial charging decision. Over the next half century, more prosecutors offices would begin doing this but not without resistance from the police and the defense bar.

One other important change in the administration of criminal justice that occurred in the nineteenth century began shortly after the American Revolution. Defendants in criminal cases were permitted for the first time to plead guilty rather than to go to trial. One of the first cases in Massachusetts of a defendant's entering a guilty plea occurred in 1804 (Nelson, 1974:124). By 1839 about 24% of all the convictions in the state of New York were by guilty pleas (Moley, 1929:164). By 1860 that percentage had doubled. By 1929 the figure was 90% and commentators were referring to "the vanishing jury," "justice by compromise," and "criminal law administration through and by the prosecutor" (Moley, 1929:169). A transformation had occurred. Plea bargaining had replaced the jury trial as the mechanism for securing conviction; and to the extent that the prosecutor was involved in plea bargaining, his domain had been further expanded.

In summary, by the end of the nineteenth century the criminal justice system had been transformed from a system of private disputes initiated by individual victims to one operated by publicly paid officials on behalf of the community at large. The victim's role in the criminal justice process had been greatly reduced and replaced by an expansion of the role of the police and the role of the prosecutor.[11] The early stages of the criminal justice process and the lower courts were dominated by the police. The public prosecutor's domain was largely restricted to the middle stages of the criminal justice process. These included the formal accusatory process, i.e., presenting cases to the grand jury or filing informations;

dismissing cases filed by the police; plea bargaining; and prosecuting cases at trial. The domains of the grand jury, the petit jury, and the judge had been considerably reduced. Finally, a totally new enterprise was added to the process, namely, an elaborate correctional system.

CRIMINAL JUSTICE TODAY

Plea Bargaining

The shift to a system of criminal justice in which 90% of the felony convictions were obtained by guilty pleas did not automatically and simultaneously bring about an expansion of the prosecutor's domain. Only where guilty pleas were the result of explicit bargains in which the prosecutor played a major negotiating role was the prosecutor's domain extended. We believe (McDonald, 1978) that that domain started small and expanded greatly over the course of the last century, especially in the last decade.

To clarify this point, it is useful to distinguish three major kinds of plea bargaining: explicit bargains involving charge bargaining, explicit bargains involving sentence bargaining, and implicit bargains (which always involve sentences). An implicit bargain refers to those situations in which the defendant does not negotiate a specific agreement with anyone but learns (somehow) that if he is found guilty at trial he will be punished more severely than he would have been if he had pled guilty. This kind of bargaining is controlled by the judge. It is up to him to decide whether as a personal policy he will punish defendants convicted at trial more severely than he would otherwise have done if they had pled guilty. In contrast, charge bargaining is within the exclusive control of the prosecutor (although judges may occasionally pressure prosecutors to engage in this type of bargaining). A third type of bargaining, namely, sentence bargaining, is a mixed case. It is not in the exclusive control of the prosecutor or of the judge. Prosecutors can sentence bargain by agreeing to drop all charges in exchange for some consideration from the defendant. Judges can sentence bargain through open negotiation with the defense over the specific sentence that would be given in exchange for a guilty plea. A third possibility is that both the prosecutor and the judge cooperate in a system of sentence bargaining. This occurs in jurisdictions where judges have permitted prosecutors to make sentence recommendations as part of their plea negotiations and virtually always follow the prosecutors' recommendations.

In its national survey of plea bargaining in thirty American jurisdictions conducted in 1977, the Georgetown University Institute of Criminal Law and Procedure (Miller et al., 1978) found no jurisdictions where the dominant form of plea bargaining was either implicit or explicit sentence bargaining by judges acting alone. The most common pattern of plea bargaining for a jurisdiction was one in which some portion of the bargaining involved charge bargaining and another portion involved sentence bargaining. The second most common pattern was one in which most plea bargains involved charge modifications. In only one court, the county court in Greenville, South Carolina, was implicit bargaining the dominant means of securing guilty pleas.[12] In the eighteen jurisdictions where sentence bargaining occurred, it involved the prosecutors' making sentence recommendations which were usually followed by judges.

The historical record is not entirely clear about the relative proportions of the various kinds of implicit and explicit bargaining during the late nineteenth and early twentieth centuries. However, some evidence suggests that the form of plea bargainig has changed in the direction of expanding the prosecutor's role in the plea bargaining process. The change has been in the form of a reduction in the relative importance of implicit bargaining and an increase in the frequency of sentence bargaining by the prosecutor, particularly in the form of making sentence recommendations which are accepted by the judge (McDonald, 1978; Moley, 1929).

These changes signal the subtler refinements that have occurred within the criminal justice process after it had assumed its new shape by the end of the last century. For some time in the new system of conviction by compromise, the judge had continued to play a central role through implicit bargaining or direct participation in plea negotiation. But that system has been of declining importance, and the rate of decline has increased in the last few decades. During the course of the Georgetown national survey of plea bargaining, we were told by older lawyers about how plea bargaining had been done in the 1940s. In Henrico County, Virginia; St. Louis (city), Missouri; New York City, New York; Delaware County, Pennsylvania, and other places, the story was pretty much the same. Judges either engaged in implicit bargaining or played active roles in negotiating with defendants for guilty pleas. In St. Louis they referred to it as "burning the black candle." Judges negotiated directly with defendants in their chambers. In New York judges simply warned defendants that if they pled guilty they would get mercy whereas if they went to trial they would get justice. But these practices were rapidly disappearing. In ten of 25 states studied (Miller et al., 1978:214), explicit judicial participation in plea bargaining has been prohibited. In those and other states, judges have become more guarded about direct participation in negotiations. When it comes to implicit bargains, judges today are more careful to invoke an acceptable rationale for punishing defendants who go to trial more severely than those who plead guilty. Many judges use the American Bar Association (1968: § 1.8 [ii]) rationale that they are not punishing a defendant for going to trial but are merely giving the defendant who pleads guilty a break because he had taken the first step towards rehabilitation.

In some jurisdictions the transition from implicit to explicit negotiations dominated by prosecutors was in progress at the time of our visit. In Greenville, South Carolina, for instance, the process was partially completed. There are two court systems there with separate but almost identical concurrent jurisdiction. The same prosecutor's office serves both court systems. Until the early 1970s all plea bargaining in both court systems was done either through charge bargaining or by implicit bargaining. The judges in neither court would accept sentence recommendations from the prosecutor as part of a negotiated plea. Then a new prosecutor was elected and began making sentence recommendations. The judges in the circuit court went along with the change. The judge in the county court regarded it as an unacceptable encroachment on judicial territory and refused to honor any recommendations. Local observers believe that when the present county court judge retires his replacement will accept sentence recommendations from the prosecutor. In Kalamazoo, Michigan, in 1976, the chief prosecutor told us that his office was not at that time permitted by local judges to make sentence recommendations as part of plea bargaining. But, he was hoping to change their minds. In the majority of other jurisdictions studied, sentence bargains by the prosecutor had already become an established way of doing business.

Such sentence bargains are indeed an encroachment by the prosecutor on judicial terrain. It is part of the blurring of roles that exist in the contemporary administration of justice. Our Greenville judge was only echoing the traditional formalist view of the hard and fast division of labor among criminal justice agencies described in 1913 by Justice Emery. In those days that view prevailed and any encoachment by one agency on the terrain of the others was quickly condemned. In his article defending the authority of the prosecutor to dismiss cases, Justice Emery (1913) also took strong exception to a form of sentence bargaining by prosecutors that had developed. Cases arising under the liquor laws were being nolle prossed if the defendant would pay a certain sum of money to the state. This practice was widespread. Some prosecutors who engaged in it justified it on the grounds that the county needed the money and the courts might impose imprisonment rather than a fine. In deploring this practice, a Rhode Island court (State v. Conway, 20 R.I. 270) had said that "the practice is a vicious one and meets with our entire disapproval. There is no law authorizing a sentence or any legal substitute therefore by consent of parties, without the imposition thereof by the courts." Justice Emery (1913:202) called the practice "a plain, inexcusable usurpation of a power entrusted to the court, the power of determining what the penalty should be within the limits fixed by the legislature." He was contemptuous of both the argument that the county's need for money was superior to the full enforcement of the law and the argument that prosecutors are more able than the courts to dertermine what penalties are appropriate. But his views are no longer as dominant as they once were. There is widespread acceptance today for the proposition that saving the county money is a legitimate grounds for not fully executing the law. We also found fairly common among judges and some senior prosecutors the view that in most, if not all, cases the prosecutor is in a better position than the judge to determine the sentence. One of the main justifications for this later view is the recognition of the importance of the strength of the case in determining the terms of the plea bargain. Judges in several cities said they rarely question the prosecutor's sentence recommendation, even when it does not appear appropriate given the nature of the crime or the criminal. They assume that the discrepancy lies in the fact that the prosecutor has a weak case. Since assessing the prosecutor's case is not something they want to get involved in, they do not question these sentence recommendations. They subscribe to the prevalent philosophy that a half-a-loaf is better than none at all. They would prefer to see a serious criminal get at least a lenient sentence than to risk a trial and the possibility of no sentence at all.

In addition to the expansion of the prosecutor's role into sentence bargaining through the making of sentence recommendations, the prosecutor has further expanded his sentencing role through various analogs of the practice so roundly deplored by Justice Emery. In restitution and early diversion programs, charges are dropped if the offenders either repay the victim or accept some kind of penalty.[13]

Habitual Offender and
Mandatory Sentencing Legislation

Another important factor in the confusion of roles between prosecutor and judge has been the enactment of penal codes containing mandatory sentencing provisions. This has been particularly relevant to the habitual offender laws. These laws transferred power from the judiciary to the prosecutor and established him in the sentencing business. This was immediately recognized and protested—but to no avail—by the judiciary when it happened in New York in the early 1900s (Moley, 1929).

Habitual offender laws provided for enhanced sentencing of repeat offenders. These sentence-enhancing provisions, however, were under the control not of the judge but rather of the prosecutor. From a formal legal point of view, this made sense. Initiating these habitual offender proceedings was simply a special kind of charging decision, i.e., charging the defendant with being an habitual offender. Since in legal theory charging belongs to the prosecutor, he should be given this new charging power. But as the New York judges who protested Baume's law knew, such logic places form over substance. When mandatory sentences are involved, the charging decision becomes the sentencing decision.

If legislators had wanted to, they could have kept the prosecutor out of the sentencing business. They could have provided that the sentence—enhancing proceeding be initiated by an agency of the court, for instance, the probation department. Giving this power to the prosecutor maintained the neat formal division of labor between executive and judicial branch but in practice established a substantial confusion of roles.

Habitual offender legislation is just one illustration of how features in the penal code affect the prosecutor's domain. Several scholars have clarified this relationship (Ohlin and Remington, 1958; Lagoy et al., this volume). The prosecutor's domain and his general influence over the sentencing process tends to be greater when penal codes have the following characteristics either alone or in combination: (1) when they contain mandatory sentencing provisions; (2) when they provide for indeterminate sentences with the final release decision determined not by the judge but by a separate sentencing authority; (3) when there is a presumption or requirement that sentences for multiple charges and/or offenses be served consecutively; (4) when there is a graded system of punishment linked with a graded system of offenses and the differences among the grades entail substantial differences in the severity of the punishment. In short, when the penal code is such that the prosecutor's charging decision can make a major impact on the type of sentence that will be served and this cannot be substantially altered by the judge, the prosecutor's domain is expanded into the traditional judicial prerogative of sentencing.[14]

The Initial Screening Decision

While the police may have dominated the front end of the criminal justice system in many jurisdictions, they did not dominate in all. The crime commissions of the 1920s revealed that in some urban jurisdictions the prosecutor was very much in control of the initial charging decision. In 1926 the Missouri Crime Survey (1926:290) reported that the prosecutor's office in St. Louis (city) was rejecting 40% of the arrests brought to it by the police. The Jackson County prosecutor was rejecting 18% of the arrests in his jurisdiction. But in other states the initial screening decision was either fragmented among several agencies of justice or dominated by an agency other than the prosecutor. In Chicago, the police (not the prosecutor) presented cases at the preliminary hearing and the judge (not the prosecutor) performed the initial screening function. The Illinois Crime Survey (1929:209) found that 56% of the incoming felony cases were eliminated at the preliminary examination. Judges continued to dominate the initial screening process in Chicago until the early 1970s when because of unusual political circumstances a Republican was elected state's attorney and altered the initial screening process. Under the new system the prosecutor's office has taken over the initial screening function.[15]

In the early 1920s in Cleveland, Ohio, the initial screening mechanism was fragmented among a number of separate agencies. The Cleveland Crime Survey (1922:236) reported that of every thousand persons arrested for felonies, 13% were released by the police themselves, an additional 8% were either "no-papered" or "nolled" by the police prosecutor, 14% were "no-billed" by the grand jury, and 11% more were nolled by the county prosecutor. A total of 46% of the felony arrests were dropped from prosecution. The Cleveland Crime Survey concluded that this fragmentation was a major source of inefficiency. It criticized both the municipal prosecutor and the municipal court for their failure to take a more active role in screening. Significantly, it chastised them for using the traditional legal charging standard, viz., probable cause (1922:209). It wrote: "[The municipal prosecutor,] having no responsibility for the ultimate result, . . . feels no responsibility for preparing a case for that ultimate result. In this attitude he is supported by the court, which generally proceeds upon the assumption that the hearing need not be thorough, since all that is required is the discovery of some indication of a violation of law, with just enough evidence to point toward the defendant as the responsible party, thus enabling the whole matter to be passed on to the grand jury." It recommended that (1922:209) legislation be obtained "to place all state cases, both misdemeanors and felonies, in the exclusive charge of the county prosecutor from the beginning, including the presentation of the cases to the municipal or examining court. That would involve the enlargement of the force of that office, but correspondingly relieve the municipal prosecutor's office. The present division of the work in state cases is wholly illogical and harmful" (1922:209). A decade later the Wickersham Commission (National Commission on Law Observance and Enforcement, 1931:20) noted that "much of the growth of the prosecutor's power of disposition has been due to the slipshod way in which cases are initiated by the police or other investigating agencies and the tendency to arrest first, and find a case, if at all, afterwards, which unhappily prevails in too many localities. The sifting which must be done somewhere, and in a proper system should be done at the outset, had to be done by the prosecuting attorney." The Commission (1931:87) pointed out the importance of the emerging new role of the initial screening mechanism: "As the capacity of the [court system] to handle its task efficiently is obviously related to the size or volume of the load thrown thereon, an efficient system for determining upon the instituting or beginning of prosecution is obviously a matter of great importance." It was clear in the Commission's mind that this decision should be made at the earliest point, but it was less clear who should make it and how. The Commission (1931:88-89) wrote:

> Despite the obvious importance of the instituting of prosecution as bearing on the workload, . . . none of the [crime commissions of the 1920s] had searchingly faced . . . this problem of whose function it should be to determine the instituting of prosecution and what should be the working methods and principles which govern its administration. Should the clerk of the court be the official in whom this function is placed, and using clerical methods, or the prosecuting attorney using methods appropriate to that office, or the magistrate using methods of a judicial nature? What, if any, should be the part of the accused in the procedure? These, and other questions which will occur to the mind, present important problems which must be studied thoroughly, before we could feel that there exist adequate data on which to base conclusions or recommendations.

The Wickersham Commission hesitated to endorse the prosecutor as the actor in the system who should have control of the initial screening apparently for two reasons. First, the 1920 crime commissions had shown that in some states where the power to institute prosecutions legally belonged to the prosecutor he had not exercised that power with much care or discrimination. Those commissions had "amply demonstrate[d] that the mere statutory locating of this function in the prosecuting attorney will not necessarily produce efficient administrative methods or a careful sifting of the cases at that stage" (1931:88). Consequently, the Wickersham Commission did not join in the Illinois Crime Survey's recommendation that the power to institute prosecutions be placed in the hands of the prosecuting attorney.

Secondly, there was the Commission's concern for the possible blurring of roles which that would create. The Commission (1931:108) declined to endorse the recommendation of the Cleveland Crime Survey that "the county prosecuting attorney be a sort of local attorney general directing the whole process of criminal prosecution somewhat analogously to the Federal Attorney General." It (1931:108-109) felt that before making such a recommendation one had to face the "complex and intricate problems of structrual organization of the county's prosecutor's office, if he were to perform such a function, and the relationship between it and the police (1931:108-109). In its conclusion, the Wickersham Commission (1931:157-158) made clear its overriding concern to establish and maintain a clear division of labor between the prosecutor and other agencies. It wrote:

> In regard to the prosecution, the lesson to be drawn . . . is that the work of the prosecution locally (that is, the work of the State's attorneys) needs to be simplified in its organization and consolidated, with a definite location of the field of functional responsibility, and in the more populous districts particularly, with definite provision for executive direction.

The need is that of defining and delimiting the field of the prosecuting attorney so as, on the one hand, not to invade the field appropriate to the police and, on the other hand, not to invade the field appropriate to the jury and the court, and then, within that delimited and defined field to concentrate the work and the responsibility in one official who has executive direction of a staff amply manned and amply equipped, with systematic coordination between presecution and police and the other organs of administration. So far as the (crime commissions of the 1920s) show, no such condition exists anywhere. While the problem is stated in many of the (reports of these crime commissions) in none of them is it thought through. The relationship of the prosecuting attorney to the issue of warrants and the institution of prosecution, the relationship of the prosecuting attorney to the conduct of the gathering of evidence, identifying the offender and ascertaining the circumstances of the offense, the machinery or work-methods which will coordinate the work of the prosecuting attorney with that of the police; questions such as these spring from the surveys, but have not as yet been exhaustively analyzed.

Four decades later there was no doubt in the minds of any of the several criminal-justice-standards-setting commissions regarding who should control the decision to institute criminal proceedings. It was unanimously agreed that the county prosecutor should control. The American Bar Association's Committee on Standards Relating to the Prosecution Function (American Bar Association, 1970:84) noted that historical changes had occurred in who had control over the power to initiate prosecution. But it added, "Whatever may have been feasible under conditions of the past, modern conditions require that the authority to commence criminal proceedings be vested in a professional, trained, responsible public official, [namely, the prosecutor]." Moreover, it argued that where a magistrate still had power to issue a warrant on a complaint of a citizen, provisions should be made to allow the public prosecutor to share in that responsibility. Furthermore, it recommended that the prosecutor should have a role in the issuance of arrest warrants. It endorsed the federal practice of requiring the police to secure the approval of the United States Attorney before application is made to a magistrate for issuance of an arrest warrant..

The President's Commission of Law Enforcement and Administration of Justice (1967a:5) had reached the same conclusion. It wrote: "In some places particularly when less serious offenses are involved, the decision to press charges is made by the police or a magistrate rather than by the prosecutor. The better practice is for the prosecutor to make this decision, for the choice involves such factors as the sentencing alternatives available under the various possible charges, the substantiality of the case for prosecution, and limitations on prosecution resources—factors that the policemen often cannot consider and the magistrate cannot deal with fully while maintaining a judicial role." The Commission was in favor of the early elimination of as many cases from the criminal justice as possible without sacrificing the proper administration of justice. It recommended:

> Prosecutors should endeavor to make discriminating charge decisions, assuring that offenders who merit criminal sanctions are not released and that other offenders are either released or diverted to noncriminal methods of treatment and controlled by:
>> Establishment of explicit policies for the dismissal or informal disposition of the cases of certain marginal offenders.
>> Early identification and diversion to other community resources of those offenders in need of treatment, for whom full criminal disposition does not appear required [1967b:134].

Despite these recommendations, the movement of county prosecutors into full control of the initial screening business had been slow.[16] Tracing this movement is all the more difficult because of the deceptiveness of formal appearances. In some jurisdictions there is no doubt about the matter. The prosecutor simply does not staff the early charging process. In other jurisdictions, however, the prosecutor may be physically present at initial charging and be in formal control but not real control. In their study of the initial charging process in Los Angeles County, Graham and Letwin (1971:674ff.) reported that nearly one-third of those arrested on felony charges in Los Angeles were never charged. Formally these cases were rejected by the prosecutor, but in fact they represented case screening by the police. The local police had a policy of never releasing persons, even those arrested without sufficient evidence to justify prosecution. The police maintained that the release decision had to be made by the prosecutor. Accordingly, the police would bring cases to the complaint deputies and tell them the cases should be rejected. Graham and Letwin (1971:675) note that this arrangement had organizational benefits for both agencies. It allowed the police to close the case and to blame the prosecutor and through him the court for the failure to prosecute. It allowed the prosecutor to claim that these cases demonstrated that the office was not simply counsel for the police but was in fact exercising the responsibility for screening cases imposed on the prosecutor by law.

Graham and Letwin (1971:669) were impressed with how little sophistication or self-awareness Los Angeles prosecutors had about the charging process, viewing it almost entirely in terms of evaluating the strength and admissibility of the evidence. They found a marked disparity among deputy prosecutors regarding the standards to be used in judging the strength of the case. Some accepted cases only if there were a prima facie case; others only if they thought the case would result in a conviction; but most viewed the complaint-issuing function as one of simply deciding whether the police "had a case."

Graham and Letwin had perceptively analyzed the imprecise phrase, "case screening," into ten distinct functions: (1) the summary judgment function; (2) the demurrer function; (3) the litigant control function; (4) the abuse-of-process control function; (5) the predictive function; (6) the directed verdict function; (7) the allocation of resources function; (8) the limitation of jurisdiction function; (9) the sentencing function; and (10) the community judgment function. They found, however, that the complaint deputies in Los Angeles had little appreciation of these distinctions. The deputies rarely engaged in any of the potential screening functions other than those of summary judgment and demurrer functions. That is, most cases that were dropped were done so either because they lacked probable cause or because the conduct involved did not appear to constitute a crime under the applicable statutes. Prosecutors did not exercise the litigant control function as they could do, for example, by attempting to control abuse of police practices. There was little conscious use of the allocation of resources function. Cost benefit analysis was never applied to the charging decision. The jurisdictional function was not performed; i.e., prosecutors rarely thought it proper to suggest misdemeanor prosecution if they could find grounds for a felony. Similarly, it was never suggested that the sentencing function should be performed by declining a prosecution because of the inappropriateness of punishment in a particular case. In general, prosecutors in Los Angeles in 1970 were still taking a very narrow view of the screening function.

But the winds of change were in the air. In other jurisdictions prosecutors were beginning to develop a broader view of their role at initial screening. They began taking real control over the screening process and establishing systematic, officewide charging standards to achieve certain explicit policies.[17] When this happened in Alaska, New Orleans, Louisiana, Phoenix, Ariz, and DeKalb County, Illinois, the prosecutor's move was met with resistance from the police.

Aside from the long-standing concern about overcrowded court dockets, one of the major stimuli for the recent move by prosecutors to take real control over the initial screening process has been the concern over plea bargaining. Although explicit plea bargaining has been around for decades, it became a heated political and scholarly issue only in the late 1960s. Even though the American Bar Association (1968) and the U.S. Supreme Court[18] had endorsed the practice of plea bargaining, prosecutors found themselves on the defensive with both the general public and the scholarly community. In 1972 the National Advisory Commission on Criminal Justice Standards and Goals recommended that plea bargaining be abolished by 1978. The movement to eliminate or minimize plea bargaining was well underway and took various forms. In Florida legislation was proposed to make plea bargaining a crime.[19] In numerous jurisdictions total or partial no-plea-bargaining policies were established.[20]

In many places the no-plea-bargaining effort led the prosecutors back to the initial screening mechanism and a recognition of the functional interdependency between initial screening and plea bargaining. Historically, prosecutors had used their nolle prosequi powers of dismissal to screen out cases put into the system by the police. It had been an easy step from there to plea bargaining. As Justice Emery's (1913) article suggests, the prosecutors had quickly learned that they could get something from defendants in exchange for dismissing the case. The nolle prosequi with or without strings attached became the solution to the new criminal justice system's need for screening. But, as the crime commissions of the 1920s pointed out, a more rational and efficient system was to have all screening done at the earliest point in the process, namely, at the charging decision.

Plea bargaining, as it had developed, proved to have many benefits to the new system of justice administered by professional organizations. The police came to rely upon it to secure the services of informants (whose cases would be dismissed or reduced after they had performed satisfactorily); it assured the prosecutor of a politically beneficial high rate of conviction; and particularly important, it provided a way to obtain convictions in cases that might have been lost at trial because of inherently weak evidence, sloppy police work, incompetent prosecution, or biased or unpredictable juries.[21] When plea bargaining came under attack in the 1960s, the propriety of the various "benefits" that plea bargaining provided were challenged. Plea bargaining had been justified as necessary to deal with overwhelming caseloads. But if this were so, then an alternative solution was to reduce the flow of cases entering the system. This could be done by making the threshold standards used for accepting a case into the system higher than they had traditionally been. The traditional standard was one of legal sufficiency. Did probable cause exist; and was the arrest lawful in other respects? But, with the crush of massive caseloads, legal sufficiency was not enough. There were too many cases that could meet that standard. A higher standard would have to be used, but no one wanted this standard imposed by law. It could be imposed, however, as a matter of policy by prosecutors. But this meant that prosecutors would have to be in real control of the initial charging decision.

The other advantages of plea bargaining were also seen in a new light. When Attorney General Gross (1978) initiated the no-plea-bargaining policy in Alaska, his purpose was in part to force the criminal justice system to drop its reliance on plea bargaining as a substitute for competent professional work. He specifically disapproved of using plea bargaining to get convictions in cases that would not otherwise have resulted in convictions. He directed that "an effective screening of cases filed . . . will have to be instituted in order to avoid filing cases which might be 'bargains' under the existing system but which could not be won at trial.[22]

One of the major criticisms of plea bargaining is the practice of "overcharging" (see, e.g., Alschuler, 1968). Although there is not yet any adequate definition of this practice, it can be partially defined as the practice of charging a defendant with the highest number and degree of charges that can possibly be supported by the available evidence. This practice had become standard procedure in the criminal justice process. It is called "overcharging," not to suggest anything illegal but to convey the notion of overkill. The charges are higher than anyone reasonably expects the defendant to be convicted of or punished for given the usual local practice for similarly situated offenders. Overcharging has the benefit of giving both the police and the prosecutor something to negotiate for guilty pleas or services of informants. Overcharging allows the prosecutor to reduce charges without really giving anything away. The defendant pleads to a sentence which is virtually the same he would have received had he been convicted at trial.

Critics of this practice are appalled by its coercive, corrupting, and deceptive qualities (Alschuler, 1968; and Chambliss and Seidman, 1971:398). Alschuler suggested that the prosecutor should charge at the level to which he would be willing to bargain down to. The Alaska no-plea-bargaining policy attempted to do this. Attorney General Gross explained:

What I am trying to prevent is deliberate overcharging. That will not be easy to change, but I want a real effort made. I know that even if the facts warrant reduction on a charge, some of you will be hesitant to make it if you do not get some sort of implied or expressed indication from the defendant that he will plead guilty. After all, if the defendant does not want to plead, why give him the break of reducing ADW to A & B. The answer lies in the fact that if it is the kind of case that should be reduced to A & B, it is the kind that should be filed as an A & B.[23]

The New Charging Policies

One of the basic changes in the new charging policies has been the increase of the threshold level of case acceptability from the traditional legal sufficiency standard. In some jurisdictions this has been to the higher standard of a prima facie case. In others it has been to the even higher standard of requiring the case be winnable at trial. An additional feature of these new policies is their selectivity. Threshold standards will be lowered back to the traditional legal sufficiency level for cases involving either serious crimes or dangerous defendants. These prosecutors are consciously using the screening function to selectively ration the limited available court resources. In so doing, they act in the capacity of quasi-legislators. They decide which laws will be enforced, against which defendants, and with what degree of vigor.

The new charging policies raise important philosophical and empirical issues which have not yet been fully recognized, much less adequately addressed. Professor Brunk (1978:31) is quite correct in his observation that "there seems to be no even theoretical standard of proper charging derivable from the penal philosophy underlying the (criminal justice) system as there is in the case of normal sentencing." The questions raised by the new policies are several. In somewhat oversimplified terms the fundamental question seems to be, "Is it better to have a system in which a lot of people are given a little punishment or a few people are given a lot of punishment?" From this follows several additional questions. If only a few defendants are to be punished, what criteria should determine who is selected for punishment, who should set these criteria, and how should they be implemented? Which system would have the greater certainty of punishment; and the greater deterrent, rehabilitative, and retributive values? Which would cause the greater amount of public dissatisfaction? Which would operate more evenhandedly? Which is more just? A jurisprudence of initial charging is needed. It is not yet available, because the initial charging decision has only begun to be taken seriously in the last few years.

INTERORGANIZATIONAL
CONFLICTS OVER DOMAIN

The historical evolution of the office of public prosecutor had extended the boundaries of his domain into territories formerly held by the police, the grand jury, the petit jury, the defense bar, and the judiciary. The police and the judiciary have not allowed this to happen without a protest. The defense bar has also lost some territory but more importantly has been forced to change its method of operation as a result of the changes brought about by prosecutors in the extent of their domain and the way they are performing their function. The defense bar has also resisted the prosecutorial changes. As for the grand jury and the petit jury, there is no contest because no vested interests were at stake. Below, we illustrate some of the conflicts which have accompanied the growth of the prosecutor's domain.

The Police Versus The Prosecutor

As noted earlier, when prosecutors have taken real control in initial screening decisions, it has been accompanied by strong reaction from the police. In Alaska the police loudly protested and resisted the no-plea-bargaining policy. This came as a surprise to Attorney General Gross (1978), because the police there—as elsewhere—have long been critical of the prosecutor's use of plea bargaining. It should be noted, however, that where police have objected to no-plea-bargaining police policies their objection has not been so much focused on plea bargaining as on the new role the prosecutor is playing at the initial screening. Formerly, prosecutors' offices had been largely rubberstamps for the police at initial screening. But this was going to change. Attorney General Gross told his assistants, "Merely because you are brought a police file does not mean that you are required to file a criminal charge. . . . I am not interested in seeing the office file on Assault with a Deadly Weapon charges and then reduce them to Simple Assault with suspended impositions of sentence with no fine or jail time purely because we never had a case in the first place."[24]

The American police have not been very discriminating in what they let into the criminal justice system. In their minds if a fellow police officer felt the case was good enough to make an arrest then it was good enough to go to trial. Every case rejected is an implied criticism of the arresting officer. When the tough screening policy was established in New Orleans and the case rejection rate went up to 46%, the police response was that they refused to believe they were "wrong" in almost half the arrests they make (Times-Picayune, 1974).

In some jurisdictions the police have come to rely on the initial charging policies of the prosecutor to protect them from civil suits for false arrests. Accommodating prosecutors have done one of two things to cooperate. They file charges in cases they might otherwise reject just to convince the defendant the arrest was lawful; or they require the defendant to sign a release waiving any claim of false arrest. The defendant's case is not dropped unless he signs a release. Tough screening policies would disrupt these informal arrangements.

In addition, the police have come to rely on overcharging as a means of obtaining the services of snitches. They promise to have charges reduced or dropped once the services of the snitch have been rendered. The importance to the police of securing these services cannot be overstated as suggested by the police axiom that "a policeman is as good as his snitch." A policy of "honest" charging is a threat to this system.

Aside from securing snitches, police will not be able to manipulate the charging decision because it affects other aspects of police work. It interferes with their ability to perform their "peacekeeping" (Bitner, 1970) functions. In some situations in order to maintain order on the street, they have to make arrests that they do not intend to have prosecuted. But where prosecutors have taken full control of the charging decision it is not always possible for the police to control what happens to these cases. In New Orleans, for example, one experienced police officer complained to us that under the strict charging policies of District Attorney Connick he was not always able to get cases dropped that he had arrested but did not intend to see prosecuted.

Another concern is that the police like to be able to control the doing of substantive justice as they see it. This has two sides to it—both to reduce and increase the punishment that some offenders get. For instance, our ten-year veteran in the New Orleans police department complained that under the charging and no-plea-bargaining policies of Connick, he was not able to charge certain types of cases in the way he thought they deserved. He mentioned the "hypothetical" case where the police officer arrests a second-time offender for possession of a gun. The officer may want the man charged with the misdemeanor of possession of a weapon because the person has been "toeing the line for quite a while." Under Connick's policies, however, the police officer's wishes would not prevail. Instead, the offender would be charged with the felony and with being a habitual offender.

In other cases the police want to increase the punishment a defendant gets. They have long since learned that arresting someone even when they know the case will subsequently be dropped imposes an informal, unofficial penalty. A person may have to raise bail money, spend time in pretrial custody, and pay substantial attorney's fees. The philosophy here is that though "he may beat the rap, he won't beat the ride." This handy little informal sanction, however, will not amount to much if "the ride" ends a few hours after arrest at the initial screening.

A final source of police dissatisfaction with the new charging policies is that the police have become committed to the old system of a little punishment for a lot of people. They believe at a visceral level that it is better than the alternative policy of a lot of punishment for a few people. They are unhappy at the thought that cases which formerly would have been accepted and resulted in conviction will now be rejected outright. They fear that certain classes of offenders or offenses will go unpunished altogether. One chief of police in Alaska complained that the no-plea-bargaining policy there meant, in effect, that the prosecutor had declared "open season on misdemeanors." Other Alaskan police officers had the same complaint. The Alaska Judicial Council (1977:54) reported:

> Police investigators often objected strongly to dismissal of charges by prosecutors. Investigators working with bad check cases cited several examples of cases in which charges had been dismissed, giving the reasons they believe that caused the dismissals. "If a guy pays up on a check case charges are dropped." "We had a recent forgery case involving numerous checks. The D.A. and defense attorney got together, the defendant pled guilty to two charges and the others were dropped." "In the old system [of plea bargaining], they pled guilty to three out of five charges. Now, no deals are made, but they still drop charges, without talking to defense counsel." "If there aren't enough judges to go around at calendar call or the D.A.'s are busy, they only take more serious cases and dismiss the others." "If they eliminated plea bargaining entirely, it would be O.K. but if we've got four counts, some shouldn't be dropped." Police were indignant that charges were dropped without any concessions in return by the defendant.[25]

The Judiciary Versus The Prosecutor

The trend in the relationship between the prosecutor's domain and that of the judiciary has been steadily in the direction of increasing the former at the expense of the latter. Before the American Revolution the judge interrogated the defendant (Nelson, 1974) and served as prosecutor at the trial (Langbein, 1978). Thereafter those functions were assumed by the police and the prosecutor. The judiciary once controlled the initiation of prosecutions through its control of the issuance of warrants. That function has since been steadily taken over by the prosecutor. In the heyday of the jury trial the judiciary had a major influence in the process of determining guilt and innocence and the sentence (Langbein, 1978). But that system was replaced by the system of administrative justice in which over 60% (see, e.g., Forst et al., 1977) of the incoming cases are disposed of by the prosecutor without a finding of guilt or innocence, and in which 90% of the convictions are obtained by plea bargaining in which the prosecutor usually plays a key role. Even in the bail decision the prosecutor now plays an influential role (Suffet, 1969). Some of these transfers of domain from the judiciary to the prosecutor have been accompanied by strong protests from the judiciary (Moley, 1929); and there are still some judges resisting this trend. But their efforts are in vain. Today's criminal justice industry is big business with large case volumes being processed through multi-judge courts. As the Wickersham Commission realized, that kind of system must have a central executive officer if it is to achieve any degree of efficiency at all. Although the chief judge in a multi-judge court system can perform this function to some extent, the officer in the best position to do it is the chief prosecutor.

Today many judges do not seem to be resisting the growth of the prosecutor's domain. In fact, with the decline of the grand jury and petty jury as institutions available to take the brunt of public criticisms for unpopular decisions, judges appear to be happy to have the prosecutor share in their decision making. It diffuses responsibility. Of particular interest in this regard is the experience in El Paso, Texes, where the prosecutor decided to stop plea bargaining. This left the judges with the responsibility of setting the appropriate (but unpopular) sentences. Within a short time, however, the judges got out of that sentencing function by establishing a no-plea-bargaining policy.

The Defense Bar Versus The Prosecutor

Inasmuch as the prosecutor and the defense attorney are adversaries, one might suppose that there is little opportunity for their domains to come into conflict. One would not expect to find prosecutors performing services for defendants that their attorneys might perform. But to some limited extent this has happened. One illustration will make the point.

Defense attorneys in many jurisdictions have reported that they sometimes are able to have prosecutors reject cases at initial screening or dismiss them at a later point as the result of new information brought to light by the defense attorney. This frequently is information that could have been discovered by a diligent prosecutor's office bent on careful case screening. For instance, a Greenville, South Carolina, attorney with a long-established reputation of trust among the local prosecutors reported he was once able to telephone the prosecutor's office and have a case not charged. He told them that the defendant, his client, was out of town on the date in question and that he (the attorney) had the airline and hotel receipts to prove it. For getting this case dropped, this attorney received a fee.

In New Orleans, the prosecutor's office has placed a heavy emphasis on initial case screening (see Wessel, this volume). Assistant prosecutors are given financial and other incentives for being innovative and diligent in finding the kind of information that would show that a case should not be put through the system. If our Greenville attorney's case had occurred in New Orleans, there is a good chance the prosecutor's office might have established the defendant's alibi themselves and dropped the case. Of course, this would have been at public expense. No attorney's fee would have been paid.

This example, however, is the exception. The expansion of the prosecutor's domain has not usually been at the expense of the domain held by the defense bar. The conflict that has occurred between the two components of the system has more often been the result of the fact that in expanding his domain the prosecutor has changed the way in which the functions he has taken over are performed. This has posed a threat to the interests of the defense bar. Vigorous initial screening is a threat because every case rejected from the prosecution is a potential client lost. Furthermore, the stronger and the more serious the cases are that are accepted for prosecution, the less the defense attorney is going to be able to do for his client, the more often he is likely to have to go to trial, the more often his client is going to be convicted at trial, the more often his client is going to be severely sentenced either after trial or at plea bargaining, the less outstanding the defense attorney's reputation will be, and the less pleased the attorney will feel about his ability to serve his clients.

The no-plea-bargaining policies are a threat because the defense attorney will no longer be able to function as he once did; he will have to go to trial more often; he will be less able to show his client that he has gotten something for him; he will be less able to maintain the image of manipulator, wheeler-dealer, or fixer; and (as with the police) he will be less able to ensure that substantive justice as he sees it will occur. Little wonder that in jurisdictions such as Alaska, New Orleans, and El Paso (Texas) where tough screening and/or no-plea-bargaining policies have been instituted, there have been strong protests from the defense bar. The prosecutors in these jurisdictions did not usurp domain but forced the defense bar to change the performance of its functions.

CONCLUSION

The traditional formal view of the division of labor among criminal justice agencies is misleading. Legal pronouncements about the clear distinction between the functions of these agencies obscure the reality of the overlapping and constantly changing roles they perform. It is more useful to regard each component of the criminal justice industry as having a domain, i.e., a claim to control performance of certain parts of the process. Those claims are always open to negotiation. The domain of any particular component may be expanded either because the criminal justice process itself had been enlarged or because the existing domain of some other component of the process has been usurped. Furthermore, changes in the way one organization performs its part of the work will cause changes in the way other components perform. Encroachment on domain and the forcing of changes in performance of one's function will be resisted if vested interests are at stake.

Over the course of the last two centuries, the American criminal justice industry had been transformed from a small amateur operation into a sprawling bureaucratic machinery operated by full-time professionals. The old system consisted of three main components: the victim, the judge, and the jury; and the major form of disposition was trial by jury. Today the main components in the system are: the police, the public prosecutor, the judge and the correctional agencies; and the major form of disposition is by the prosecutor's decision to decline or dismiss cases. In addition, most convictions are obtained from negotiations in which prosecutors are usually involved.

In this transformation the office of the public prosecutor has grown from virtually a nonexistent role to the position of central actor in the system. Much of this growth has been by displacing other components of the criminal justice system. The public prosecutor has virtually replaced the private complainant or the complainant's private prosecutor, and the grand jury. The public prosecutor is also continuing to extend real control over the initial parts of the process, i.e., initial screening process. In so doing, the prosecutor has displaced the police, the judiciary, and the defense bar from territory that was once theirs. The public prosecutor has also continued to displace the judge and jury as determiners of guilt and of sentence. The increase in the size and complexity of the criminal justice industry brought with it the need for a centralized chief executive to bring some efficiency and coordination to its operation. The public prosecutor was the only component in the system able to do this. Today's system is one of criminal law administration through and by the prosecutor, and it is likely to become even more so in the future.

NOTES

1. All references to "the prosecutor" are to the public prosecutor unless otherwise specified.

2. Although we will not attempt such a definition we point out that trying to work through such an effort for each of the various criminal justice officials is a useful exercise for recognizing the points we are trying to make. One quickly finds that various tasks which are traditionally identified with one or another particular role are not inherently a part of that role. One rapidly finds that the role of a particular official usually cannot be identified with any particular act. The same act may be performed by different officials in different jurisdictions. Also, one comes to recognize that an action or decision may be formally made by one official but in fact has been made by another. These discrepancies will reveal the blurred and negotiated nature of all the roles in the system. One is sensitized to the inadequacies of the formal, textbook description of the division of labor in the criminal justice system.

3. Elsewhere in this volume (Sigler) an international comparison is made between the domains of prosecutors from various countries.

4. See, for instance, the report on the transformation that occurred as recently as the 1970s in New Orleans, La. (Wessel, in this volume).

5. Interested observers can regard the latter type of jurisdictions as a kind of convenient historical laboratory where part of the history of the evolution of the prosecutor's domain is being recapitulated in a concentrated time frame.

6. For the sake of convenience, we shall refer to individual private defense attorneys and to individual judges as if each group were an "organization." Although this stretches the usual sense of this term, it avoids a cumbersome construction, "organizations and other actors or participants in the criminal process."

7. That dual system continues today in most states (McDonald, 1976).

8. Professors Langbein (1978) and Alschuler (1978) have chosen to conclude that no "plea bargaining" existed at this time. In none of the cases studied by Langbein was a guilty plea entered. In support of his statement that he could not "find a trace of plea bargaining in the Old Bailey in these years," Langbein (1978:278) reports a case which he and Alschuler regard as illustrative of the fact that *plea bargaining* did not occur at that time. In this case, one Stephen Wright, caught robbing a physician in his surgery at gunpoint, informed the court that he was willing to plead guilty in order to spare the court the trouble of trying him. He hoped he might "be recommended to his Majesty's mercy by the court and the jury." However, the court advised him to plead not guilty and go to trial. Although, Langbein notes, a few defendants did insist upon pleading guilty, the usual procedure was for the court to advise defendants to plead innocent and stand trial.

While I agree with Langbein and Alschuler that the Wright case may illustrate the view at the time that the preferred legal procedure was a full trial and that guilty pleas were a rarity, I draw the opposite conclusion about whether this indicates that *plea bargaining* was not a common practice at the time. For one thing, I would be suspicious of defendants offering to do the court favors when there is nothing in it for them and especially in this case, when the penalty would undoubtedly be death. Furthermore, in those days of ten-minute trials and minimal legal process, the defendant was not doing the court much of a favor by pleading guilty. Why would he not do what the big losers do today, go to trial and hope for an acquittal? Furthermore, this defendant is even suggesting the nature of the bargain. He wants a recommendation from the court to the King for mercy. Such commutations and pardons were a regular part of the ordinary criminal procedure of the 18th century (Langbein, 1978:297). We would suppose that the commutation power of the King was the mechanism through which plea bargaining was done at that time. We would further speculate that that is why Beccaria in his famous treatise, *An Essay on Crimes and Punishment,* published in 1764, specifically singled out the use of clemency powers by the chief executive as a means by which the harshness of the criminal law of the time was being mitigated—in European systems of justice.

9. Interestingly, these checks were built into the system without the police in mind. For instance, the delegates to the California Constitutional Convention apparently intended that the prosecutor should do his case screening after the preliminary hearing. Graham and Letwin (1971:669) report that this was undoubtedly because extensive increase in the police use of inquisitorial powers had not yet developed. The delegates assumed that the prosecutor would get the facts through the inquisitorial powers vested in the magistrate as prosecutors had formerly gotten them from the grand jury. (The delegates had replaced the grand jury system with formal charging by way of the information system.)

10. This system continues today. A national survey conducted in 1976 by the U.S. Bureau of the Census (1978:5) found that 74 agencies in 23 states employed police prosecutors. Thirty-three percent of them are in Massachusetts. This finding was regarded as an underestimate because a large number of municipal-level prosecution and legal services indicated in their survey report that police agencies also act as prosecutors in their jurisdiction.

In seven states some police prosecutors indicated that their prosecutorial jurisdiction covered the full range of crimes, including felonies. In half of the police prosecutor agencies reporting, the police officers serve as prosecutors.

11. However, the transition from private to public prosecution was never complete, and by 1929 Moley (1929:231) reported that "the plain fact is that no group and few individuals have any considerable amount of confidence in public prosecutors or public prosecution. Whenever a case arises in which they have a genuine stake they prepare their own cases and conduct, so far as they can, their own prosecutions. Public officials are permitted to act as formal agents of the state and to take public credit for their formal acts but the actual work is done by private individuals."

12. That was not the dominant form for the entire jurisdiction, because another court had concurrent jurisdiction and did not rely on this method of plea bargaining.

13. A similar transfer of judicial power to the prosecutor in connection with first-offender type cases has occurred in West Germany (see Sessar, this volume). For a further description of this trend of transferring judicial power to the prosecutor in other European countries, see Felstiner and Drew, 1978.

14. For an analysis of how the new trend toward determinate sentencing will affect this relationship, see Lagoy et al., this volume.

15. McIntyre's (1968) description of the judicial dominance of the preliminary hearing in Chicago is now outdated.

16. This is true, even though the movement has been stimulated to some extent by early screening projects funded by the Law Enforcement Assistance Administration.

17. See Jacoby (this volume) for analysis of the explicit and de facto policies that result from different types of charging standards.

18. Santobello v. New York (1971) 404 U.S. 257.

19. State of Florida, H.R. 1108 (Regular Session, 1976).

20. A partial listing of the jurisdictions is as follows: Alaska; Blackhawk County, Iowa; El Paso County, Texas; Kalamazoo, Michigan; Maricopa County, Arizona; New Orleans, Louisiana; State of New York, for narcotic offenses; and the U.S. Attorney's Office, Southern District, California.

21. The nineteenth century advocates of a professionalized criminal justice system had clearly seen the corruption attendant upon the existing system of private prosecution. Justice, they argued, in their system was too often subject to the self-interest of individual victims. What they did not fully appreciate, however, was that organizations also act in their own self-interest. They are all subject to the phenomenon of goal displacement (Chambliss and Seidman, 1971:266). That is, they attempt to depart from officially prescribed goals and substitute the unofficial goal of minimizing strain and maximizing

rewards. This tendency is most likely to succeed in organizations with certain characteristics. The role occupants in the organizations must have considerable discretion and incentives for exercising that discretion in such a way as to cause goal displacement; and there must be weak or nonexistent sanctions to prevent occupants from so acting. All three conditions exist in the organizations that constitute the criminal justice industry, but they existed to a greater extent in the nineteenth century than they do today. Prosecutors have the legal authority to exercise discretion to decline or dismiss prosecution or modify the nature of charges. As organizations, both police and prosecutor agencies were motivated to use methods disposing of cases that would simultaneously hide their mistakes, inefficiencies, and incompetencies; lighten their work load; and allow them simultaneously to do political favors with little risk of being caught.

22. Avrum Gross, Attorney General, Alaska, Memorandum of July 3, 1975.
23. Avrum Gross, Attorney General, Alaska, Memorandum of June 30, 1976.
24. Avrum Gross, Attorney General, Alaska, Memorandum of July 24, 1975.
25. A year and a half later Attorney General Gross (1978:11) reported that police fears that the new intensive screening policy would mean that prosecutors would "only take some convictions" and would "[screen] out other offenses which merited trial . . . seem to have been misplaced." (1978:11). He cited the fact that the number of charges filed had not substantially declined and most of the decline could be attributed to the decline in the oil pipeline construction activity and the crime associated with it.

REFERENCES

Alaska Judicial Council (1977). Interim Report on the Elimination of Plea Bargaining. Project report. Anchorage: AJC. (mimeo)

ALSCHULER, A. W. (1978). "Plea bargaining and its history." Presented at the Special National Workshop on Plea Bargaining, French Lick, Indiana, June, 1978. (forthcoming in Law and Society Review)

———(1968). "The prosecutor's role in plea bargaining." University of Chicago Law Review 36:50-112.

American Bar Association (1970). Standards Relating to the Prosecution Function and the Defense Function. Chicago: ABA.

———(1968). Standards Relating to Pleas of Guilty. Chicago: ABA.

BITNER, E. (1970). The Functions of the Police in Modern Society. Washington, D.C.: U.S. Government Printing Office.

BRUNK, C. G. (1978). "The problem of voluntariness and coercion in the negotiated guilty plea." Presented at the Special National Workshop on Plea Bargaining, French Lick, Indiana, June, 1978. (forthcoming in Law & Society Review)

CHAMBLISS, W. J. and R. D. SEIDMAN (1971). Law, Order, and Power. Reading, Mass.: Addison-Wesley.

Cleveland Crime Survey (1922). Criminal Justice in Cleveland. Cleveland, Ohio: Cleveland Foundation.

EMERY, L. A. (1913). "The nolle prosequi in criminal cases." Maine Law Review 6(February):199-204.

FELKENES, G. T. (1973). The Criminal Justice System. Englewood Cliffs, N.J.: Prentice-Hall.

FELSTINER, W.L.F and A. B. DREW (1978). European Alternatives to Criminal Trials and Their Applicability in the United States. Washington, D.C.: U.S. Government Printing Office.

FORST, B., J. LUCIANOVIC, and S. J. COX (1977). What Happens After Arrest?
    Washington, D.C.: Institute for Law and Social Research.
GRAHAM, K. and L. LETWIN (1971). "The preliminary hearings in Los Angeles: Some
    field findings and legal-policy observations." UCLA Law Review 18(March):636-757.
GROSS, A. M. (1978). "Plea bargaining: The Alaska experience." Presented at the
    Special National Workshop on Plea Bargaining, French Lick, Indiana, June, 1978.
    (forthcoming in Law and Society Review)
HALL, J. (1936). "Legal and social aspects of arrest without a warrant." Harvard Law
    Review 49:566-592.
HIBBERT, C. (1963). The Roots of Evil. New York: Minerva.
Illinois Crime Survey (1929). The Illinois Crime Survey. Chicago: Illinois Association for
    Criminal Justice.
JOHNSON, E. H. (1974). Crime, Correction, & Society. Homewood, Ill.: Irwin.
KALMANOFF, A. (1976). Criminal Justice. Boston: Little, Brown.
KRESS, J.M. (1976). "Progress and prosecution." The Annals 423 (January):99-116.
LANE, R. (1971). Policing the City: Boston, 1822-1885. New York: Atheneum.
LANGBEIN, J. H. (1978). "The criminal trial before the lawyers." University of Chicago
    Law Review 45(Winter):263-316.
———(1973). "The origins of public prosecution at common law." American Journal of
    Legal History 17(October): 313-335.
LEVINE, S. and P. E. WHITE (1961). "Exchange as a conceptual framework for the
    study of interorganizational relationships." Administrative Science Quarterly 5:583-
    601.
McDONALD, W. F. (1978). "From plea negotiation to coercive justice: Notes on the
    respecification of a concept." Presented at the Special National Workshop on Plea
    Bargaining, French Lick, Indiana, June. (forthcoming in Law and Society Review).
———(1976). "Towards a bicentennial revolution in criminal justice: The return of the
    victim." American Criminal Law Review 13:649-673.
McINTYRE, D. M. (1968). "A study of judicial dominance of the charging process."
    Journal of Criminal Law, Criminology and Police Science 59:463-490.
MILLER, H. S., W. F. MCDONALD and J. A. CRAMER (1978). Plea Bargaining in the
    United States. Washington, D.C.: U.S. Government Printing Office.
Missouri Crime Survey (1926). The Missouri Crime Survey. New York: Macmillan.
MOLEY, R. (1929). Politics and Criminal Prosecution. New York: Minton, Balch.
National Advisory Commission on Criminal Justice Standards and Goals (1973). A
    national Strategy to Reduce Crime. Washington, D.C.: U.S. Government Printing
    Office.
National Commission on Law Observance and Enforcement [Wickersham Commission]
    (1931). Report on Prosecution. Washington, D.C.: U.S. Government Printing Office.
NELSON, W. E. (1974). "Emerging notions of modern criminal law in the revolutionary
    era: An historical perspective," pp. 100-126 in R. Quinney (ed.), Criminal Justice in
    America. Boston: Little, Brown.
OHLIN, L. E. and F. J. REMINGTON (1958). "Sentencing structure: Its effect upon
    systems for the administration of criminal justice." Law & Contemporary Problems
    23:495-507.
President's Commission on Law Enforcement and Administration of Justice (1967a).
    Task Force Report: The Courts. Washington, D.C.: U.S. Government Printing Office.
———(1967b). The Challenge of Crime in a Free Society. Washington, D.C.: U.S.
    Government Printing Office.
REISS, A. J. (1975). "Public prosecutors and criminal prosecution in the United States of
    America." Juridical Review 20 (April);1-21.

RICHARDSON, J. F. (1970). The New York Police: Colonial Times to 1901. New York: Oxford University Press.

SUFFET, F. (1969). "Bail setting: A study of courtroom interaction," pp. 292-307 in R. Quinney (ed.), Crime and Justice in Society. Boston: Little, Brown.

TAPPAN, P. (1960). Crime, Justice and Corrections. New York: McGraw-Hill.

THOMPSON, J. D. (1967). Organizations in Action. New York: McGraw-Hill.

Times-Picayune (1974). "DA refusals of charges said 46 PCT." (cited by D. W. Neubauer and G. F. Cole [1976]. "Court reform: A political analysis," pp. 182-201 in R. Wheeler, and H. Whitcomb [eds.], Judicial Administration—Text and Readings. Englewood Cliffs, N. J.: Prentice-Hall).

United States, Bureau of the Census (1978). State and Local Prosecution and Civil Attorney Systems. Washington, D.C.: U.S. Government Printing Ofice.

Van ALSTYNE, W. F., Jr. (1952) "Comment: The district attorney—a historical Puzzle." Wisconsin Law Review:125-138.

Chapter 2

THE PROSECUTOR:
A COMPARATIVE FUNCTIONAL ANALYSIS

JAY A. SIGLER

Comparative criminal procedure is still an undeveloped field into which only the most venturesome have probed. The decisions about which systems to compare and about the nature of the comparisons seem almost unlimited, for "on the professor of comparative law the gods have bestowed the most dangerous of all their gifts, the gift of freedom" (Kahn-Freund, 1966:40-41). Even so, the perspective provided by the comparative approach may yield important insights into the most vital characteristics of the prosecutor's functions by revealing analogous features and unique conditions. Careful control of the type of comparisons should prevent more anecdotal assemblages. So, a strict scheme of comparison, discussed below, will be imposed upon the information collected.

This is by no means the first such comparative endeavor. Ploscowe's writings (1932, 1933, 1935) are still landmarks. Professor Mueller and Le Poole-Griffeths (1969) have attempted to provide guidelines, as has Schlesinger (1970). Yet Schlesinger (1977) has also noted the inadequacy of most research in comparative criminal procedure. The World Center for Peace Through Law has recently undertaken, through its prosecutor's section, an international survey of prosecutors to determine what functions are performed by prosecutors in different countries. Perhaps such a survey, if it is completed, will greatly add to the observations to be made here.

AUTHOR'S NOTE: The preparation of this research was, in part, supported by a grant from the Penrose Fund of the American Philosophical Society.

The most significant shortcoming of Anglo-American comparative criminal procedure research is the pervasive tendency to assume a dichotomy between the supposedly "inquisitorial" civil law systems and the familiar "adversary" criminal process. This misleading imagery still influences most researchers, even though the justifications for the distinction have long ago been eroded. In a historical sense, it is appropriate to speak of a distinction between an inquisitorial and adversarial approach. Yet we know that the American criminal justice system is often nonadversarial (Blumberg, 1967). Indeed, elements of the American system are inquisitorial (Goldstein, 1974). Probably the common law system has been moving away from the adversarial ideal while the civil law countries have evolved away from the essential elements of the inquisitorial approach, leading toward a convergence of systems.[1] So it seems tiresome and fruitless to dwell upon the supposed differences between the two systems, which have some features in common and other quite dissimilar characteristics.

A broad outline of the similarities and divergences of prosecuting structures is an ambitious undertaking. Some would say that only a firm empirical foundation can provide a true picture of the operational reality of each system (Grosman, 1970), but in only a few nations have such studies been made. Considering the few empirical studies outside of America, such as Grosman's own for Canada (1970) and some suggestions of my own about the actual operation of the English system (Sigler, 1974), there seems to be little reason to expect the appearance of empirical studies of many other systems. An attempt based upon the best available empirical studies combined with an examination of the provisions of criminal codes and scholarly comments upon those codes may be sufficient material for our broad survey. In any event, that is the best we can do at this moment in time.

Comparative law scholars have generated several new models of criminal procedure to supplant the standard inquisitorial versus adversarial description. Damaska (1975) suggests that a "hierarchical" and a "coordinate" model are closer to reality and provide a better means of analysis, but he also seems to admit that his framework does not work very well. A systems approach was championed by Rosett (1972) and holds some promise. Two well-known scholars seem to believe that continental pretrial criminal procedures are quite similar to American procedures (Mueller and Le Poole-Griffeths, 1969:159-175). Indeed, a review of the literature suggests that a fresh and simple approach may be best at this stage of our understanding, and such an approach will be used here.

There are many differences among prosecutorial systems which are interesting. For example, the French prosecutor is a civil servant, the American prosecutor is elected or appointed on a political basis, and the English prosecutor is separately hired by the police as a solicitor (the barrister typically is selected by the solicitor typically). Do these selection processes affect the outcomes? The question, while important, awaits the collection of large amounts of empirical data and the control of numerous institutional and cultural variables. The public policy implications of such a study are obvious, but the magnitude of the undertaking is overwhelming.[2]

A structural and functional approach to the prosecutorial role will be used here to cut across the boundaries of national systems. In 1976 the U.S. Supreme Court made one of its rare examinations of the actual operation of the prosecutor's office (Imbler v. Pachtman [1976] 423 U.S. 817). Although the case concerned the issue of the prosecutor's immunity from civil suit for damages, the Court was compelled to review the scope of the prosecutor's authority in order to determine the extent of the immunity.[3] Justice Powell listed a number of varying functions, including the obtaining, reviewing, and evaluating of evidence. These functions, which were less than judicial, were not necessarily covered by civil immunity. Some courts have classified the prosecutor as a member of the judicial branch; others, the executive branch. Questionnaires mailed to selected prosecutors showed that 15 of 36 prosecutors responding regarded themselves as judicial officers whereas fourteen others saw themselves playing police-like roles and 7 regarded themselves as independent of either branch of government.[4] In analyzing plea bargaining, Alschuler (1968) identifies an administrative, a judicial, a legislative, and an advocate component. The multiple functions of the American prosecutor have never been fully explored. A comparative functional approach will disclose the uniqueness of the American system of prosecution and at the same time suggest differences among other systems. Robert H. Jackson, once the Attorney General, stated (1940: 18-19) that the American prosecutor "has more control over life, liberty, and reputation than any other person in America." It will be shown that the scope of prosecutorial functions is greater in America than in any other democratic nation. Other lessons can also be learned from this functional analysis.

The following structural and functional considerations and categories will be applied in examining the comparative aspects of the activities of public prosecutors:

(1) Private/public or mixed prosecution
(2) Centralization or decentralization of organization (these two are not so much functional as structural)

(3) Detection of alleged offense
(4) Investigative functions
(5) Quasi-legislative functions
(6) Charging
(7) Plea negotiation
(8) Trying cases
(9) Sentencing

These slices of prosecutorial behavior seem to account for almost every important aspect of official activity. In no country is every function performed by the prosecutor. Nations vary greatly in the number of functional activities assigned to prosecutors—formally or informally. These variations can only be suggested because of the many gaps in information about the actual operation of non-American systems. Nonetheless, this functional approach allows a beginning, at least, in the framing of comparisons which are meaningful. Because of the scattered condition of the available information, the American system will be most frequently mentioned and other systems to the extent permitted by space and available data.

PRIVATE/PUBLIC PROSECUTION

Nations vary considerably in the extent of private, public, and mixed prosecutions. These variations set boundaries to the functions of prosecutors. In America, where public prosecutors have a near monopoly on criminal prosecution, the range of prosecutorial functions is very large. In England, operating within a theoretical private prosecution framework, the prosecutors have a narrow range of functions. Most nations have adopted mixed systems permitting some private prosecution either in combination with public prosecution or, limitedly, as an alternative to the failure of the public prosecution to act. The extent of public prosecution power sharply conditions the extent of prosecutorial activity.

Private prosecution is generally used on the European continent as a means of guarding against the inaction of the public prosecutor. In West Germany a citizen may file an administrative complaint (*Dienstaufsichtsbeschwede*) against a prosecutor who neglected to file criminal charges in an appropriate case. Parties injured by a crime may compel the initiation of prosecution (*Klageerzwingungsvefahren*, StPO, sec 172 et seg.). For petty offenses the injured party may sue by himself in a private complaint (StPO, sec. 374), although in serious cases the public prosecutor must be solely in charge of the case.

Pure private prosecution is virtually unknown in civilized society. In England what is called private prosecution is really prosecution at the initiation of the police. The decision to bring formal charges may be made by a designated police official or, more commonly, by a professional solicitor hired by the local police authority (Sigler, 1974). Trials of serious criminal cases are conducted by barristers selected by the solicitors or by the police officials. In practice, the police solicitor is the major figure in forming prosecution policy, but, as agent of the police, his decisions are subject to the ultimate review and control of the head of the police. Rights of private prosecution are still pursued by victims of assault, minor theft, fraud, and damage to property (Dickens, 1974). Otherwise, unfettered private prosecution by non-police officials is discouraged by statutes which place power to check private prosecution in the hands of the Director of Public Prosecutions or the attorney General. Indeed, persons bringing private prosecutions may be required by a court to show the extent and quality of their interest in the action (R. V. Metz [1915] 11 Cr. App. R. 164).

Israeli criminal procedure permits private parties to initiate criminal charges, but the private complainant must forward a copy of the charges to the public District Attorney who may, if he chooses, conduct the prosecution (Israel, 1967:ch. 4, nos. 62-65). Turkish criminal procedure is quite similar but numerous criminal offenses may be sued directly without the public prosecutor. Breaking into a house, disclosing secrets to third parties, unfair competition, violations of patents and copyright, minor assaults, and most libels and slanders may be treated as strictly private criminal actions (Turkey, 1967:Book 5.,ch.1).

Even in America most states accept the English common law view which permits private prosecution (Sidman, 1975). In the prominent Joan Little murder trial, a private prosecutor was hired by the family of a deceased jailor and was permitted, over defense objections, to take an active part in the case (Following State v. Page [1974] 22 N.C. App. 435, 206 S.E. ed. 2d 771). However, a number of states have specifically prohibited private prosecution. Trial judges have considerable discretion to interfere with private prosecution, especially if abuse can be shown. Private prosecutors are not permitted to appear before grand juries because of the "prejudice and lack of impartiality inherent in private prosecution"(Nicholas v. State, [1916] 17 Ga. App. 873, 87 S.E. 817). Thus, the private prosecutor, where permitted at all, has much narrower functions in America than do public prosecutors; and, in practice, private prosecutions are extremely rare in America, since public prosecutors are approaching a near monopoly on all serious crimes. However, half the states do not require the participation of a public prosecutor in minor crimes. In general, many American and Canadian legal scholars favor the complete elimination of private prosecution, and the trend seems to be

going in that direction (Burns, 1975; Sidman, 1975). Private prosecution
for American federal crimes seems to be permitted, but it is virtually
unheard of (Powers v. Hauck [1968] 399 F. 2d 322 5th Cir.).

CENTRALIZATION/DECENTRALIZATION

According to the American Bar Association (1970:18), the chief
distinguishing feature of the American prosecutor as compared with his
European counterparts is that the American official is a local official.
Certainly, among the states this is true, because most prosecutors are
county officials, and state attorneys general have little control over their
activities. Some state attorneys general have substantial criminal power,
including powers to regulate criminal appeals, but generally they are not
involved in decisions to bring criminal charges. The U.S. Attorney, who
prosecutes violations of federal criminal law, is much more subject to the
supervision of the U.S. Attorney-General, and uniform policies are
announced in the U.S. Attorney's Bulletin while procedures are found in
the U.S. Attorney's Manual. America has a prosecution system which is
decentralized in the states and centralized at the national level.

The English system is more decentralized than the American, permitting the exercise of more discretion in the enforcement of national
legislation. Although there is a national Director of Public Prosecutions
and an Attorney General whose consent is required to institute certain
kinds of suits, their supervisory role is quite limited. The D.P.P. is
required to prosecute cases punishable by death (Prosecution of Offenses
Regulations 1946, S.R. O., No. 1467), and he may prosecute any case
referred to him by a government department. He may also take over a
case from another prosecutor if the case is deemed to require his
intervention, but this is an exceedingly rare event. Corruption cases are
sometimes tried by the Director of Public Prosecutions (Public Bodies
Corrupt Practice Act, 1889; Prevention of Corruption Act, 1906-1916).
Otherwise, cases may be prosecuted directly by government departments
with their own prosecuting staffs. The remainder, which is the bulk of
criminal prosecution in England, is left to local authorities.[5] Effectively,
most English criminal prosecution rests with the chief constable of the
boroughs, counties, and municipalities. In more rural areas this means
that prosecution decisions may belong to police officers assigned to the
task (Police and Constabulary Almanac, 1975). Approximately 88% of
all criminal proceedings are brought by the police or their solicitors
(Devlin, 1958:21).

Across the channel in Ireland all prosecutions are at the suit of the
Attorney General, except where a criminal prosecution is instituted in a

Court of Summary Jurisdiction by a Minister, Department of State, or a person otherwise authorized by statute (The Criminal Justice [Ad.] Act, 1924, S.9). Moreover, the Attorney General has the power to nolle pros at any time, and the court may not interfere with his judgments (Killian v. Attorney General [1955] 92 I.L.T.R. 182. "Common informers" among the public have a limited authorization to prosecute (Wedick v. Osmond & Son [1935] I.R. 820).

The Japanese prosecuting system is even more highly centralized. The Supreme Public Prosecutor General is the head, and his subordinate offices are organized in parallel fashion to the court structure. The Prosecutor General, the Deputy Prosecutor General, and eight Superintendent Prosecuting Officers are appointed by the Cabinet, whereas all others are appointed by the Minister of Justice with the recommendations of the Public Prosecutor Selection Committee (Koshi, 1970:190-191).

The most highly centralized prosecution systems are generally found among communist governments, many of which are patterned after the Soviet Union. Mainland China's system even exceeds the centralization of other communist regimes. In China the People's Procurate is accountable only to the People's Congress, and it has supreme supervisory power to ensure the strict observance of the law (China Documents, 1955:131-163). Intervention in civil suits is also possible—an extreme of centralization, supposedly available only when the state or public interest are involved (Hsien-tien, 1957:55-59). The procurators are supposed to be the eyes and ears of the Communist Party, itself a highly centralized entity. The institution of the tightly centralized procuracy is nearly universal in communist governments, probably because a chief function of the procuracy is as a control mechanism for dominant forces within the Communist Party.

Centralization may also be consistent with democracy. For example, Denmark's prosecutors are all subordinate to the Minister of Justice and subject to the Minister's inspection in the discharge of their functions. The supreme prosecuting authority is the Chief Public Prosecutor (*Rigsadvocaten*), who argues for the public all cases brought to the Supreme Court. Although local public prosecutors actually make their own decisions in most criminal proceedings, the Chief Public Prosecutor has authority over them and his decisions are final (Denmark, 1970:197-198). Obviously, centralization in Denmark is intended to foster consistency rather than some repressive goal.

DETECTION

Crime detection, a function frequently assigned police in most countries, has, in some instances come under the vast ranging duties of public prosecutors. In America many states have given prosecutors detective-like powers. For instance, Hawaii statutes (Title 6 Sec. 62-78 Hawaii Rev. Stat.) state that county prosecutors may appoint investigators and "any investigators shall have the powers and privileges of a police officer in the county." Pennsylvania statutes permit the district attorney to appoint detectives to "investigate and make reports to him as to the conduct in office of magistrates . . . and other officers connected with the administration of criminal law" (Pa. Stat. Anno. 16 Sec. 1440). Many states have created special prosecutors with detective powers to deal with official corruption. Of course, the federal Watergate special prosecutor is a familiar example of this merged detective-prosecutor function. Even without any special prosecutor, the Justice Department has the statutory power to institute investigations into criminal activity and electoral misdeeds within the states (28 U.S.C. Sec. 515). However, at the federal level it appears that detective work is still performed by the FBI, the IRS, or other investigatory agencies.

It is hard to find other national examples of the merger of detective functions into the prosecutor's office. In the Soviet Union the investigators are now members of the procurator's office, especially concerned with serious crimes (Anashkin, 1971:21). Particularly dangerous crimes against the state may be unearthed by investigators for state security (KGB), but the lines between the two investigative staffs are not clearly drawn.

Two centuries ago in England justices of the peace used to serve as detectives, police, and public prosecutors. Since 1856 magistrates, by law, "abandoned completely the role of detectives and prosecutors" (Williams, 1955:601). After that time the police took over the detective function, as well as assuming the prosecuting function. Today, the two functions are being separated again as prosecuting solicitors gradually replace police prosecutors throughout the country.

In England, as in many other nations, various administrative agencies possess combined detective and prosecuting functions. Thus, the Board of Inland Revenue, the Department of Health and Social Security, and the Post Office, as well as other public agencies, blend the detective and prosecuting functions when they directly press criminal charges for violation of various statutory provisions.

But the American system is quite distinctive. In it, administrative agencies do not themselves institute criminal actions. Federal prosecutors hold a virtual monopoly on criminal prosecutions. In general, the same holds true in the states. Yet, in spite of the possibility of police and prosecutor conflict, state after state has chosen to create a corps of investigators attached to prosecutors' offices, or to create special investigating prosecutors, with a few conferring upon prosecutors the whole responsibility for investigating all crimes in their counties (New York: People v. Dorsey [1941] 29 N.Y.S. 637, 644). The American Bar Association's proposed guidelines also give the prosecutor "an affirmative responsibility to investigate suspected illegal activity when it is not adequately dealt with by other agencies" (ABA, 1970:30).

INVESTIGATION

The investigation of crime after it has been detected is a stage which usually follows arrest. However, in the Soviet Union and most nations which follow its example, investigation and detection are not clearly distinguished. Not only does the procuracy make preliminary investigations prior to arrest or detention, but it also may intrude into the investigatory processes of other agencies, including police agencies. The procuracy may remove cases from other agencies of inquiry, may require these other agencies to follow its instructions regarding investigations, and "may commission agencies of inquiry to fulfill particular investigative actions in cases being conducted by investigators of agencies of the procuracy, namely: to detain, bring in, or arrest the accused, to conduct searches and seizures to discover concealed criminals" (Berman, 1972: 102-103). Apparently, the Soviet system combines policing and arresting with the investigatory function.

In the west only the Scottish system begins to approach this aspect of the Soviet system. In Scotland the police may make preliminary investigations but the Lord Advocate may, from time to time, issue instructions to local chief constables regarding the reporting of crimes (Crim. Justice Act Scotland 1949, S.33). Police may be required to institute investigations upon the call of a public prosecutor (Police Scotland Act 1967, S.17). Because of the central control of the Lord Advocate and the Crown Office, antiquated or unpopular laws can go unenforced (Kirkland v. Cairns [1951] J.C. 61); the Crown Office for years, for example, has simply not prosecuted sexual offenses between consenting males, save in very unusual circumstances, thus discouraging arrests for such activities.

In America the prosecutor also performs quasi-police functions at times. In some communities, especially in rural areas, the prosecutor may be the primary investigating officer. He is often more competent for this work than the local sheriff or constable. But beyond this casual arrangement some state legislatures have cast upon the prosecutor the chief "responsibility for detection, arrest and conviction of criminals in his county (State v. Winne [1953] 12 N.J. 152, 96 A. 63). As a practical matter, most American prosecutors are hesitant to use detective-like powers or to initiate their own investigations. Most commonly, detection is confined to improving upon cases already brought by the police to the prosecutors' attention. However, in certain classes of offenses, such as white collar crimes, vice, drug traffic, and political dissidence, American prosecutors have developed their own investigations. In the run of the mill prosecutorial investigation, the prosecutor seems to be compensating for inadequate police investigation.

This trend to spread the American prosecutor's functions into policing activities has been deplored by some leading criminologists who believe that it produces friction between police and prosecutors (Sutherland and Cressey, 1974:423). Yet the trend continues, and in certain urban areas the prosecutors have absorbed some of the regular police, employing them on original and supplementary investigations (Smith, 1960:93-94). Distrust of police (and trust in prosecutors) has grown so great in Pennsylvania that a special commission recommended the appointment of a permanent autonomous special prosecutor with primary jurisdiction over police corruption and other corrupt official acts (Pa. Crime Commission, 1974).

Of course, the French system of the juge d'instruction does for the judiciary what some other notions have done for the prosecutor. The juge d'instruction had great authority to gather facts and to determine the weight of the evidence preliminary to trial. But the juge d'instruction is a judge from the *tribunal correctionel*, a French criminal court, not a prosecutor, and French law keeps separated the three functions of prosecution, investigation, and judgment (Languier, 1968:33), although the juge d'instruction, too, has access to his own investigators, and had been known to be subject to the influence of the French prosecutor.

QUASI-LEGISLATIVE FUNCTIONS

Legislative activity by prosecutors often goes unnoticed, yet prosecutors are often important actors in the formation of substantive criminal policy. For example, in 1964 the District Attorneys' Association of New York successfully opposed a group composed of law school deans, experts from psychiatric associations, other state agencies, and even key committees of the state and local bar associations. The prosecutors' organization wanted to retain the M'Naughten test for the legal insanity defense. The district attorneys won (Sherry, 1973:212-214). The opposition of prosecutors to laws changing the insanity defense was also successful in California and Texas. The District Attorney for El Paso County, Texas, a Mr. Simmons, has been actively lobbying his state legislature to impose a speedy trial rule in Texas. His unusual position is due to internal political struggles. In Oregon the state District Attorney's Association has been active in past lobbying efforts (see Miller, 1970). In Louisiana District Attorney Harry Connick has actively, and successfully, lobbied to confine the parole board's powers.

No thorough review of American legislative politics in the criminal law exists. Thus, the extent and scope of prosecutor lobbying can only be speculated about. However, one of the few empirical studies of this subject suggests that prosecutors (at least in Illinois) are major sources of proposed criminal legislation and major forces in the eventual passage or defeat of proposed criminal legislation (Heinz, Gettleman, Seeskin, 1969). This one study also contends that criminal laws are written by a legal elite and are heavily weighted in favor of the prosecution.

Japan, which has a highly organized, centralized prosecution, also has an effective prosecutor's lobby (Suzuki, 1973:302). In France, on the other hand, where the public prosecutor's powers are generally weak, prosecutors appear to have had little influence on the reform of criminal law. In West Germany legal scholars, not prosecutors, have taken the lead in criminal law revision (Eser, 1973:247-249). Information on this topic is scanty, as legal scholars and political scientists alike have neglected it. Nonetheless, that prosecutors may help create the laws which they subsequently enforce is an important subject worthy of greater attention.

CHARGING

The decision to charge, or not to charge, a suspect with a crime remains the central aspect of the prosecutor's functions. The control of abuses of this function is still the critical problem. A comparative treatment of this topic reveals that in every system controlling abuses of charging decisions is very difficult, although external checks upon the prosecutor are sometimes employed for this purpose with some success.

The most exhaustive study of this subject was made in America by F. W. Miller (1970). He concedes that there are few external limits upon the charging decisions of the American prosecutor. Charge selection and adding or dropping charges are acts of virtually unchallenged discretion. Miller (1970:166) finds that there has been "no substantial agitation to restrict the prosecutor's discretion by giving that discretion to some other official." Miller then proceeds to produce an extensive listing of factors which influence prosecutors' decisions not to proceed further or to pursue charges. Some of the factors seem to disclose a lack of concern with equal treatment before the law. Miller (1970:174) notes that in a large majority of cases involving assualts between blacks, the offender is released without trial. Statutory rape cases are generally not charged (Miller, 1970:175), and victimless crimes (gambling, drug use, and so on) are often not charged. Charges may be dropped because of the costs of pursuing the charge (i.e., extradition), the popularity of the suspect, or the unpopularity of the law. Important public policies may be avoided deliberately, such as by failing to invoke the provisions of habitual offender statutes. There seems little the American citizen can do other than repose confidence in the judgment of the prosecutor, as long as the prosecutor is not guilty of gross misconduct in office or of flagrant corruption, since it seems to be agreed "that no one else is in a better position to make charging decisions which reflect community values as accurately and effectively as the prosecutor" (Miller, 1970:294-295).[6]

In 1977 Joan Jacoby produced an interesting study on charging. Looking at the charging decision from an administrative perspective, she examined its impact on the rest of the criminal justice system. Jacoby suggests that greater internal managerial control would eliminate many of the abuses of charging by reducing some of its personal aspects.

The situation seems better in England, and judges "will not hesitate to express their disapproval if they feel that a prosecution is ill-advised" (Wilcox, 1972:114). Judges may be pointedly critical, characterizing prosecutorial decisions as "monstrous," "scandalous," or "ridiculous."[7] Since all prosecutions are essentially managed by the police or their prosecuting solicitors, parliamentary supervision is possible either through the Home Office or through special parliamentary committees such as the famous Wolfenden Committee of 1957 which recommended different approaches toward the prosecution of homosexual offenses. The Director of Public Prosecutions or the Attorney General may also scrutinize prosecuting patterns and suggest approaches to important prosecutions. All these restraints, though more extensive than in the American system, are still usually unavailing because of the absence of a national control over the police and the basically local, low-level visibility of most decisions to charge or not to charge. In fact, the English prosecuting system is extremely decentralized and manned by widely varying policies toward the charging decision (see Final Report of the Royal Commission of the Police, 1962, Cmnd. 1782).

According to Glanville Williams (1955:226-227), the police do not show favoritism in prosecution or seek popularity in making charging decisions, unlike in the United States. Williams also points up the well-understood rule which prohibits the withdrawal of a prosecution once it is started without obtaining leave of court. Thus, nolle pros is supervised in Britain, and dropped cases are scrutinized by the Director of Public

Prosecutions. Moreover, the charging decisions are in the hands either of professional prosecuting solicitors, who are remote from public pressures, or in unusual cases, of the Chief Constable, a politically rather secure person. There is, then, extensive discretion in charging decisions in England, but less than in America. There is more external scrutiny in England. It should be noted that individuals not charged are often given a police warning instead, and that such warnings are kept as official records, even though no judicial proceedings are invoked.

In West Germany charging decisions are much more constrained, especially by the basic statute which obliges the prosecutor to take action against any activities which may be prosecuted, and which are punishable in a court of law, to the extent that sufficient facts may be obtained (StPO, sec. 152II). So the prosecutor must proceed if facts are presented to him or if he has evidence sufficient to press charges. Even the Ministry of Justice itself is limited by this so-called "legality principle" and may not bypass it. Another check upon the prosecutor is the statutory right of a citizen to file an administrative complaint for neglect of duty and the right of injured parties to insist upon prosecution (StPO, secs. 171 and 172 et seq.) with court scrutiny of the latter right.

The West German prosecutor must disobey an order to drop a prosecution from his political supervisor, the minister, if there is sufficient factual basis to proceed. Then "the rule of compulsory prosecution frees him from demands of partiality from within the executive, while opening him to demands for impartiality from without" (Langbein, 1977:92). The role of compulsory prosecution applies with vigor only to serious crimes. Petty infractions are selectively prosecuted. As we shall see, the effect of the legality principle is virtually to eliminate plea bargaining in serious crimes.

Although most communist systems vest fairly complete charging powers in the public prosecutor (sometimes shared with police), the Yugoslavian model presents interesting variations. The Code of Criminal Procedure (Article 60) requires the prosecutor to notify the injured party if the prosecutor decides not to press charges. The injured party may continue the proceedings on his own. Another restraint upon the Yugoslavian public prosecutor is created by an elaborate set of requirements about the contents of the charge sheet. The basic elements of the offense, the theory of proof, and the names of witnesses and experts to be summoned must be disclosed in the basic charge sheet (Article 241).

In closing this section, we should take note of the highly limited role of the public prosecutor under the French and the similar continental procedure.[8] The French prosecutor is an agent of the executive, and he "is obliged to make his written demands in compliance with the instructions given him by his superior" (C. Proc. Pen. Art. 33). The Minister of Justice may issue orders to the attorney general of the appellate district, who in turn may issue instructions to the state's attorney (*Procureur de la Republique*). The state's attorney may issue instructions to the state's counsel in the police courts (C. Proc. Pen. Acts. 36, 37, 44). The state's attorney is regarded as the "judge of the advisability of the prosecution," whereas the examining magistrate, once having heard the evidence presented, "decides what measures are to be taken" (C. Proc. Pen. Art. 40). In practice, this means that the public prosecutor is required to adhere to the prosecuting policies of his superiors for the most part; he is further restricted by the determination of the advisability of prosecution made by a magistrate (of the *parquet*). Thus, the French prosecutor plays a most limited role, hardly "inquisitorial" in character (see Vouin, 1970), although some magistrates are influenced by strong-willed public prosecutors.

PLEA NEGOTIATION

"Plea bargaining," as it is usually called, is the subject of heated debate, having its defenders and detractors throughout the American legal system, but generally deplored as a practice in most other nations. If the ideal for a criminal proceeding is a jury trial, then a negotiated plea of guilty is a departutre from the legal norm (See Skolnick, 1967). But if "plea bargaining" is perceived instead as a species of pretrial negotiation to settle or resolve a dispute without resorting to trial, then it resembles civil trial negotiation functionally (Neubauer, 1974:223). The advantage of this perspective is that it removes the peculiarly American flavor of "plea bargaining," allowing for cross-cultural comparisons based upon the ability of the public prosecutor to function in the criminal system in a similar manner to the civil system insofar as settlement is concerned.

In truth, the American system tolerates more plea bargaining than most other systems, although data on this issue is suspect because plea negotiation in other countries tends to be concealed from view. Typically, plea negotiation in America consists of an accommodation between the prosecutor and the defendant's attorney resulting in an exchange of a plea of guilty for an agreement by the prosecutor is press a less serious charge than he might have pleaded or a promise by the prosecutor to recommend a more lenient sentence then he might otherwise have recommended to the judge. Such negotiations require a relatively cooperative defense and prosecuting attorney and a fairly passive judge. That institutional setting seems to exist in America in many places, amounting to a bureaucratic rather than an adversarial model of criminal justice (Blumberg, 1967).

Casper (1977) contends that "plea-bargaining" has become essential to the system, but it depends upon the willingness of judges to wink at the process so as to pretend that the negotiated guilty plea was the result of a free choice by the defendant. It is the abdication by the judge of an active part in the processing of trial negotiations which makes the negotiated plea so prevalent in America. The general rule on plea negotiation seems to be that courts should disturb the results of plea bargaining only when the prosecutor "unfairly burden(s) or intrudes upon the defendant's decision-making process" (Brady v. United States [1972] 397 U.S. 742). But since judges usually assume that guilty pleas are voluntary, bargains once struck are almost impossible to break, and the defendant is unlikely to take the risk of recanting his bargain. Judicial participation in plea negotiation might facilitate a more open process, but such a reform (adhered to in only a few courts) runs counter to the generally approved model of the judge as a silent ratifiers of the negotiations (See Neubauer, 1974:93-94).

The incidence of American plea negotiations resulting in guilty pleas varies considerably from one jurisdiction to another. Between 80% and 90% of all felony convictions in America are produced by guilty pleas, many of them not negotiated. Formerly it was believed that plea bargaining was more prevalent in urban areas.[9] A few cities, because expedited trial procedures, have had markedly lower rates of guilty plea convictions (Alschuler, 1968:61), suggesting that when pressures for mass-produced convictions are reduced the adversarial trial is more likely to be used. The American resort to a bureaucratically produced guilty plea seems to be a response to urbanization, high crime rates, and a desire on the part of prosecutors for high conviction rates.

In most other nations the phenomenon of plea negotiation has been largely overlooked. Yet there is evidence that such negotiation may be widespread even though the institutional setting may be different. Plea bargaining in Canada probably bears some resemblance to the American situation because Canadian courts have nearly absolute control over sentencing but little control over the withdrawal or reduction of charges, a situation similar to the American.

Over 70% of accused persons in Canada plead quilty before trial, but the extent of negotiating pleading is uncertain (Canadian Committee on Corrections, 1966:134). Canadian prosecutors rarely make explicit sentencing promises, because to do so seems to require that the judge be made a party to the bargain. Yet bargains do occur even though Canadian courts have not been willing to discuss and analyze the practice or to consider the voluntariness of guilty pleas resulting from plea bargaining (Ferguson and Roberts, 1974). Possibly, there is a lower incidence of guilty plea negotiation in Canada than in the United States. Canadian prosecutors are not elected and may not be as concerned with "win-loss" ratios as their elected American counterparts. No one can say for sure, although the incentives for American bargaining—heavy caseloads and the politicization of the office—seem less significant in Canada. In England, the conventional view is that plea bargaining "is exceptional" (Jackson, 1967:113-114). Other studies show that plea negotiation plays "a large part in the day-to-day administration of criminal justice, yet it is kept from the public eye" (Thomas, 1969:70). The English plea negotiating system is markedly different from the American or the Canadian because of the lack of a permanent professional prosecutor, because of the greater independence of the higher judiciary in the sentencing process. The English practice of hiring barristers to prosecute serious cases on a case-by-case basis mitigates against American style negotiations (Purves, 1971:470-474).

The most striking fact about the system in England and Wales is that approximately 98% of all criminal cases are tried at the Magistrate court level, well below the visibility level of the Crown Courts. Magistrate Court proceedings may be treated summarily, and the police or their prosecuting solicitors have no need to hire barristers. Supposedly, the practice of reducing charges so as to treat them summarily is frowned upon by higher courts, even when agreed to by both prosecution and defense (R. v. Bennett [1928] 20 Cr. App. Rep. 188). But magistrates seem to encourage plea negotiations (Gabbay, 1973:6-7). The decision by the police to choose the Magistrate Court rather than the Crown Court as a forum is probably the major negotiating counter. Consequently, there is a strong suspicion that plea negotiation is rampant in England below the level of the Crown Court (see Bottomley [1973], who suggests that it may be quite prevalent, in spite of official judicial views strongly to the contrary; see also La Cheen, 1975).

The failure of many commentators outside the United States to take note of plea bargaining in their own systems is easy to understand. In many cases the American definitions of plea bargaining do not apply because negotiations take place at a different time and place and between different actors. There is also an unwillingness to admit that formal rules have been breached. But haggling over pleas prior to trial may be a nearly universal event and involves, at least, an implicit bargain. The recent furor in England about a Home Office study which revealed some sort of plea bargaining system was deeply resented by many English lawyers (Baldwin and McConville, 1977).

Concealment of facts concerning the prevalence of plea negotiation prevents tentative conclusions about this important subject. Nonetheless, it does appear that some significant amount of plea negotiation probably takes place in every system, regardless of the crime rates and in spite of conventional theory. Bargains of some sort are struck in every criminal justice system. Criminal codes are never literally enforced. Usually, the prosecutor is the chief bargainer, although that is less true in England or France, for example, than in America.

TRYING CASES

The forensic activity of the public prosecutor is his most familiar function. In America, visions of Hamilton Burger and Perry Mason in forensic combat provide a stereotypical, if exaggerated, depiction of the trying of criminal cases. At this level the distinction between the adversarial and inquisitorial system comes closest to being meaningful.

In all criminal systems which are not based upon the Anglo-American model, the presiding judge conducts the trial, examines the accused, and takes the evidence. The public prosecutor may do little more than read the accusation in open court under the so-called inquisitorial system. The prosecutor may ask the witnesses a few questions after the judge's examination is finished, but the prosecutor will be hesitant to ask additional questions for fear of irritating the judge. So passive is the public prosecutor in Germany that some have been observed reading novels while the judge is conducting the examination (Langbein, 1974: 448).

Those steeped in the Anglo-American legal culture may find it difficult to envision such a diminished role for the advocates. The production of witnesses, introduction of evidence, direct and cross-examination, selection of the jury, and summation are, under the Anglo-American systems, functions of the attorneys. But under the inquisitorial system the facts are first screened by the examining magistrate (juge d'instruction), and the trial itself is later conducted before a criminal trial judge or panel. Because the trial, under the inquisitorial system, lacks the same presumption of the innocence of the accused so cherished (if only in theory) by Anglo-American lawyers, some observers have falsely concluded that there is an operative presumption of guilt at the trial (see Radin, 1948:99).

SENTENCING

The vast majority of American district attorney's offices participate in the sentencing process to some extent. They may present arguments concerning the nature and severity of the crime, give opinions on probation, or even, quite often, make specific recommendations regarding the sentence (Teitelbaum, 1972). Of course, in America, as in all other nations, sentencing authority belongs to the judge, but there is considerable evidence that in many parts of America the judge defers to the prosecutor's recommendations. (Teitelbaum, 1972:80).

One of the most careful American studies of a particular community concluded that in most criminal sentencing "the prosecutor's initial offer is the one that is agreed to eventually" (Neubauer, 1974:97). However, the dominance of the American prosecutor in sentencing has been disputed (Green, 1961). Certainly, it appears clear that heavy sentences are regarded as a symbolic victory for the prosecutor (Eisenstein and Jacob, 1977:269).

Little is known about the extent of prosecutor's influence on sentencing elsewhere. However, in England there are numerous cases in which sentences were reduced for informing (See R. v. James and Sharman [1913] 9 Cr. App. Rep.) or for pleading (See R. v. deHaan [1967] 3 All E.R. 618), and sentence reduction in the public interest is advocated by the leading English text on the subject (Cross, 1971:153-154). Since most sentencing is done by magistrates and very little is known of police prosecutor influence over magistrates, no assertions can be made with confidence.

At least tentatively, it appears that among democratic nations America is the only place where prosecutors play active roles in the sentencing process. This seems a fair assumption, considering the probable greater incidence of plea bargaining in America. In the Soviet Union prosecutors supervise the legality of judgments in an active way, even supervising the treatment of prisoners, performing roles far beyond the influencing of sentencing (Berman, 1972). The same expansive quasi-judicial and quasi-administrative powers in the procuracy typify most communist systems (see Szilbereky, 1961).

CONCLUSIONS

Comparative studies of criminal procedure are still in their infancy. Yet most previous studies have been based upon superficial distinctions, especially the familiar accusatorial versus inquisitorial dichotomy. Clearly, a more penetrating view discloses the inappropriateness of that approach.

Beyond this negative finding is a strong suggestion of the major differences among the world's systems. These differences do not amount to totally discrete systems for each nation. One could construct a scale along which each nation might be placed functionally, if the information were available.

Frankly, the study also displays some huge gaps in information. There is very little empirical information available on the actual functioning of prosecutors in places other than America, Canada, England, and West Germany. For most other countries the codes of criminal procedure and the impressions of prominent jurists provide a very crude hint of the prosecutor's activities.

On the most general level, the American and Soviet prosecutors appear to have the widest range of functions. In America the prosecutor's authority seems to be much broader than that in other democratic nations. Of course, the Russian procuracy is intended to have social significance far beyond that of public prosecutors in non-socialist nations. Its supervisory powers over the courts, over the prisons (and labor colonies), over acts of social and political organization permit oversight over virtually every aspect of Soviet life, except for the higher reaches of the Communist Party. The American prosecutor does not have the power of the Soviet procurator, but the tendency to expand the functions of the American prosecutor are significant, and the temptation to create "special prosecutors" (See Cutler, 1975) to investigate official corruption has a faint resemblance to the "inspector general" approach to law enforcement found in Soviet criminal procedure.

NOTES

1. Merryman (1959) suggests this convergence. The theory would require a lengthy proof, perhaps, but the historical record tends to lend support to Merryman's view.

2. Those so inclined would have to deal with rudimentary data, outside America. There seems to be no French research to provide empirical support, and very little in England. For Germany, there is an interesting beginning. See Bristen (1974). For an American study, see Johnson (1973).

3. Interestingly Judge Warren Burger, when on the District of Columbia federal appellate bench, held (Newman v. United States [1967] 382 F. 479 D.C. Cir.), that the judiciary was powerless to review the discretion of United States Attorneys because they were employees of the executive branch.

4. This and related aspects of the investigative functions are treated by Aspin (1958).

5. In the English system the Director of Prosecutions is given sufficient powers to persuade police forces of his views of prosecution policy over certain classes of cases, such as sedition, bribery of public officials, and other political kinds of crimes. Most other serious crimes must be reported by local police to the DPP. This reporting is for the purpose of attaining uniformity, but regional variations in prosecuting patterns still persist. See Justice (1970).

6. Actually, in some American cities police practically make charging decisions or at least insist that the prosecutor file charges. Judges, too, may influence charging.

7. English trial judges may terminate "oppressive" prosecutions at will (Connelly v. D.P.P. [1964] A.C. 1254). If a prosecuting authority wrongly declines to prosecute, judges may issue a writ of mandamus requiring prosecutions (R. v. Comm r. of Police of the Metropolis ex. p. Blackburn [1967] W.L.R. 902). The judiciary seems concerned with a pattern of nonprosecution of particular types of offenses.

8. Before 1808 the French system was truly inquisitorial in that the prosecutor had been a royal official who served the king with an almost unlimited power to locate wrongdoers, to interrogate them, and even to define crimes. This was changed by the 1808 Code of Criminal Examination which shifted many of the functions of prosecutors to jurors and to judges. In many ways the pre-1808 French prosecutor resembles the current American prosecutor.

9. Current research by Miller, McDonald, and Cramer (1978:16-24) for LEAA suggests that there may be little distinction in plea bargaining between urban and rural jurisdictions. This important research indicates that more powerful forces such as distrust of the jury system may be at work.

REFERENCES

ALSCHULER, A. W. (1968). "The prosecutor's role in plea bargaining." University of Chicago Law Review 36:50-71.

American Bar Association (1970). Standards Relating to the Prosecution Function and the Defense Function. Chicago: American Bar Center.

ANASHKIN, G. (1971). "Basic provisions of the Soviet legislation on criminal procedure and some aspects of its application." International Review of Criminal Policy 29:20-28.

ASPIN, M. E. (1958). "The investigative function of the prosecuting attorney." Journal of Criminal Law.

BALDWIN, J. and McCONVILLE, M. (1977). Negotiated Justice: Pressures on Defendants to Plead Guilty. London: Martin Robertson.

BERMAN, H. J. (1972). Soviet Criminal Law and Procedure. Cambridge: Harvard University Press.

BLUMBERG, A. (1967). "The practice of law as a confidence game; organizational cooptation of a profession." Law and Society Review. 1:15-39.

BOTTOMLEY, A. K. (1973). Decisions in the Penal Process. London: Martin Robertson.

BRISTEN, M. (1974). "Polizei-staatsanwaltschaft-Gericht." Monatschrift für Kriminologie und Strafrechtsreform 57(3):129-150.

BURNS, P. (1975). "Private prosecutions in Canada: The law and a proposal for change." McGill Law Review 21:269-2997.

Canadian Committee on Corrections (1966). Report. Ottawa: Government Printing Office.

CASPER, J. (1977). American Criminal Justice: The Defendant's Perspective. Englewood Cliffs, N. J.: Prentice-Hall.

CROSS, R. (1971). The English Sentencing System. London: Butterworth's.

CUTLER, L. N. (1975). "A proposal for a continuing public prosecutor." Hastings Constitutional Law Quarterly 2:5-23.

DAMASKA, M. (1975). "Structures of Authority and Comparative Criminal Procedure." Yale Law Journal 84:483-520.

Denmark (1970). An Official Handbook. Copenhagen: Krak.

DEVLIN, P. (1958). The Criminal Prosecution in England. New Haven: Yale University Press.

DICKENS, B. (1974). "The prosecuting roles of the attorney general and the director of public prosecutions." Public Law 50-73.

EISENSTEIN, J. and H. JACOB (1977). Felony Justice. Boston: Little, Brown.

ESER, A. (1973). "Criminal law reform: Germany." American Journal of Comparative Law 21:245-268.

FERGUSON, G. A. and D. W. ROBERTS (1974). "Plea bargaining: directions for Canadian reform." Canadian Bar Review 5:497-576.

GABBAY, E. (1973). Discretion in Criminal Justice. London: White Eagle.

GOLDSTEIN, A. S. (1974). "Reflections on two models: Inquisitorial themes in American criminal procedures." Stanford Law Review 26:1009-1025.

GREEN, E. (1961). Judicial Attitudes in Sentencing. London: Macmillan.

GROSMAN, B. (1970). The Prosecutor: An Inquiry into the Exercise of Discretion. Toronto: University of Toronto Press.

HEINZ, J. P. and R. W. GETTLEMAN and M. A. SEESKIN (1969). "Legislative politics and criminal law." Northwestern University Law Review 64:277-358.

HSIEN-TIEN, K. (1957). "The chief procurator's participation in civil actions." Fa-hsuen (Jurisprudence, China) 4:55-59.

Israel (1967). Criminal Procedure Law. South Hackensack, N. J.: Fred B. Rothman.

JACKSON, R. H. (1940). "The federal prosecutor." Journal of the American Judicature Society 24:18-25.

JACKSON, R. M. (1967). The Machinery of Justice in England. Cambridge: Cambridge University Press.

JACOBY, J. (1977). "The Prosecutor's Changing Decision: A Policy Perspective." Washington, D.C.: Law Enforcement Assistance Administration (NILECJ).

JOHNSON, J. M. (1973). "The influence of politics upon the office of the American prosecutor." American Journal of Criminal Law 2:187-195.

Justice Educational and Research Trust (1970). The Prosecution Process in England and Wales. London: JERT.

KAHN-FREUND, O. (1966). "Comparative law an academic subject." Law Quarterly Review 82:40-46.

KOSHI, G. M. (1970). The Japanese Legal Advisor. Rutland, Vt. Charles E. Tuttle.

La CHEEN, S. R. (1975). "First impressions: A Philadephia lawyer's view of English justice." Shingle 38:31-35.

LANGBEIN, J. H. (1977). Comparative Criminal Procedure: Germany. St. Paul, Minn.: West.

———(1974). "Controlling prosecutorial discretion in Germany." University of Chicago Law Review 41:439-455.

LANGUIER J. (1968). "The preliminary investigation by the French judge d'instruction." Northern Ireland Legal Quarterly 19:32-47.

MERRYMAN, J. (1959). The Civil Tradition. Standford: Stanford University Press.

MILLER, F. W. (1970). Prosecution. Boston: Little, Brown.

MILLER, H. S. (1970). "Criminal law reform in Oregon." Willamette Law Journal 6:357-430.

MILLER, H. S., F. W. McDONALD, and J. A. CRAMER (1978). Plea Bargaining in the United States: Phase I. Washington, D.C.: U.S. Government Printing Office.

MUELLER, G. and F. Le POOLE-GRIFFETHS (1969). Comparative Criminal Procedure. New York: New York University Press.

NEUBAUER, D. W. (1974). Criminal Justice in Middle America. Morristown, N.J.: General Learning Press.

Pennsylvania, Crime Commission (1974). Report on Police Corruption and the Quality of Law Enforcement in Philadelphia. Harrisburg: PCC.

Police and Constabulary Almanac (1975). London: R. Hazell.

PLOSCOWE, M (1935). "The investigating magistrate (juge d'instruction) in European criminal procedure." Michigan Law Review 33:1010-1040.

_____(1933). "Administration of criminal justice in France." Journal of Criminal Law and Criminology, 24:712-730.

_____(1932). "Development of inquisitorial and accusatorial elements in French procedure." J. Crim. L. & C. 23:372-382.

PURVES, R. F. (1971). "The plea bargaining business: Some conclusions from research." Criminal Law Review (England) 470-477.

RADIN, M. (1948). The Law and You. New York: Mentor Books.

ROSETT, A. (1972). "Discretion, severity and legality in criminal justice," Southern California Law Review 46:12-50.

SCHLESINGER, R. (1977). "Comparative criminal procedure: A plea for utilizing foreign experience." Buffalo Law Review 26:361-381.

_____(1970). Comparative Law: Cases, Text and Materials. St. Paul, Minn.: West.

SHERRY, A. H. (1973). "The politics of criminal law reform." American Journal of Comparative Law 21:200-216.

SIDMAN, A. (1975). "The outmoded concept of private prosecution." American University Law Review 25:754-794.

SIGLER, J. (1974). "Public prosecutions in England and Wales." Criminal Law Review (England) 642-651.

SKOLNICK, J. (1967). Justice Without Trial. New York: John Wiley.

SMITH, B. (1960). Police Systems in the United States. New York: Harper & Row.

SUTHERLAND, E. H. and CREESEY, D. R. (1974). Criminology. New York: J. P. Lippincott.

SUZUKI, Y. (1973). "Criminal law reform: Japan." American Journal of Comparative Law 21:245-262.

SZILBEREKY, J. (1961). "The principles of the organization and activity of the procurator's office in the Hungarian People's Republic." Hungarian Law Review 1:37-45.

TEITELBAUM, W. J. (1972). "The prosecutor's role in the sentencing process: A national survey." American Journal of Criminal Law 1:75-82.

THOMAS, P. (1969). "An exploration of plea bargaining." Criminal Law Review (England) 69-75.

Turkey (1967). Criminal Procedure Law. South Hackensack, N.J.: Fred B. Rothman.

Von BAR, C. L. (1916). History of Continental Criminal Law. T. S. Bell (trans.). London: John Murray.

VOUIN, R. (1970). "The role of the prosecutor in French criminal trials." American Journal of Comparative Law 18:483-497.

WILCOX, A. F. (1972). The Decision to Prosecute. London: Butterworth's.

WILLIAMS, C. (1961). "The justices and the police," in Justices of the Peace Through Six Hundred Years. Chichester, England: Justice of the Peact Ltd.

WILLIAMS, G. (1955). "The power to prosecute." Criminal Law Review (England): 600-605.

Chapter 3

THE CHARGING POLICIES OF PROSECUTORS

JOAN E. JACOBY

The key to understanding the nature of prosecutorial policy is understanding the nature of the prosecutor himself. As the public official responsible for criminal prosecution in his[1] political subdivision, his nature is shaped by three distinct and important roles. They are the legal, the bureaucratic, and the political. The prosecutor is the chief law enforcement official in his district having authority to prosecute violations of the law. He is a bureaucrat because he is responsible for supervising and managing the operations and resources allocated to him to carry out his legal functions. And he is a politician because, generally, [2] he holds his office as a result of popular election.

All prosecutorial policy is made within the bounds created by these three considerations. In reality, prosecutorial policy is simply a microcosm of much larger considerations—the values that society itself places on controlling aberrant behavior among its citizens. The prosecutor's nature is discretionary. Within a general framework of state law and local economics, he is given the latitude to choose among alternative courses of actions. His policy is simply the course that he does choose. Those choices may be limited or constrained by various external influences over which he has little or no control. Some of the more important exogenous variables are the size of the jurisdiction, the type of court structure, and the amount of appropriated monies. Though they may account to some degree for his selection of policy, nevertheless once a course of action has been chosen, the policy of the prosecutor has been defined and a base upon which his performance must be evaluated has been created.

This chapter will discuss the connection between prosecutorial policy and the disposition of individual decisions which manifest that policy.

The discussion assumes that policy implies the existence of a value system used in the decision-making process to produce observable outcomes. In attempting to compare the outcomes of different policies, the concept of policy as a discretionary choice is critical. More importantly, it points out the obvious necessity of identifying policy before undertaking any evaluation, since results can only be evaluated in terms of identifiable and rational goals.

POLICY:
THE LAW AND SOCIAL CONTROL

Prior to a discussion of actual prosecutorial policies or a description of the rationales that shape them, it is important to place the concept of prosecutorial policy within the broader perspective of social control. The prosecutor is the chief practitioner of the criminal law, representing the interest of the state and thereby the interests of the public in creating and maintaining a lawful and orderly society. But criminal law is only a small part of the general mechanism of social control that operates through numerous influences in addition to the formal legal network. The family, schools, peer pressure, religious institutions, business and commercial entities all contribute to this general system of social control, and most citizens react within acceptable ranges of behavior to the pressures, overt and subtle, that are being applied constantly within society to maintain that order.

It is only when the general methods of social control fail that more specific types of action are needed. Even under these circumstances controls are often maintained in ways that never call into action the official sanctioner of society—the courts. Informal modes of arbitration among citizens with the assistance of public and private agencies (not necessarily the police) offer some of the best and most expedient methods of resolving conflicts that otherwise might find their way into the courts. Conflicts or violations that fail these types of controls are numerically rare in the world of human interactions. When they occur, however, it is the law, and most ominously the criminal law, that is called into play. From this perspective, it is clear that the criminal problems eventually reaching the courts are extreme cases and represent only a very small proportion of the population.

The law is just one component of the general apparatus of social control, albeit the most sanctified and official mechanism. It is the last line of defense, the theory that is designed to solve those problems which cannot be solved by other means. The law, as a means of social control, attempts to formalize public policy as well as possible at any moment in time.

Theorists in the law have recognized its limitations in blanket application to the diverse types of circumstances that society attempts to bring under its broad umbrella of social control. As one pointed out, the laws "are not intended to command each individual to follow a precisely prescribed path, but rather aim at an aggregate of systemic response. They are designed to control the rate of an activity by altering the costs for engaging in it" (Feeley, 1976:511). Law, under this modern view, is not a system of moralistic structures, as much as a series of cost benefit mechanisms by which society weighs the costs and effects of certain activities and attempts to develop socially economical sanctions against them.

Since changing legislation is far too slow and cumbersome a way to keep up with changing public policy, certain key actors within the criminal justice system are given discretion to decide whether the "ideal goals" of the law are being affected by the "actual practices" (Feeley, 1976:497-500). The underlying assumption of this approach is that the law is not simply a static set of public policy directives, but must contain a "dynamic" element that will allow changes in public policy to come into effect and be tested.

In the American democratic tradition, this important discretion within the framework of the criminal law is given to an elected official, whose policies are meant to reflect the attitudes and policies of his constituents and whose policy decisions are subject to voter scrutiny at the ballot box—the public prosecutor.

EXTERNAL FACTORS AFFECTING POLICY

There are numerous influences which come into play when the prosecutor attempts to formulate policy. Policy choice is clearly shaped by personal considerations such as the prosecutor's own philosophy of law and his perception of the prosecutor's purpose and duties in law enforcement. In addition, there are most certainly environmental factors which affect the equation as well. Research evidence already exists, for example, to show prosecutors' offices can be classified on the basis of a number of external factors beyond their immediate control. The extent of external influences, however, is yet undetermined, and raises questions for further study.

Research done by the National Center for Prosecution Management (1972) identified population as the most influential factor in characterizing a prosecutor's office. The urban, suburban, or rural character of the prosecutor's jurisdiction affects the amount of crime that has to be handled and the level of effort required to do the work. If policy is defined

as a result of a choice among possible alternative courses of action, it may
be that offices serving large urban populations find themselves more
restricted in their possible choices than offices handling smaller caseloads. The answer at this time remains speculative, and additional
research is needed.

A second environmental factor is the economics of the local government unit in which the prosecutor operates. The overall tax base of the
community, the priority structure within which prosecution services
compete for a part of the total budget, or the community's perception of
the threat of crime may limit or support the development and expansion of
prosecutorial policy. As a result, the amount of funding for the office may
affect either the selection of a course of action or limit its implementation.
Since some policy decisions are intimately tied to the ability to implement
programs or provide organizational support, inadequate funding will
preclude some courses of action from consideration. Prosecution is, if
nothing else, the occupation of the realist; most prosecutors adopt the
most practical approaches when confronted with a lack of resources.
Innovative programs or techniques generally require higher levels of
funding; when those funds are not available, the prosecutor tends to make
choices that are oriented toward efficiency rather than experimentation.

Other factors such as the existence of branch offices, the type of court
and defense systems, the characteristics of the police, and even the length
of term of office may also influence the formation of prosecutorial policy.
At the present time the power or significance in determining policy
choices is undetermined. At best it can be said that policy determinations
should be and probably are influenced by the socioeconomic characteristics of the community and its value system. Since the prosecutor is a result
of the local political process, his policy about enforcement of the law
should reflect the opinions of the community at large.

If an adequate analysis of the prosecutive process and function is to be
undertaken, it requires a recognition of the existence of external variables
and their possible effects on policy. Notwithstanding this caveat, the
focus of this chapter will be on those aspects of prosecutorial performance over which the prosecutor has control—namely, his policy and
its implementation.

A CONCEPTUAL MODEL
FOR POLICY ANALYSIS

Prosecutorial policy is best examined through a conceptual frame
which assumes that the local environment affects prosecutorial policy;
that it shapes and colors the policy of the prosecutor and his perception

of this role, and restricts the extent to which he may select policies not acceptable to the community he represents.

It also assumes that the prosecutor's policy is implemented through an organizational structure that can be described by its resource allocation pattern, management, and operational procedures and controls to ensure the implementation of policy.

Various strategies may be used to achieve a policy's goals. Of those available to the prosecutor, there is generally little variation from one jurisdiction to another. Although statutes, the constitution, or court rule may preclude the use of some of these strategies in certain states, it can be assumed that each will be selected or rejected on the basis of its consistency with the policy.

The dispositions that result from the implementation of a policy will, when aggregated, produce a dispositional pattern that is distinctive to the policy. Thus, if one knows the policy of the prosecutor, one should be able to predict an expected dispositional pattern.

Underlying all of these assumptions is a basic (though controversial) one. We assume that the prosecutive function is rational and that what may appear to be irrational behavior to the observer is only so because the purpose of an action is not clearly specified or placed in proper perspective.

Figure 1 illustrates the conceptual framework within which the prosecutive function will be examined and the power of policy explored. The potential environmental effects on prosecutorial policy are recog-

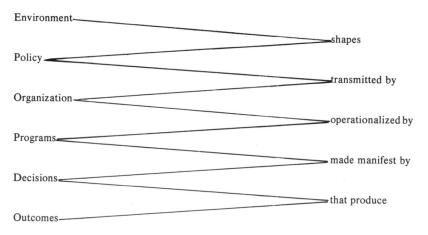

Figure 1: A Schema for Examining the Dimensions of Policy

nized, but will not be examined here. Instead, this chapter will focus on the factors under prosecutorial control that can be used to implement a selected policy. These include the organization and management of the office and the procedures used to control and monitor the decision makers who implement the policy. As the prosecutor exercises authority over factors such as these that are under his control, his policy and the power of that policy on the operations of the office as well as on the broader universes of criminal justice and society are illuminated.

A POLICY TYPOLOGY[3]

In 1975, the Law Enforcement Assistance Administration (LEAA) supported through its National Evaluation Program a Phase I Evaluation of Pretrial Screening Projects[4] to determine the feasibility of a nationwide evaluation. Based on an examination of the issues and observation in nineteen prosecutors' offices throughout the nation, the study concluded that such an evaluation was theoretically feasible but not practical until further research was undertaken. While this finding was primary to the Phase I study, another important discovery was made: that prosecutorial policy has an overwhelming effect on an office's performance as demonstrated by its disposition rates, its allocation of resources, and its use of various prosecutive strategies. Additionally, it was found that these policies could be classified and presented in a model typology format.

In his preface to the study, Lewis Katz wrote:

> The material developed by Joan Jacoby and her associates . . . offers a major breakthrough in the development and understanding of case screening. . . . The typology . . . sets forth a methodology for evaluating screening mechanisms in operation in a given office to determine whether those devised are fulfilling the purposes for which the prosecutor adopted them. Nowhere does Jacoby or her cohorts seek to dictate a policy to prosecutors, instead they recognize that there are many possible policies from which a prosecutor may choose one or more. Their role was not to evaluate or criticize those policies but to develop measures which would enable a prosecutor to determine whether his or her policies are being serviced. The typology deals with four of the policies and provides tools for measurement at each stage of the criminal process [Jacoby, 1976:vii-viii].

The purpose of this paper is to (1) summarize the findings of this study, (2) show that the identification of policy is a primary requirement in evaluating prosecution, (3) illustrate how differing strategies and allocation patterns are needed to support different policies, and, finally, (4) indicate the policy choices available and some of their effects on local communities as well as on their budgets.

The latter purpose is important. Already trends are occurring that give priority to questioning the type of prosecutorial services we can afford. As a result, policy criteria have to be stated so that sound decisions can be made on prosecutorial procedure. The workload created by the demand for improved delivery of legal services, the increased utilization of public defender agencies, the impact of Argesinger v. Hamlin (1972) 407 U.S. 25, and the increased system efficiency could result in one response, an increase of staff at additional public expense. More likely, however, it will require the prosecutor to become increasingly selective in accepting cases for prosecution.

As states examine the possibility of abolishing plea bargaining (as has occurred statewide in Alaska and locally in New Orleans, Kalamazoo, Portland, Boulder, and Prince George's County, Maryland), success can be fostered only if court capacity is increased to meet trial needs, alternatives to criminal justice processing are expanded and, screening of cases for proper charging is accorded its due importance. What the public should fear is not the tough prosecutor but the sloppy one. Where more intensive scrutiny of cases occurs, the probability of prosecuting the innocent defendant is diminished.

Prosecutorial policy is not circumscribed by the limits of the office. Its impact can be measured in other criminal justice agencies, particularly corrections. Depending upon the prosecution policy, the future size and characteristics of the correctional population can be anticipated. Where treatment programs are used, prosecutorial policy may well indicate the needs and requirements of such activity. This predictive power can be turned into a highly effective planning and management tool as well as a testing mechanism for attempted solutions to some of the problems confronted by the criminal justice system.

Because of their widespread ramifications, it is important to understand what types of policies exist and how they influence the distribution of justice in a community. Emphasis will be placed on prosecutorial policy as it is reflected by the charging decision. Since this decision acts as a gatekeeper for the office, it, more than any other subsequent ones, dictates the quality and tone of prosecution in a community. With this background, four "ideal" policies will be examined, representing the range of those that are likely to be found in one form or another in prosecutors' offices. The results of the policies will be discussed in terms of expected case disposition rates, and the strategies and resource allocation patterns that support the policies will be briefly described.

Prosecutorial Policies

No matter what the external environment or a prosecutor's perception of his discretionary authority, the prosecutor operates with a policy (usually either the one for which he was elected or the one he inherited) and implements the policy by various strategies. One might expect the policies of the district attorney to vary as much as the characteristics of the approximately 3,400 prosecutors. However, experience and observation has shown that only a few generalized classifications need delineation. Of the four discussed here, all have been observed operating in almost "pure" form in offices throughout the United States. The differences between offices were so marked that the abstraction of their operations into policy models was not a difficult task. The examples presented below are therefore discussed as ideals or models. It should be emphasized that the four policy types presented here are neither exhaustive nor mutually exclusive. Other policies probably exist which result in different treatment modes and disposition patterns. In some offices a mix of these policies may have been implemented. For the purpose of this presentation, however, the policy types have been abstracted and presented as pure types.

For convenience, the policies have been given the abbreviated descriptive names of Legal Sufficiency, System Efficiency, Defendant Rehabilitation, and Trial Sufficiency. The four tables that follow show the goals of the policies and the dispositional patterns each generates. Goals are equated to outcomes which should be maximized or minimized. Once the goals are established, other outcomes are logically predictable. One can expect them to occur with high frequency, others with low frequency. A few outcomes appear to occur independent of the policy and goals in some instances (shown as N in Table 5).

Legal Sufficiency Policy. Some prosecutors believe that if any case is legally sufficient (i.e., if the elements of the crime are present) then it is their responsibility to accept the case for prosecution. For example, in a breaking and entering case, if there was evidence of forcible entry and if the person arrested was found to have in his possession items belonging to the victim, the case would be prosecuted because it was legally sufficient. The elements of the case are present. However, what may on the surface seem to be a prosecutable case might ultimately be lost because of constitutional questions, such as an illegal search and seizure. Implementing this policy at the charging level requires only an examination for legal defects. If the basis for a charge is not legally sufficient, either additional investigation could be ordered or the case would be rejected. The legal sufficiency policy is prevalent in lower, misdemeanor courts processing large workloads or in offices given little attention to screening either by choice or necessity. A routine but rapid examination for obvious defects prior to court appearance generally constitutes the extent of screening that a case receives. As a result, overloads occur, plea bargaining is encouraged to reduce the volume, and, with scant case preparation time, dismissals and acquittals abound (see Table 1).

Table 1: Legal Sufficiency Policy Expected Frequency of Dispositions

Disposition Universe (Numeric Base for Rates)	Disposition	Frequency
Cases Presented	Reject for Prosecution	Low
	Accept for Prosecution	High
	Divert—Non-CJS	Not Predictable
	Refer—Other CJS	High
Cases Accepted	Dismiss at Preliminary Hearing	High
	Bound Over	Minimize
	Plea to Reduced Charge	Maximize
	Plea as Charged	Low
Cases Bound Over to Grand Jury	No True Bill	High
Trials	Guilty—Trial	Low
	Acquittal—Trial	Low
	Dismissed—Trial (Insufficient Evidence)	High

Policy: If the elements of the case are present, accept for prosecution
Goals: Maximize pleas, minimize bindovers

System Efficiency Policy. Another common policy is labeled "system efficiency" because it aims for the speedy and early disposition of cases by any means possible. The time to disposition and the place in the court process where disposition occurs are measures of success in addition to favorable dispositions. Under this policy, the breaking and entering case would have been rejected because emphasis is placed on screening as a primary technique for minimizing workload. The search and seizure issue would have been spotted and the case rejected at intake. If there were no search and seizure issue, after acceptance the case would have been charged as a felony and at the committing magistrate hearing the defendant might have pled to a reduced charge of unlawful trespassing or larceny (both misdemeanors). The system efficiency policy usually emerges when the trial court is overloaded or backlogged, or when the resources of the prosecutor are so limited that the early dispositions are a necessity if he is to move the caseload.

Under these conditions, in addition to the emphasis placed on pretrial screening, other methods of case disposal will be sought and used. The prosecutor himself may be an active searcher in the community for additional avenues of case disposition. Extensive use will be made of community resources, other agency resources, and diversion programs so that cases may be kept out of the criminal justice system. Cases will be examined for their ability to be plea bargained (to achieve this, over-charging may occur). If possible, charges will be broken down for handling in the lower courts or modified and referred to another court with a different jurisdiction (e.g., a county court case referred to another court with a different jurisdiction, perhaps a municipal court). Full utilization of the court's resources and the charging authority will be made to dispose of cases as soon as possible. Particular emphasis will be placed on the disposal of the case before a bindover to the higher court or grand jury. (see Table 2.)

Table 2: System Efficiency Policy Expected Frequency of Dispositions

Disposition Universe (Numeric Base for Rates)	Disposition	Frequency
Cases Presented	Reject for Prosecution	Not Predictable
	Accept for Prosecution	Not Predictable
	Divert—Non-CJS	Maximize
	Refer—Other CJS	Maximize
Cases Accepted	Dismiss at Preliminary Hearing	Low
	Bound Over	Minimize
	Plea to Reduced Charge	Minimize
	Plea as Charged	Low
Cases Bound Over to Grand Jury	No True Bill	Not Predictable
Trials	Guilty—Trial	High
	Acquittal—Trial	Low
	Dismissed—Trial (Insufficient Evidence)	Low

Policy: Dispose of cases as quickly as possible, by any means possible
Goals: Maximize early dispositions, minimize bindovers

Defendant Rehabilitation Policy. A third approach is a defendant-oriented policy. It incorporates some of the elements of the early and speedy disposition policy but should not be confused with it. Under this policy, the prosecutor believes that the most effective treatments for the vast majority of defendants who pass through his office can be found outside the formal criminal justice processing system. Citing the breaking and entering case again, if the defendant were a first offender or had a drug problem and if restitution were made to the victim, the defendant might very well be placed in a pretrial diversion program. If this option were not available, prosecution might be deferred or, with the court's concurrence, the defendant could be sentenced to probation without verdict. In a defendant-oriented policy, the charging and prosecution decision depends primarily on the circumstances of the defendant and secondarily on the offense that the defendant allegedly committed. Thus, the goal of a Defendant Rehabilitation policy is the early diversion of many defendants from the criminal justice system coupled with serious prosecution of those cases accepted. It is logical to expect vigorous prosecution of this latter category especially if the defendant's history includes prior convictions with no evidence of rehabilitation. Offices using this policy tend to rely heavily on the resources in the community, as well as in the criminal justice system, to move eligible defendants out of the judicial and correctional systems. Close cooperation with the court often ensues, particularly in using the sentence recommendation power of the prosecutor to ensure consistency in the recommended treatment plan for the defendant. (See Table 3.)

Table 3: Defendant Rehabilitation Policy Expected Frequency of Dispositions

Disposition Universe (Numeric Base for Rates)	Disposition	Frequency
Cases Presented	Reject for Prosecution	Not Predictable
	Accept for Prosecution	Minimize
	Divert—Non-CJS	Maximize
	Refer—Other CJS	High
Cases Accepted	Dismiss at Preliminary Hearing	Low
	Bound Over	High
	Plea to Reduced Charge	Not Predictable
	Plea as Charged	Not Predictable
Cases Bound Over to Grand Jury	No True Bill	Low
Trials	Guilty—Trial	High
	Acquittal—Trial	Low
	Dismissed—Trial (Insufficient Evidence)	Low

Policy: Divert, since the vast majority of defendants cannot benefit from criminal justice processing

Goals: Maximize noncriminal justice treatment, minimize prosecution of lesser offenders

Trial Sufficiency Policy. The forth policy is that of trial sufficiency. This policy states that a case will be accepted and charged at a level capable of being sustained at trial. Under these circumstances, the prosecutor views his responsibility stringently but not without leniency. The decisions to accept and to charge are crucial to the implementation of this policy. If a decision was made to charge the defendant of the hypothetical breaking and entering case and, again, if the constitutional questions of the search were overcome, the defendant would be charged with a felony and a conviction at this level would be expected. Since changing a charge is discouraged, implementation of trial sufficiency should be supported by either good police reporting or experienced investigative staff. It also requires alternatives to prosecution for the cases rejected. Most importantly, it requires court capacity because with plea bargaining minimized it is expected that the cases will go to trial. Finally, this policy, must rely on extensive management controls to ensure the proper setting of the initial charge and to ensure that the charges, once made, will not be modified or changed. (See Table 4.)

Table 4: Trial Sufficiency Policy Expected Frequency of Dispositions

Disposition Universe (Numeric Base for Rates)	Disposition	Frequency
Cases Presented	Reject for Prosecution	High
	Accept for Prosecution	Low
	Divert—Non-CJS	Not Predictable
	Refer—Other CJS	Not Predictable
Cases Accepted	Dismiss at Preliminary Hearing	Minimize
	Bound Over	High
	Plea to Reduced Charge	Minimize
	Plea as Charged	High
Cases Bound Over to Grand Jury	No True Bill	Low
Trials	Guilty—Trial	Maximize
	Acquittal—Trial	Low
	Dismissed—Trial (Insufficient Evidence)	Minimize

Policy: If a case is accepted for prosecution, it will be charged at a level capable of sustaining a conviction or a plea to charge

Goals: Maximize convictions, minimize results of sloppy charging

A CHARGING TYPOLOGY

From the policies just described, it is possible to develop models that (1) demonstrate the various goals that are consistent with each policy, (2) predict the expected outcomes for each policy and goal, (3) show by comparison that it is impossible to determine prosecutorial effectiveness from dispositional data unless the policy is known.

If one reads across the row for any particular disposition in Table 5, it is clear that the expected dispositional values may change drastically depending on the policy being used. For example, under the Legal Sufficiency policy, the number of cases dismissed[5] at a preliminary or probable cause hearing should be high. Since cases receive only routine screening for obvious defects at intake, other more serious problems may not surface until the probable cause hearing is reached. This policy, therefore, results in some prosecutorial responsibility being transferred to the court when it functions as the determinant of legal sufficiency. By contrast, the low dismissal rate can be expected in the System Efficiency policy and the Defendant Rehabilitation policy offices because of the fact that relatively few weak cases are permitted to proceed to a preliminary hearing. This is particularly characteristic of the System Efficiency policy, since the tendency is to screen first and then to negotiate pleas to those accepted. Since weak cases seldom survive these two processes, few have to be dismissed at a preliminary hearing for lack of probable cause. The cases that do survive are necessarily better prepared and so have a high probability of going to trial. The same occurs for the Defendant Rehabilitation policy, although the reason differs. There, all weaker cases have been handled by other means; the remaining cases involving the most serious crimes or defendants are set for rigorous prosecution. Finally, the Trial Sufficiency policy, which anticipates trial and conviction based on the initial acceptance/change decision, mandates that few dismissals occur, since each is a direct reflection on the quality of the intake division's decision and indicates possible errors on their part.[6]

A comparison of the effects of these policies reveals that prosecutorial performance varies with regard to the policy of the office. It follows, therefore, that policy must be identified before performance can be evaluated within an office. Table 5 presents the expected distribution of outcomes which are consistent with a certain policy. For example, the Trial Sufficiency policy (ensuring that the charge is correct and the case convictable) logically should result in a substantial rejection rate at intake, an indeterminate number of referrals to other criminal justice systems such as a municipal court, a low rate of dismissals both at the

Table 5: Expected Frequency of Selected Dispositions as a Function of Policy

Disposition Universe (Numeric Base for Rates)	Dispositions	Legal Sufficiency	System Efficiency	Defendant Rehabilitation	Trial Sufficiency
				Policies	
Cases Presented	1. Reject for Prosecution	L	N	N	H
	2. Accept for Prosecution	H	N	Mm	L
	3. Divert—Non-CJS	N	Mx	Mx	N
	4. Refer—Other CJS	H	Mx	H	N
Cases Accepted	5. Dismiss at Preliminary Hearing	H	L	L	Mn
	6. Bound Over	Mn	Mn	H	H
	7. Plea to Reduced Charge	Mx	Mx	N	Mn
	8. Plea as Charged	L	L	N	H
Cases Bound Over to Grand Jury	9. No True Bill	H	N	L	L
Trials	10. Guilty—Trial	H	H	H	Mx
	11. Acquittal—Trial	L	L	L	L
	12. Dismissed—Trial (Insufficient Evidence)	H	L	L	Mn

Key

Goals
Mx = Maximize this disposition
Mn = Minimize this disposition

Expected Outcomes
H = High frequency
L = Low frequency
N = Not predictable

probable cause hearing and at the trial level, a high frequency of bindovers since the goal is to try the case, a rarity of plea bargains, a large number of pleas to the original charge, and, correspondingly, a high percentage of convictions.

Under the System Efficiency policy (the earliest and speediest disposition of cases), an evaluator would measure success or failure in terms of the number of persons diverted from the criminal justice system or referred to other court systems, the number of cases disposed of by a plea, and the number of cases bound over (which should be minimal). Additionally, time to disposition and location in court process where disposition occurred also become factors in the evaluation of this policy.

The typology thus permits the examination of prosecutorial performance within a rational and logical system. Although the pattern of dispositions is expected to vary among policies, once policy is chosen, its disposition pattern should be reasonably regular and interpretable as prosecutors strive to decrease what they consider to be undesirable dispositions of their cases.

Strategies to Implement Policy

Assuming that certain policies logically lead to certain outcome patterns, one can then examine various strategies to implement policy. Strategies can be defined as choices available to the prosecutor to accomplish certain tasks, and at least three are immediately identifiable. They are plea negotiation, discovery, and diversion.

Plea Negotiation. One of the most important strategies used by prosecutors in disposing of cases is that of plea negotiation or plea bargaining. Recommendations to abolish this practice by 1978 were included in National Advisory Commission on Criminal Justice Standards and Goals (1973:46). The ethics of plea negotiation—whether or not a plea to a reduced charge is an acceptable form of case disposition—can be argued. Practically, however, plea negotiation plays an important role in the ability of an office to implement the policy.

Plea negotiation strategy is consistent with both the Legal Sufficiency and System Efficiency policies. Having little case preparation and review time, the assistants working under a Legal Sufficiency system will tend to accept pleas to reduced charges as a means of either correcting a charging mistake or reducing the time needed for more substantive case preparation if the case were to go to trial. Under the early and speedy disposition policy of System Efficiency, plea bargaining becomes the primary disposition route because it is the fastest and least costly conclusion. If the Defendant Rehabilitation policy is in effect, it is difficult to predict whether plea bargaining will be used, because it is not a consequence of the policy. Whether the more serious cases are allowed to plead to a reduced charge is both a function of court capacity as well as prosecutorial preference. However, under the Trial Sufficiency policy, it is entirely consistent to expect low plea bargaining since the initial premise for accepting a case for prosecution is that it be properly charged, capable of being sustained in a trial, and expected to produce a conviction. Consequently, to permit plea bargaining would be to contradict the policy.

Discovery. In its broadest definition, discovery is a procedure whereby the prosecutor "opens his case file" to the defense counsel and makes known the evidentiary strength of the case. Where discovery is not mandated by law, the defense counsel is usually limited to that information which has been filed in the court (usually the accusatory instrument) and that which he may glean from his client or from witnesses suggested by the client. Sometimes the defense counsel may not even see a copy of the arrest report until it is entered as evidence, nor may he know in advance who the witnesses for the state are.[7]

Where discovery is not mandated by state law, its use will vary according to the policy being followed by the prosecutor. Under what we have termed the Legal Sufficiency model, discovery is not likely to be used, precisely because that policy tends to process more marginal or weak cases. On the other hand, since discovery tends to produce a rate of dispositions by plea (either to the original or a reduced charge), one would expect its frequent use in both the System Efficiency and the Trial Sufficiency models. Under a policy of Defendant Rehabilitation, discovery is useful to assure the channeling of the defendant into a proper treatment program.

Diversion. Diversion is a third strategy useful in the implementation of some policies. Diversion, broadly defined in prosecutorial context, transfers the case to a noncriminal justice agency. Most typically cases are diverted from the criminal justice system to alternative treatment programs—for example, the drug abuser to TASC or the first offender to an employment program. Alternatively, a case may be referred from one part of a criminal justice system to another. For clarification purposes, we will call this a "referral," though it is similar to the broad category of diversion.

Diverting a case from the criminal justice system to programs such as educational training or medical treatment programs is a strategy that is consistent with all policies, even though the reasons for diversion may vary. Under a Legal Sufficiency model that deals mostly with misdemeanors, the universe of diverted defendants will more likely be first offenders and therefore most eligible for noncriminal justice diversion.

The System Efficiency model would make extensive use of all available diversion programs or facilities as a means of disposing of cases and reducing workload. The Defendant Rehabilitation policy views discretion as a treatment option. The Trial Sufficiency model does not necessarily need a diversionary exit; since its decisions are essentially binary in nature (trial or nothing), the use of diversion is more a matter of the individual preference of assistants for disposing of nontrial cases.

Table 6 summarizes the strategies likely to be employed by an office to implement policy. Since the ultimate goal of the prosecutive function is case disposition, how the case is disposed of by using these strategies reflects the policy of the office and the choices that are available and consistent with the policy.

Table 6: Expected Use of Strategies to Implement Policy

Policy	Strategies		
	Discovery	Plea Negotiation	Diversion
Legal Sufficiency	Not Predictable	Yes	Yes
System Efficiency	Yes	Yes	Yes
Defendant Rehabilitation	Yes; to expedite treatment	Not Predictable	Yes
Trial Sufficiency	Yes; to insure adjudication	No	Not Predictable

Resource Allocation Approaches

No matter what policy is implemented, work has to be distributed in a rational manner to achieve desired outcomes. *Many* resource allocation options which theoretically are available to the prosecutor actually may be precluded by external environmental factors. For example, it would be difficult to organize an office around a trial team concept (in which one or two assistants handle a case all the way from charging through trial to disposition) without a court processing system geared to support it. Successful trial teams flourish when cases are assigned to a specific judge or a specific courtroom or when the prosecutor controls the docket.

Most prosecutive resource allocation plans are created in response to external forces. The characteristics of police, defense, and courts, as well as office budget constraints, need to be taken into consideration in evaluating an organizational structure. After their constraints have been determined, the selection of resource allocation patterns should be made with respect to their consistency with the policy and priorities of the prosecutor. The different policies require a rational and consistent implementation of strategies as well as resource allocation patterns. For purposes of illustration, consider briefly three areas under the prosecutor's control—charging, case assignment and trial preparation, and sentence recommendation. For this discussion, assume the three decisions to be environmentally independent. Table 7 summarizes organizational variations with regard to the three areas among the policy models.

The timing and completeness of police reporting has been mentioned as essential to the charging process; equally important are the qualifications of the person making the charging decision. Table 7 shows how the experience level of the charging assistant may vary according to the policy of the office. For example, if the policy of the office is to examine cases only for Legal Sufficiency, then it is not necessary to use the most experienced assistant. Third-year law students or paralegals are capable of examining a case for simple crime elements. Their decisions or recommendations can be reviewed by less-experienced assistants.

On the other hand, the System Efficiency policy requires that the charging decision be made with respect to a speedy and early disposition. Thus, the charging assistant should have enough trial experience to know what is negotiable, enough system experience to know what can be diverted elsewhere (either to another court or other noncriminal justice programs) or what should be tried. There is little need for internal review of his charging decisions since either the case is sent elsewhere or the charge is expected to be changed. Problems will not occur so long as speedy dispositions are occurring. Final evaluation review should focus on the disposition of those cases that were processed through various steps in the system.

Similarly, the Defendant Rehabilitation policy requires experienced assistants to make the charging decision. Since the goal is to divert the treatable defendant from the system and to prosecute the recidivist who would not be eligible for diversion, the charging assistant not only must be trial experienced but also must have some social services training. The delicate decision of whom to prosecute and whom to divert offer potentially dangerous situations to an elected prosecutor. A defendant released to a community treatment program poses a certain level of risk to the community. Therefore, the prosecutor must feel confident that his decision maker is competent, experienced, and ideologically attuned to his philosophy. Since the operators of the diversion programs can accept or reject the referral, the need for a review of the charging decision in the prosecutor's office is reduced.

Finally, the Trial Sufficiency policy requires the utilization of the most experienced trial lawyers to make the charging decision. With this policy,

Table 7: Expected Patterns of Resource Allocations by Type of Policy

Policy	Resource Allocation Needs			
	Charging		Case Preparation for Trial	Sentence Recommendation
	Minimum Qualifications For Charging	Personnel Needed to Review Charges	Trial Experience Necessary	Personnel Needed for Sentence Recommendations
Legal Sufficiency	Paralegal; 3rd-Year Law Students; New Assistants	Yes	Minimal	None
System Efficiency	Trial and Criminal Justice System Experience	Not Necessary	Minimal	None, unless basis for plea bargain
Defendant Rehabilitation	Trial and Social Background	Not Necessary	Moderate	Yes, to ensure consistency with treatment
Trial Sufficiency	Extensive Trial Experience	Yes	Extensive	Yes, to ensure consistency with charge

once the decision is made to prosecute, the strategy is set; the case will go to trial and a conviction is expected. Under minimal conditions, the charging decision will be made by an experienced review, thereby diminishing the chances of something being overlooked at the initial step. Not only will the allocation of personnel to the charging and review process vary according to policy, but so too will the assignment of personnel for preparing and trying the case. The Legal Sufficiency and System Efficiency policies both move the cases after charging to assistants who first attempt to strike a bargain, and failing this, prepare the case or transfer this task to other assistants. Since the goal is to minimize trials, it is not necessary that the assistants have extensive trial experience.

The Defendant Rehabilitation policy, on the other hand, needs experienced trial lawyers to handle the few cases that reach this level. Since the cases accepted for prosecution would tend to include more serious, repeat offenders, case preparation, and trial, or even plea negotiation would be assigned to the more experienced assistants. A similar strategy would apply to the Trial Sufficiency policy which places strong emphasis on the trial phase.

After conviction and before sentencing, many prosecutors are able to make recommendations to the court about the length and type of sentence the prosecution feels suits the crime. Sentence recommendation, when used, may be a powerful prosecutorial tool. Its use, therefore, varies by policy. It would seldom be employed under the Legal Sufficiency and System Efficiency concepts, since so few cases are expected to be disposed of by trial and since the majority will be disposed of by plea negotiations.[8] For the Defendant Rehabilitation and Trial Sufficiency policies, one could expect sentence recommendation to be used extensively, since, for the former, it would ensure the consistency of treatment with the needs of the defendant and, for the latter, it would ensure the consistency of the charge with its expected punishment.

Consistency with goals is obviously the critical factor in this discussion. Just as it makes little sense to assign third-year law students at intake to determine whether a case can be bargained, so, too, it is unreasonable to use experienced lawyers merely to determine that the elements are present. When one examines any prosecutive process, the first question should be "What is the policy?" Then, "Are the organization, resource allocation plans, operations, and strategies consistent with the goals?" Consistency provides a meaningful measure of the degree of implementation of policy and opens up avenues for useful research and evaluation.

CONCLUSION

The critical impact of policy on dispositions, prosecutorial strategies, and resource allocation patterns cannot be discounted. When one evaluates the performance of the prosecutor, and more broadly the direction of all criminal justice activity, the first task is to determine what the prosecutor is attempting to do; the second is to assess how well he is performing; the third is to see whether the community agrees with him. It is only through systematic and objective analysis of prosecutorial policy and its implementation that we can gain the knowledge about the operation of an efficient and equitable criminal justice system.

Yet there are several caveats regarding this approach. The limited state of the art in this area requires that much more work needs to be done before solutions can be produced with reliability or validity. The policies discussed here were observed in actual operation; yet they do not necessarily represent all policies, nor are they always mutually exclusive within a single office. There is a need for further exploration and verification.

The "high" and "low" frequencies assigned to the dispositional patterns of the policies are unscaled. Output measures, limits, and tolerances need to be developed to make these rankings meaningful and testable. This is not a simple task. Additionally, the variables that describe organization, management, and operations within an office, as they apply to the implementation of policy, need identification and quantification. Without this, the true effect of a policy cannot be assessed.

Finally, a very basic question has yet to be addressed. Given the community's social order and the ideals of American society, which of the policies distribute justice fairly and in the most effective manner? There may not be a single policy or a single answer to this question. Nevertheless, the search should ultimately lead to some partial knowledge or answers if we are to make intelligent decisions about prosecutorial policy and performances.

NOTES

1. While recognizing the need for a "genderless" pronoun and objecting to the male stereotype of a prosecutor, the author has employed the masculine pronoun for the sake of convenience and consistency.

2. Only in Alaska, Connecticut, Delaware, New Jersey, and Rhode Island are prosecutors not elected.

3. This section is based on materials discussed in Jacoby (1977).
4. The major findings of this project are available in published form. See Jacoby, J. (1976). Other published materials are available on a loan basis or microfiche.
5. In some jurisdictions a nolle prosequi may be used in lieu of or in conjunction with disposition. For purposes of this discussion, this type of disposition will be called a dismissal.
6. A special note should be made about dispositions by dismissal, not all of which may be adverse measures of prosecutorial performance. In some offices the largest proportion of all dismissals is a result of the practice to dismiss other pending cases or counts after a conviction has been obtained on one case. In other instances, cases may be dismissed because a complaining witness refused to prosecute, the police officer failed to show, or the defendant was placed in a medical or health treatment facility. The dismissals that should be used to evaluate the performance of the prosecutor are those which reflect an insufficient case or lack of adequate preparation. Generally, they can be classified as "dismissal-insufficient evidence." One would expect this to be a relatively high outcome under the Legal Sufficiency policy, since only cursory examination is given to a case, and relatively low under the System Efficiency and Defendant Rehabilitation policies, since both seek other forms of dispositions based on extensive review of the facts and evidence. Of all dispositions possible, the most sensitive for evaluating prosecutor performance and the most accurate for measuring the effect of the charging would be a "purified" dismissal rate (that which attributes responsibility to the proper participants in the system).
7. See Grossman (1969) for an excellent discussion on abolishing this practice and the merits of implementing discovery.
8. A major exception to this statement occurs when the prosecutor bargains for a sentence, not charge. Under these circumstances, he would make use of this power.

REFERENCES

American Bar Association (1971). "Standards relating to the prosecution function and the defense function." Project on Standards for Criminal Justice. New York: Institute of Judicial Administration. (approved draft)

BAKER, N. R. and E. H. DeLONG (1933)."The prosecuting attorney—Provisions of law organizing the office." Journal of Criminal Law and Criminology 23:926.

COLE, G. F. (1968). The Politics of Prosecution: The Decision to Prosecute. Ann Arbor: Xerox University Microfilms.

EISENSTEIN, J. and H. JACOB (1977). Felony Justice: An Organizational Analysis of Criminal Courts. Boston: Little, Brown.

FEELEY, M. M. (1976). "The concept of laws in social sciences: A critique and notes on an expanded view." Law and Society 9(Summer):497-523.

GROSSMAN, B. (1969). The Prosecutor: An Inquiry Into the Exercise of Discretion. Toronto: University of Toronto Press.

JACOBY, J. E. (1971). The Prosecutor's Charging Decision: A Policy Perspective. U.S. Department of Justice, Law Enforcement Assistance Administration, National Institute of Law Enforcement and Criminal Justice. Washington, D.C.: U.S. Government Printing Office.

_____ (1976). Pre-Trial Screening in Perspective. National Evaluation Program, Phase 1 Report Series A, No. 2. U.S. Department of Justice, Law Enforcement Assistance Administration, National Institute of Law Enforcement and Criminal Justice. Washington, D.C.: U.S. Government Printing Office.

KATZ, L. R. (1972). Justice is the Crime: Pretrial Delay in Felony Cases. Cleveland: Press of Case Western Reserve University.

MILLER, F. W. (1969). Prosecution: The Decision to Charge a Suspect With a Crime. Boston: Little, Brown.

National Advisory Commission on Criminal Justice Standards and Goals (1973). Courts. Washington, D.C.: U.S. Government Printing Office.

National Center for Prosecution Management (1972). First Annual Report. Washington, D.C.: NCPM.

NEUBAUER, D. W. (1974). Criminal Justice in Middle America. New Jersey: General Learning Press.

Vera Institute of Justice (1977). Felony Arrests: Their Prosecution and Disposition in New York City's Courts. New York: Vera Institute of Justice

Chapter 4

TWO MODELS OF
PROSECUTORIAL PROFESSIONALISM

PAMELA J. UTZ

The argument of this paper is based on a comparative study of discretion and negotiation in two California court systems, San Diego and Alameda Counties (Utz, 1978). Field work, conducted in 1974, consisted of observations of felony proceedings all the way from charging at the municipal court level through superior court disposition; and of extensive interviews with some ninety selected informants from all branches of the criminal justice apparatus—probation officers, public and private defense attorneys, prosecutors, municipal and superior court judges. In addition, statistical data from the California Bureau of Criminal Statistics were utilized. The two court systems are quite comparable in size and volume; in 1973, they ranked third and fourth in the state in number of felony arrests (California Bureau of Criminal Statistics, 1975a), and had about the same number of judges (27-29) and prosecutors (about 100). Yet, they exhibited striking differences in the exercise of prosecutorial discretion and in the conduct of plea negotiations.

Although the crime problem was far less severe in San Diego than in Alameda,[1] San Diego prosecutors felt more threatened by the practice of plea bargaining. The DA's office indulged in indiscriminately "tough" charging, and then perceived "concessions" to the defense as a betrayal of law enforcement responsibilities. The top management imposed rigid restrictions on the discretion of deputies to respond to defense claims. The system as a whole encouraged a tactical, game-like approach to negotiation that often compelled both sides to resort to expedient weapons, and introduced considerable arbitrariness in case outcomes.

Alameda, by contrast, had a prosecutor's office strongly committed to "realistic" charging, and an internal organization that facilitated moderation and objectivity in the exercise of prosecutorial discretion at all stages. Alameda had evolved a pattern of "bargaining" that resembled a process of inquiry, where outcomes were reached by "settling the facts" and reasoning from shared and objective standards of seriousness.

This report is an attempt to account for those differences. My argument is that their root is traceable to different conceptions of the institutional role and professional ethic of the prosecutor. I shall begin by introducing briefly the dilemmas that inform the exercise of prosecutorial discretion. The paper moves on to characterize the two contrasting models of prosecutorial function, the *adversary* and the *magisterial*, which underlie the patterns found, respectively, in San Diego and Alameda. The argument concludes by considering the conditions that may move a prosecutor's office to espouse one or the other model.

THE PROSECUTOR'S DILEMMA

A main focus of scholarly interest in criminal justice is the broad responsibility and corollary discretion of the prosecutor. He wears many hats. The prosecutor is a law enforcement officer, charged with protecting the community against crime; as an elected official and member of the executive branch of government, he is the People's representative (and hence policy maker) in the formal and informal processes that constitute "doing justice"; as an officer of the court, as well as administrator in his own right, he shares an obligation to the efficiency and integrity of the criminal justice system. It has long been recognized that the prosecutor, in attempting to perform his multiple roles, wields considerable discretion, especially in deciding to charge a suspect with a crime and in negotiating pleas of guilty. Although dependent on the police for the flow of cases, he has the (at most imperfectly checked) power to "do nothing" or to file charges at any level that can claim support from the evidence (Davis, 1969:164; Southern California Law Review, 1969:521-523). He is the sentry at the gate of the criminal court system. Once criminal charges are initiated, the prosecutor arranges for most to be either dismissed or reduced at very early stages of processing, or at later stages he reaches agreement with the defense on the type and seriousness of conviction, and sometimes even on the sentence. Such "plea bargaining" between prosecution and defense is the rule today; proportionately few cases travel the procedurally ordered path of adversary adjudication.

Despite public expectations that the state's attorneys prosecute "without qualification" and despite the absence of express provisions for prosecutorial discretion (Goldstein, 1960:586; Kadish and Kadish, 1971:941), discretion is unavoidable. What is more, it ordinarily serves as a moderator of the criminal law. Its inevitability stems from the material impossibility of full enforcement of all criminal statutes, as well as from the harsh, often irrational character of penal codes. Codes are "notorious" for their "repetitive and overlapping" provisions, which permit multiple liability for single acts (Johnson, 1970:360); poor draftsmanship in "setting out specific elements of crimes" (Southern California Law Review, 1969:533); intentional overgeneralizations, aimed at casting the largest net (Kadish, 1962); archaisms, obscurities, and "unrealistic moral idealism" (Remington and Rosenblum, 1960: 493-494). In addition, some criminal statutes contain severe mandatory provisions that deny flexibility to individualize sentences and are therefore frequently circumvented; excessive and impractical prison terms; and little guidance on the standards to be applied in mitigation. Only major code reform, leading to more realistic and economical statutes, could begin to make prosecution less discretionary in the United States (Davis, 1969). However, such characteristics of the criminal law may be intractable. Not only is the legislature susceptible to expedient political considerations that make clarity and specificity, shorter and more reasonable terms, and less recourse to mandatory provisions imprudent; but it also has a legitimate concern for the symbolic worth of punishment in upholding moral and legal standards.

This peculiar combination of ambiguity and rigidity in the criminal law assures that much will be left to the discretion of criminal justice officials. It is the task of officials to interpret, temper, and adapt rules to accommodate the concrete individual cases that pass through the system. Only they, if anyone, can see to it that the artificial labels of conviction will correspond to substantially equitable dispositions. To do so, they must employ whatever explicit grants of discretion exist, depart from or circumvent rules, and draw on the great silences and implicit delegations of authority to be found in codes.

The problem of course is that adjustment operates covertly, away from public view and judicial review. In this shadowy area of unregulated power, the well-known dangers of discretion—"the unequal, the arbitrary, the discriminatory, and the oppressive" (Breitel, 1960:427)—are likely to emerge. There is a high risk that not only will the rights of defendants be abused but the social values at stake in apprehending and punishing criminals will be undermined. In part, the problem of invisibility lies in the persisting illegitimacy of the policy-making role of the prosecutor. By speaking in absolutes and resisting delegations of authority, the criminal law places officials at risk for their discretionary judgments, however unavoidable and desirable the judgments may be. In contrast to the regulation of economic activity, "in the field of criminal law, the regulation of social behavior, there has been little explicit recognition given to the role of administrative expertness in determining, within a legislative framework, what conduct ought to be treated as criminal" (Remington and Rosenblum, 1960:491). Penal codes do not recognize the necessity of adjusting blanket criminal provisions to the needs of communities with variable crime problems, divergent values, and variable but always insufficient resources for law enforcement. Usually, no provision is made for negotiating pleas, or for prosecution and defense sharing of judicial sentencing authority.

In addition, invisible discretion is preserved because it helps the prosecutor accommodate his multiple and conflicting roles. Prosecutors are very sensitive to their image in the community and defensive toward any suggestions of laxity. Screening and bargaining are particularly troublesome sources of unease. "Most prosecutors are elected officials, and their discomfort with an ameliorative role may be an attempt to accommodate the political demands of an electorate that tends to be vindictive toward the malefactor" (Rosett, 1967:78). Crime arouses powerful fear and ambivalence in the public. There is the evident desire to have criminals apprehended, to give them their due, and to deter crime. But there is great naivete about how these ends can be accomplished and about the limitations under which officials operate. Not surprisingly, prosecutors fear the interest of the media (California Law Review, 1971; Miller, 1969), attempt to shield themselves from public view, and strive to manage and contain public criticism. However, this fear of publicity cannot be "attributed to such a simple and obvious fact as the periodic requirement of reelection. Indeed, reelection seemed to be taken for granted, and an observer would be hard put to relate prosecutorial decisions directly to electoral requirements" (Skolnick, 1967:57). More important is the fact that prosecutors themselves are ill at ease with practices which appear to betray their law enforcement responsibility, and for which they cannot invoke any firm official warrant.

Thus, prosecutors are faced with a continuing dilemma: required to use discretion, they expose themselves to censure for doing what they must. Willy-nilly, they must remake a criminal law that they have no authority to make. Their discretionary judgments are at once unavoidable and fraught with illegitimacy.

In picturing this dilemma, the social sciences have characteristically tended to focus on the pathologies and abuses to which invisible discretion is conducive. This critical impulse has produced a now all too familiar stereotype of the prosecutor as a creature of administrative convenience and political opportunism, bent on subverting the ideals of fairness associated with formal adversary procedure. Like all stereotypes, this one obscures variations. However universal the prosecutor's dilemma may be, not all prosecutors respond to it in the same way. Furthermore, I shall argue, the stereotype tends to misrepresent the sources of the abuses it criticizes. A key to variations in the exercise of prosecutorial discretion, including the variable incidence of abuses, lies in the prosecutors' own conceptions of their professional role and responsibilities. Paradoxically, as the following paragraphs attempt to show, prosecutorial arbitrariness can be traced to an "adversary" professional ethic that aggravates the one-sidedness of law enforcement responsibilities, and hence diminishes the prosecutor's own sense of legitimacy when he seems to moderate that commitment—as in plea bargaining.

THE ADVERSARY MODEL

This prosecutorial ethic—conservative, embracing law enforcement values and identifying the prosecutor's duty with the protection of the community against offenders—manifests itself in a distinctive professional self-image. In Skolnick's view, the prosecutor "seeks to maintain, insofar as possible, a reputation for utter credibility, inevitable truth, almost of invincibility" (Skolnick, 1967:57). Whatever might puncture that reputation, including defeat in the courtroom or evidence of a conciliatory stance toward criminals, must be avoided. This posture is in part principled—in that it is based on a defensible concept of prosecutorial responsibility—but it is also fraught with expedience, for in the embrace of a law enforcement ideology, the ethic pays homage to the prosecutor's political vulnerabilities. It approves all the qualities— toughness, hardheaded bargaining, bluff, punitiveness—the exercise of which would minimize occasions for political risk.

The dilemma for the prosecutor is that his work, most notably the practice of plea bargaining, forces constant departure from this traditional ethic. The "People's advocate has arranged the great majority of sentences lumped by politicians and the press as 'lenient' " (California Law Review, 1971:968). Plea bargaining is thought to be both a threat to the innocent, since it rewards the waiver of constitutional rights, and an undeserved break for the guilty. These criticisms are not without grounds: prosecutors hold such views themselves. Thus, a gap opens up between the ethic by which the prosecutor measures his achievements and the reality of practice. The gap accounts for prosecutorial "paranoia"—a heightened sensitivity to any suggestion of doing less than his duty. Self-protection becomes imperative. The prosecutor is discouraged from openly acknowledging negotiated justice, tempted to indulge in posturing, and pressed to evade responsibility for outcomes inconsistent with his public image. Commitment to such a professional ethic conflicts with the ever pressing imperatives of managing the caseload. But both needs can be accommodated, as long as a wide area of invisible discretion is maintained. Where discretion is unaccountable, a course can be run allowing one or the other need to prevail as pressures require. In this uneasy state of reconciliation, the prosecutor's charging and bargaining practices are highly susceptible to arbitrariness.

Presuming seriousness. San Diego prosecutors revealed this adversary orientation in their approach to felony charging and screening. Charing policy was governed by a presumption of seriousness: ambiguities or evidentiary questions unresolved at the time a case was brought in by the police were deferred to preserve the office's option to prosecute at the highest level of seriousness. The chief of charging continued to believe that cases should be charged, and charged as felonies, unless there were solid reasons not to do so; by contrast, prosecutors elsewhere in the state, who had collaborated on recommendations for uniform charging standards, had come to the view that cases should not be issued unless the evidence "warranted conviction" (California District Attorney's Association, 1974:7-10). Explicit charging standards were thought too inflexible, and the office was reluctant to adopt "case-weighting," i.e., standardized case evaluation at the time of charging. The complaint rejection rate was consistently low over the years.[2] The screening of felony cases in the lower court followed a low-risk policy: cases were dismissed or reduced to misdemeanors[3] only if doing so posed little threat to the prosecutor's image of tough law enforcement. It was established office practice that such screening was directed only at cases that fell at the bottom of the scale of seriousness or in the clouded area between civil disputes and criminal offenses (e.g., petty drug possession, family quarrels, neighborhood disputes, bad rent checks). This whole approach strained against the pressure of ever-growing volume,[4] for once the presumption of seriousness is indulged, it invests cases with a potential gravity that blocks efforts at early compromise and presses the office to defer disposition to the next higher level. Indeed, superior court judges complained of many "cheap" cases that managed to move up from the lower court.

Artful charging. The adversary prosecutor's interest in projecting an image of responsible law enforcement has a major impact on the character of plea bargaining. His approach to bargaining is foreshadowed in his exercise of the charging function. Charging is closely connected to bargaining because it establishes the "asking price" in negotiation (Alschuler, 1968:85). Many observers have argued that charging discretion provides the prosecutor with a powerful instrument to satisfy the expectations of defendants for leniency while in substance making few concessions. The instrument is "overcharging," charging more, or more serious counts than those on which the prosecutor truly wants conviction. Overcharging permits the prosecutor to fulfill both his administrative need for guilty pleas and his commitment, real or expedient, to tough law enforcement and minimal leniency. At its worst overcharging is a "crude form of blackmail—accusing the defendant of a crime of which he is clearly innocent in an effort to induce him to plead to the 'proper' crime" (Alschuler, 1968:85). But in extreme form it is hardly ever practiced, because without evidence, the prosecutor is missing the leverage to induce a plea. Bargaining power shifts to the defense, which can call the prosecutor's bluff. In fact, were a prosecutor to try such a crude tactic with any frequency, he would aggravate his administrative problems, since baseless cases would go to trial or be retained in the system longer than their seriousness merited. More generally, charging is restrained by expectations of success at trial. Because the prosecutor must attend to his trial record, trial outcomes are bound to influence charging practices: "Almost invariably the charging pattern is related to a play-back effect of past trials on similar charges under similar circumstances from which prosecutors have derived experience enough to realize that to charge would be a futile gesture" (Miller, 1969:43).

The form of overcharging that is most commonly observed and most likely to aid plea bargaining does not depend on fabrication. Rather, it involves charging at the highest level the evidence will permit, with the expectation that an appropriate plea for the behavior in question would be to a somewhat lesser charge. In San Diego this practice is known as "artful charging." It requires considerable skill and intimate knowledge of the penal code, since overlapping provisions can make a range of charges formally appropriate. The charger must creatively draw out of a particular fact situation those offense counts that bring the heaviest sentence. One example will illustrate. The defendant had strong-armed a bar girl, robbing her of the night's receipts. Because he had no weapon, the prosecutor noted:

> We're talking about 1-to-life—a second degree robbery. You can't charge him with theft in addition to robbery, because of the singular circumstances. But you can charge burglary intent and assault. "Entry with intent to commit a felony" then equals burglary, meaning you can get a first degree burglary conviction, which is 5-to-life and better than second degree

robbery. Hence we can say to the guy: "We'll nail you at trial on first degree burglary, so you had better plead to second degree robbery"—which is what we know the crime is factually.

In short, the prosecutor obtains what he thinks the case deserves by trading off an excessive but technically fit charge. Provided only that the prosecutor does not drop his standard of proof too low, he has both an incentive and the legal justification to charge "the highest and the most." The practice encourages plea bargaining; it affirms the prosecutor's image as a conscientious law enforcer but does not prevent him from engaging in a "cooperative" enterprise with defendants later; and it is a lawful exercise of prosecutorial discretion.

Adversary bargaining. Judged by the logic of our adversary system of justice, overcharging is simply one of a legitimate arsenal of weapons available to the prosecution in its legal contest with the defense. Under the adversary system, the adjudication of penal cases is governed by a "formal combative theory of the criminal law, involving in effect a legal battle between prosecution and defense" (Newman, 1956:788). Each side is expected to strive as "hard as it can in a keenly partisan spirit, to bring to the court's attention the evidence favorable to that side" (Frank, 1963:80). The corollary of the adversary principle is that neither party need be concerned with the entire truth; each side is expected only to make the most compelling presentation of its view (Temple, 1976:44-45; Curtis, 1954:17-21). Overcharging is a tacit admission by the prosecutor that he does not expect the defense to be reasonable and objective in negotiations and must therefore attempt to stack the cards in his favor. True to the adversary system's metaphor of battle, he extends to bargaining—the new battlefield that has replaced trial—his familiar adversary role. He has adapted by a kind of noncooperative participation in the potentially cooperative enterprise of negotiation: he espouses a tactical game theory of bargaining. The defense in turn, witness to the display of prosecutorial partisanship, doubts the objectivity and reasonableness of the prosecutor's evaluation of cases. Hence the defense demands a quid pro quo for pleading, regardless of the possible merits of the state's case, thus futher deepening the prosecutor's belief that it is impossible to deal straightforwardly with the opposition.

Many accounts of plea bargaining in the literature testify to the calculating, self-protective, adversary stance of the prosecutor (Alschuler, 1968; Blumberg, 1967a, 1967b; Chambliss, 1969; Cole, 1970). Besides artful charging, he will take advantage of aspects of the defendant's condition, such as bail and incarceration status, that enhance the state's bargaining position. Or he will exploit the inexperience, laxity, or incompetence of the defense counsel. The concepts that populate the literature—"stronger" or "weaker" bargaining position, "taking one's advantage," "getting something out" of the opponent, and so forth— reveal the extent to which the parties to negotiation act as if each will try to "win" at the other's expense. In this game, winning is framed in penal terms. It means maximizing one's advantage in sentencing. Guilt of some sort is taken for granted; acquittals or dismissals and long mandatory prison terms simply stand at opposite ends of a continuum of possibilities (Mather, 1974).

The prosecutor's pursuit of maximal sentences is consistent with his traditional professional ethic. It is further heightened because sentences are prominent indicators of his public performance. In addition, prosecutors are highly sensitive to their most immediate audience, the police, who persistently advocate strict treatment of offenders. For those reasons, in San Diego the DA felt impelled to resist any explicit sentence bargaining. A 1970 California statute permitted sentences to be stipulated by agreement between prosecution and defense, subject to approval by the court (California Penal Code, Section 1192.5). But stipulated sentences frustrated the prosecutor's need to conceal his role as a negotiator adjusting sentences through give and take. The DA preferred a regular "plea" bargain, in which he could obtain a plea without having to specify the sentence; this left him free later at the sentence hearing to impress upon the court the need for a severe sentence. With a stipulated sentence, he was faced with the unacceptable possibility that the court might find the terms insufficiently severe, thus calling into question his professional competence and public responsibility.

The strategies and calculations for "winning" in bargaining take account of the main parameters affecting the strength of the case, that is, the seriousness of the offense and the triability of the case (Mather, 1974). The stronger the prosecutor's case, the more bargaining leverage he has against the defense, up to a limit. His leverage ceases to increase at the point where the defendant has "nothing to lose" by taking the case to trial; negotiations are then aborted if the "seriousness" of the case prevents the prosecutor from offering a negotiated outcome less severe than what the defendant is liable to receive upon trial conviction (Mather, 1974:205). How large that "nothing to lose" category is tells how much of a partisan the prosecutor is determined to be. In San Diego that category was large. In contrast to the stereotype of the expedient prosecutor, the San Diego DA was ready to make more trial work for himself out of a reluctance to "give too much away."[5] Office policy formulated at the top was to make terms for pleas so high for certain offenses (e.g., robbery or drug sale) that no negotiated settlement was possible. As a deputy explained, "There are a certain number of cases where unreasonable dispositions are offered and we go to trial because the defendant balks."

On the other hand, the weaker the prosecutor's case, the less leverage he has to obtain favorable bargains. Cases made problematic by conflicting evidence, unreliable witnesses, technical difficulties, and the like are not likely to end in trial, for defeat in the courtroom would puncture the professional self-image the prosecutor seeks to maintain (Skolnick, 1967). A number of studies have found that prosecutors, despite contrary office policy and despite a professional interest in trying difficult cases, "will offer substantial concessions rather than risk losing a jury trial" (White, 1971·65; Alschuler, 1968). Hence, the often made and only partly true observation that the prosecutor's weak cases are bargained out and his strong ones go to trial.

Unfortunately, extending the perspectives of adversary battle to the circumstances of bargaining encourages well-known abuses. First, questions arise about the fairness of the fight. Are the contestants equally well situated on the "battlefield" of bargaining? If favorable consideration of the defendant's legitimate claims depends on the leverage gained by a skilled and diligent attorney, there is unfairness to defendants whose resources are weak and not up to the task of "keeping the prosecution honest." Uneven bargaining opportunities and differential sentencing will be the result.

Second, the adversary prosecutor, highly vulnerable to public criticism, is ill-equipped to assume the role of a responsible policy maker. Charging and bargaining policies remain hidden and weak, protecting the prosecutor's ability to react expediently to the imperatives of management or to transitory political demands to "get tough." Thus, damaged is the potential of self-regulation, informed by legitimate community values and concerns, to structure and rationalize the exercise of discretion. In addition, uneven treatment will result from uncontrolled variations among individual deputies, such as variable relationships with police and defense attorneys. Finally, it should be noted that objectivity and fairness are not well served when negotiation is bound to the factors that determine probability of conviction at trial. Trial forms are designed to protect procedural justice, but truth is sometimes a casualty (Curtis, 1954; Frankel, 1975; Nagel and Neef, 1974). The strict rules and procedures of the adversary system can give no guarantee of substantive justice. On the contrary, they legitimate such a partisanship that limits the prosecutor's ability to be objective and reasonable.

*   *   *

Although the influence of adversary tactics in plea bargaining has seldom been recognized, the adversary prosecutor—without that label—has captured virtually all the attention of scholarly research, to the point where it seems suggested that he is the only model to be found in criminal justice today. Yet precisely because the adversary model of prosecution is founded on the prosecutor's attempt to manage conflicting pressures—such as volume, public criticism, professional self-conception—we should expect its applicability to be variable. "Accommodation" presumes the possibility of tensions working themselves out in differing ways, depending on context and conditions. Particular combinations of such variables as local history, court structure and organization, and community politics and values are likely to be critical in determining the character and strength of the imperatives to which the prosecutor must respond. As we shall see, the pattern of adversary bargaining may be attenuated as opportunities are presented for the prosecutor to reconstruct his traditional ethic of prosecution in a form compatible with more principled, less gamelike negotiation.

THE MAGISTERIAL MODEL

In a competing model of prosecution, aspects of which are illustrated by the Alameda County court system, the prosecutor qualifies his commitment to the perspective of "law enforcement." There emerges a new professional ethic that departs from both lawyerly partisanship and the legal absolutism of the "full enforcement" ideology. That ethic may be characterized as at once managerial and magisterial. The new professionalism is managerial insofar as it emerges from the prosecutor's obligation to administer his resources. Rational management is not satisfied by reliance upon ad hoc departures from hard-nosed practices to keep the caseload moving; rather, it strives for a more realistic appraisal of law enforcement needs and resources, the development of stricter standards of what counts as serious, and a corresponding openness to prompt, no-nonsense disposition. But the new ethic does not remain managerial only. Because a tough-minded concern for rational resource allocation compels the prosecutor to take a more objective and detached look at law enforcement claims, it spurs a moderation of prosecutorial partisanship. Managerial professionalism therefore results in strengthening a sense of magisterial responsibility that is often only latent in the prosecutor's office. The rational prosecutor must allow himself to be guided by the merits, and hence to assume a posture that elevates him above his own initial claims. Fairness to defendants is enhanced as he becomes willing to listen to defense objections and to cooperate in tempering an indiscriminately harsh penal code. And management priorities come to form institutionalized policies that help assure more even-handed outcomes.

Undercharging. In Alameda a reorientation of this kind was noticeable in the DA's reform of charging early in the 1970s. The office on its own initiative implemented strict standards of felony charging that were being debated by other prosecutors throughout the state. Under that policy, the evidence on which a felony is charged was to prove "beyond a reasonable doubt"—that is, "be of such weight that it would *warrant* conviction"—rather than to only point to a "probable" conviction by the trier of fact (California District Attorneys Association, 1974:7-10). To realize the new policy, charging in all offices was placed in the hands of experienced trial deputies who accepted the premise of a tighter standard. A case-weighting system was developed to force early evaluation of the seriousness of cases, and, in part, to counter police resistance to tightened charging. The net result was what diverse participants called a pattern of "undercharging." The prosecutor was charging at the misdemeanor level cases which legally could have been charged as felonies. To many defense attorneys, it was a movement of the DA away from the filing of inflated charges as a weapon in plea bargaining. The Alameda DA's office had come to the view that cases must be differentiated early on the basis of seriousness, for the sake of effective law enforcement as well as for office management. Undercharging is *not* a policy of leniency. As a deputy explained,

> We see very serious, violent crime around here—unlike some other systems—and there are people we want in the joint. We have x amount of energy to expend, so we're not going to waste it on these other fellows. When it comes to these other guys, we'll bargain at all levels and accept offers.

Undercharging meant the decision to press a felony would be based on a careful evaluation of whether a case truly warranted prison, and on the practical likelihood of later sustaining the charge. Realism about what cases deserve and what can be accomplished took the place of earlier illusions that law enforcement values triumph only if cases are charged as seriously as legally possible. This is not leniency or capitulation, but a recognition of limits. And it has to be understood in the light of the penal code's punitive sentence provisions,[6] which often exceed what the prosecution finds reasonably proper and which compel desperate defense resistance. Undercharging helped assure that, "when we want a guy in prison, 99 percent of the time we'll get him there." Overcharging always carries the risk of backfiring if defense attorneys call the prosecutor's bluff: there may be loss at trial, or, as volume pressure builds, cases may have to be arbitrarily bargained out at less than their real worth. Thus, by abandoning the strategy of overstating his claims, the prosecutor may sacrifice some easy "wins," but more importantly he protects serious cases from the danger of loss.

"Undercharging" also meant more cases were not charged at all. Alameda's felony complaint rejection rate was markedly higher than San Diego's, despite the fact that San Diego had a higher volume of arrests and about the same prosecutorial resources.[7] Alameda prosecutors were thus yielding less to the police on flawed, minor cases, even though they experienced less volume pressure than their southern colleagues.

Facilitating negotiation. Prosecutorial realism in Alameda extended beyond charging to facilitating negotiation in the lower court. Case weighting at the charging stage permitted early identification of felonies that could be disposed of before they reached superior court, or even before the preliminary hearing. Unlike in San Diego, early discussion with the defense was encouraged by permitting full "informal discovery": both sides would get together to review the case before the preliminary hearing. Defense attorneys attested to the prosecutor's willingness to assess the evidence, even in cases where there was a risk prosecutorial claims would be undermined, and they believed they could convince DA's to dismiss poor cases, in all but troublesome "political"[8] circumstances. Even "cold" felony cases, in which the prosecutor could press for a serious conviction, might be disposable as misdemeanors. From the defense point of view, some types of cases are most favorably bargained at an early stage, because case worth may increase as the case rises in the system. If the defendant has a prior record, is on parole, or is caught "cold," the earliest conviction may be the least severe, even though jail time or revocation of parole will be the outcome. From the prosecutor's point of view, these outcomes may seem realistic and fair; for a serious sanction is imposed, although not formally the most severe disposition possible. And the resolution is practical: it saves resources. Because most felony cases disposed of in lower court are disposed of as misdemeanors without a prison sentence (unless there is parole revocation),[9] the prosecutor often appears to give too much away. However, these outcomes in Alameda follow a hard, unsentimental appraisal of the potential sentences that such cases would receive in superior court. A prosecutor noted: "If you can't get prison commitments at trial because judges aren't giving them, say, in forgery cases, you aren't going to be considering in negotiation that you have to try for prison." So, he reasons, "Why send up even good cases if they are going to get probation? You can do that down here, too."

In the upper court, on which community scrutiny is likely to focus, the temptation is greater for the prosecutor to display the form of tough, uncompromising law enforcement. Manifesting that tension, superior court prosecutors in Alameda, as in San Diego, would rather not dismiss cases or render them misdemeanors, or go on record for a "no prison" deal. Nevertheless, a commitment to realism and openness to negotiation can still be found in Alameda. By contrast with San Diego, no strict antibargaining policies were promulgated, nor was there strong office policy against sentence bargaining. The DA's terms for a plea are not so high that the two sides cannot discuss factors of the individual case that may discount its worth, even when the case-weighting system has pegged its seriousness at the top grade. Office policy does not impose specific limits in bargaining but only points to a desired end, which may require treating cases of the same broad type differently, that is, according to finer variations. The policy is that cases which are not "prison material" should not end up on trial; hence, there must be careful individual evaluation of each case. Inevitably some cases are too serious for fruitful discussions between the parties, no matter how open the prosecutor is to the search for negotiated outcomes. These are the cases which are worth long prison terms and in which the defense has "nothing to lose" by going to trial. However, that category is smaller in Alameda than in San Diego, where the prosecutor more quickly concludes that a case is non-negotiable.

Settling the facts. The individual prosecutor in Alameda County comes to plea bargaining less as a partisan advocate than as a fellow professional ready to share in reviewing the case. Using the facts of the case, including what is known about the offender, the two sides try to determine "what really happened," and what is an equitable disposition for the particular defendant. In that process there emerges between negotiators a set of principles of mutual accountability. The principles that emerge from what can be called substantive justice negotiation are separable into steps. In the first step, "settling the facts," it is recognized that (1) the assessment of the defendant's criminal culpability will depend on all available facts, not just on evidence admissible in court under rigid procedural restraints; (2) the assessment will extend to culpability for any offense found in the discrete fact situation before the negotiators, not simply culpability for the offense as formally charged; and (3) the assessment shall bind both sides. That evaluation controls all ensuing decisions, thus restraining the impulse of the defense to "play the probabilities" and reap the benefits of procedural rules by threatening a trial, as well as the impulse of the prosecution to nurture its law-enforcement image by a show of toughness. Accordingly, technical criteria of the strength of the case, interpreted with reference to what would succeed or fail at trial, are given less authority and the negotiation process is freed from the restrictions that frustrate the rendering of truth at trial. Although the negotiators have before them a potentially wider range of relevant facts, it does not follow that standards of judgment are weaker than at trial. Quite the contrary. The parties must assess the evidence according to the norms of rational inquiry, and each side is there to hold the other accountable. Thus, negotiation continues to presume vigorous advocacy.

If, after settling the facts, the defendant is judged to be guilty of some offense, the case proceeds to the dispositional phase of negotiation. Here, the emergent principles of substantive justice are (1) that the seriousness of the offense be judged according to demonstrable social goals and authentic community values and interests; (2) that the penalty be realistically related to seriousness and not bound by the inflated prescriptions of a punitive penal code; and (3) that mitigating or aggravating factors in the particular case be rationally assessed on the basis of supportable claims. Thus, the prosecutor is restrained from demanding the maximum to "set an example" or to curry his image in the community. He must be able to support his claims by reference to documented problems and realistic concerns in the community, to authoritative legal and penal goals, or to legitimate interests of the defendant.

In practice, these principles come to be embodied in specific, though implicit, norms of seriousness or case worth. In effect, a flexible tariff informed by an accumulated experience tends to replace the abstract, harsh, and rigid prescriptions of the penal code. Those norms are sensitive to changing social perceptions of offenses and penalties, and they evolve over time. Hence, different county court systems may negotiate according to the same principles and yet vary in how they assess the severity of different offenses. In this substantive justice model, negotiation is not tied to any one scale of severity, but rather to a process that helps assure that weightings are grounded in demonstrable claims and authentic interests. For example, a justifiable "disparity" in law enforcement can result from variable community urgencies or changing conceptions of what offenses constitute important crimes. Prosecutors in one county, responding to community alarm at drug use among teenagers, feel constrained to take drug offenses seriously, while in another county, they must take account of local juries that refuse to convict even on misdemeanor drug charges. These conceptions, which are accessible to prosecutors, judges, and defense attorneys in numerous ways, provide a legitimate resource for developing the norms of seriousness that will operate in a court system.

For the prosecutor, the magisterial ethic helps resolve the apparent tension between his actual way of doing business—plea bargaining—and his ideal responsibility for law enforcement. As the process of substantive justice negotiation is experienced, he discovers that his fundamental obligations can be met even as he responds to defense interests. The new legal professionalism integrates work and duty. Because negotiation is conducted in a principled way, plea bargaining acquires a legitimacy that the adversary ethic was incapable of supplying. Not only the results, but also the character of the process permit participants to affirm its worth. In addition, when responsibility for "full" enforcement is eased, the "concessions" imposed by administrative imperatives can be viewed as opportunities for enhancing the effectiveness of prosecution. Thus, tighter charging and the unsentimental jettisoning of cases that do not meet standards of seriousness and strength are "concessions" that can be "noble means" of rationalizing enforcement. "If charging is good," Alameda deputies explain, "there should be a very good conviction rate." A good trial conviction rate will in turn discourage unnecessary trials and strengthen the habit of negotiation. And the office can concentrate resources on the prosecution of cases that count. If the prosecutor gauges his fulfillment of duty by such standards, he is less likely to judge himself derelict in bargaining pleas. Negotiation is legitimized, and there need not be shame in the attenuation of adversariness. The more the actors themselves can justify what they do, the less need there is for cover and deception, and the less opportunity there is for expediency, uncontrolled discretion, and arbitrariness.

INSTITUTIONAL CONDITIONS

It is tempting to regard the political context as the most important factor in shaping the basic orientations of a prosecutor's office. San Diego, which has not yet entirely shed its small-town ethos, is a deeply conservative community. The crime problems attendant on rapid growth have heightened public alarm and demands for "law and order." Alameda, in comparison, has a strong liberal community, and its major city, Oakland, is a tough urban core with a long experience of hard crime. But political context alone is not enough to account for the character of an organization as complex as the prosecutor's office. It is quite possible for a liberal county to harbor a "conservative" adversary prosecutor like San Diego's. Indeed, at the time of this study, Alameda's liberal neighbor, San Francisco, had all the hallmarks of just that pattern: tough and indiscriminate charging, gamelike bargaining, and opportunistic adaptations to volume pressure.

The autonomy of the DA. More important than political context are the institutional relations between the prosecutor's office and other agencies of county and city government, especially law-enforcement agencies. A key difference between the San Francisco and Alameda DAs was the former's subjugation by the one combined city-county government under which his district falls. The office was kept on a budget considerably below the level of other California cities with similar crime problems, while also being periodically pressed by vigorous "clean up" campaigns. The San Francisco DA had about half the staff of Alameda and San Diego. Yet its 1972 crime rate was significantly higher than that of the other counties.[10] In addition, the office had to contend with the monolith of an old-fashioned, big-city police department.

By contrast, the Alameda prosecutor was able to remain independent of the many weak and dispersed county and municipal governments of the district, as well as of the scattered sets of local police departments. Left to pursue its own course, the office has long had a strong professional orientation and a reputation for progressive methods. Over the past fifty years, it has had few of the patronage or tenure problems associated with political control. All of the only four DAs who held office during that time were assistants to their predecessors. The office's professional reputation is a strong source of self-esteem for deputies and an important hedge against hostile criticism from "law-and-order" groups.

The organization of defense. In addition, key differences in structure and organization in the Alameda and San Diego court systems help account for the contrasting models of prosecution that dominate them. Perhaps the chief institutional variable is the strength of the defense. With appropriate resources, the defense can play an important role in moderating prosecutorial partisanship. When it can neither be bullied nor duped and can keep the prosecution "honest," the defense joins in developing the new professional ethic that supports magisterial negotiation. In this respect Alameda had what San Diego lacks: a public defender's office with the staff and budget that enabled it to approach the DA's office and impact on the court system. San Diego, however, had no public defender but had developed a hybrid system for providing counsel to indigent defendants. Three-quarters of the indigent caseload was assigned to private counsel selected from a court-approved list, and the other quarter was handled by Defenders, Inc., a small nonprofit corporation with a staff of 20-25 attorneys, mostly young and inexperienced. In size, the Alameda PD compared favorably with the DA's office, and it far surpassed the San Diego defenders as an institutional match for the prosecutor.

Institutional parity moderates the adversary instincts of the prosecutor, forcing him to be reasonable and responsive. Under parity conditions, the DA's office holds no disproportionate leverage in bargaining, and must accept negotiation as a process that is not conducted on prosecutorial terms only. The prosecution is up against opponents who have inside knowledge of the DA's management problems, can exert "nuisance power" (Skolnick, 1967:63), and are as experienced in manipulating the system as the prosecution. A strong defense is not threatened by prosecutorial claims. Since it can readily question them, it is also more open to acknowledging their merits, and more easily disposed to accepting its own claims being questioned. That responsiveness in turn is crucial in convincing the prosecution that it can afford to relinquish inflated charges and threatening sentence demands. And having to live with the PD's capability tends to discourage those restrictive bargaining policies prosecutors like to formulate for public consumption.

Responsive administration. The internal structure of authority within the prosecutor's office conditions the relations between prosecution and defense. A tight chain of command, in which rigid rules circumscribe the judgment of individual deputies, is neither the only nor always the best way to achieve uniform dispositions. Deprived of discretion, deputies may in fact be prevented from responding appropriately to such factual and legal considerations as they may learn in the process of negotiation. Thus, bureaucratically enforced rules will interfere with the careful weighing and evaluation that genuine uniformity of treatment requires. The alternative to bureaucratic control is delegation within the framework of shared conceptions of policy. The Alameda DA's office had a compartively diffuse authority structure. Branches were relatively independent and cohesive, and each branch chief had multiple duties and wide authority. Although he periodically looked over disposition sheets, the felony deputies were essentially on their own. But they were expected to—and did—bring problems to the chief and to the few highly experienced deputies who did the charging and negotiated the more difficult or sensitive cases. This arrangement was part of a deliberate effort by the District Attorney to capitalize on the flexibility of a decentralized administrative structure while assuring professionalism and minimizing the disparities of practice that too much autonomy can bring. The "older hands" also brought to the lower court offices an appreciation of the court system as a whole, and offered a model of prosecutorial pragmatism. Although the Alameda superior court office was more formal and rigid in organization, nevertheless the experienced deputies who handled pretrial negotiations had the authority to respond to defense arguments that warranted a change in the evaluation of a case and thus to reach agreements without prior authorization by top-level management. Rather than fixing an unbending office position, the management's injunction to deputies was: "Never take a plea you can't explain." The chief significance of such agreements is to permit a more genuine participation by the DAs in the process of negotiation, that is, a participation less hampered by the one-sided expectations generated before the process begins. By contrast, a more centralized, hierarchical office structure can block the natural flow of negotiation and the formation of a shared professionalism between prosecutors and defense attorneys. This was apparent in the San Diego office, where a strict chain of command restrained deputies' departure, in the course of negotiations, from the severe bargaining demands set in advance by management.

The inner dynamics of negotiation. The conditions of suspicion and tension engendered by adversary prosecution are deeply frustrating and unstable. Rigidly partisan tactics tend to be self-defeating because they bring only more of the same. A process of escalation results in undermining all sides' attempts to secure their fundamental interests. Rampant arbitrariness and uncertainty about one's ability to obtain the other side's recognition of even the most legitimate claims increase the pressure to respond in kind—to use more tactical leverage, bluffs, threats, to play the odds, to engage in distortion and inflation, to trade favors. The effect is to aggravate the arbitrariness and uncertainty that were to be countervailed. Thus, inherent in negotiation, especially because for the official actors there will always be a next time, is a strong incentive to bring some order and regularity to it (Eisenberg, 1976). Pressure builds to reduce arbitrary outcomes and to fashion rules that will forestall adversary tactics. Shared standards offer a means for both sides to assess each other's claims, to rationalize acceptable arguments, and to rule out purely tactical moves, thereby enhancing the probability of outcomes that satisfy their basic interests and are substantively just. Furthermore, administrative imperatives favor a model that promises greater economy and efficiency. Administrative needs are poorly met by the ad hoc, hidden accomodations a "full-enforcement" ideology compels. The magisterial ethic of prosecution permits, and is sustained by, a more rational allocation of resources.

The structure of the court. Finally, the organization of criminal courts has a decisive, though in some respects inadvertent, role in either hindering or facilitating rational negotiations. In Alameda, the emergence of a shared professionalism among DAs and PD's was in part fostered by the organization of work in the lower court. The largest Alameda County municipal court processed its felony cases through two specialized departments. To each felony department Deputy DAs and

PDs were assigned for six-month tours of duty. They, the judge, and the probation officer attached to the department became a team highly skilled in the initial processing and early disposition of felony cases. This organization favored a blurring of identities. Trust and colleagueship were encouraged. Working partnerships laid the foundation for a collaborative assessment of factual issues and for shared understandings about appropriate outcomes, with minimal formalism and rigidity.

Even more important was the willingness and ability of the courts to "mediate." Even a strong defense may have to lean on judicial support in order to bend the prosecution. Because the public stance of a prosecutor is always vulnerable to the political environment of law enforcement, he is likely to need periodic prodding, no matter how "progressive" the community or how rational his management. There is always a risk of regression to prosecutorial partisanship, especially in sensitve cases or in times of perceived crisis. In Alameda, for example, the DA's office, mindful of its dependence on the continued collaboration and good will of the police, would occasionally feel compelled to indulge exaggerated claims all the way to defeat at trial. More often, self-protection may impel the prosecutor to let the court assume responsibility for some outcomes. For instance, he might privately acquiesce to sentencing terms that he would resist having explicitly included in a plea agreement for fear they might appear too lenient to an uninformed public. Under such conditions, judicial intervention may be the last chance for a resolution. Alameda judges tried to urge each side to be "reasonable about what has happened and what the disposition should be. . . . We encourage full-disclosure. . . . Full participation of the judge is needed." A judge can prod the DA out of his defense posture, temper the defense need for an overly explicit agreement, and steer both sides to an acceptable outcome. Such a mediating approach has prevailed in the Alameda court system, in part because the court instituted a specialized pretrial system; two departments, staffed from among the most competent, experienced, and respected judges, were made responsible for supervision of the bulk of plea agreements. These two departments conduct negotiation sessions in chambers, reduce the diversity of judicial styles, and help train skilled, knowledgeable judges.

In contrast, at the time of this study, the San Diego court had no firm commitment to mediation, and no specialized pretrial departments to oversee negotiations. Official opinion has generally been opposed to the judge's involvement in plea negotiation (Gallagher, 1974; American Bar Association, 1974; University Pennsylvania Law Review, 1964). The chief reason for opposition is that, under current practice, mediation requires the judge to play a dual role. On the one hand, he must be a facilitator of negotiations who stimulates dicussions between the two sides, supports the demands of each side for justification of the other's claims, and bears witness to the norms of seriousness or case worth that are invoked. On the other hand, he is expected to exercise his own independent authority to fix the sentence. These two functions are in tension, especially when the judge is pressed to reassure the parties that the sentence will not frustrate expectations that condition the plea. Conventional wisdom has it that the proper response to this tension is for the judge to keep aloof from the process of bargaining. But, whatever prevents the parties from controlling the sentence—their most vital interest in the bargain—must also diminish the openness and rationality of negotiations. Both sides are compelled to resort to indirect and covert ways of reducing uncertainty, such as "judge-shopping" or distorting the charges, and these tactical maneuvers frustrate the quest for a more objective and responsible process. A principled system of negotiation ultimately may depend on a more explicit recognition of sentence bargaining, which is in fact the central object of any "plea" bargaining. This may require that judges be ready to share their sentencing authority openly and retreat to the more modest role of true mediators, upholding the standards of mutual accountability upon which genuine negotiation depends.

* * *

In conclusion, let us return to the problem of prosecutorial discretion. The fashionable view of criminal justice reformers today is that discretion is inherently abusive; hence, the goal of reform should be to narrow discretion by elaborating procedural rights, tightening rules, and subjecting prosecutorial decisions to judicial review (Davis, 1969; Packer, 1964). The main point of this study has been to show that abuses of prosecutorial authority are not inherent in discretion; rather, they are contingent upon the context and the manner in which discretion is exercised.

If this argument is correct, there should be roads to reform other, and perhaps indeed better, than formal restrictions on prosecutorial discretion. The latter are excessively costly, in part because their effect is often only to drive discretion underground (Damaska, 1973; Abrams, 1971). In a world of limited resources and variable crime problems, too many decisions must depend on how officials set their priorities: penal codes can set guidelines, but it is unavoidable that prosecutors make policy within them. More important, discretion is of great value in the quest for justice. No system of fixed rules, however finely detailed, can assure balanced judgments of the seriousness of what concrete offenders do under particular circumstances, and of what penalties will best serve the human and social interests at stake in particular situations. Even equal treatment is frustrated by rule-bound systems that cannot take account of the nonroutine, ungeneralizable, idiosyncratic factors whose recognition often spells the difference between a just result and a bureaucratically "correct" one. From the standpoint, there may be no adequate alternative to a discretionary system that has flexibility, responsiveness, and sufficient resources for informing competent judgments.

The alternative to narrowing discretion is reform that builds upon the institutional contexts and social dynamics that shape the responsibilities and the professional aspirations of the prosecutor. This study suggests that supports for a responsible exercise of prosecutorial discretion *can* be found in the organizational fabric of criminal courts. An institutional approach to reform offers no clear or instant legal cure to abuses of official discretion.[11] But perhaps it has the merit of being grounded in a more sober and realistic appraisal of the limits of formal accountability, of the requirements of genuine change, and of, last but not least, the inherent complexity of "doing justice."

NOTES

1. The California Bureau of Criminal Statistics (1975b) reported crime rates of 1072.6 per 100,000 population in San Diego and 2097.0 in Alameda in 1966; 2288.3 and 4223.7 in 1972; and 3003.2 and 4658.7 in 1974. The rates are based on seven major offenses against persons and property. The most marked difference between the two counties is in rates of personal violence crime: in 1973, the San Diego rate was 309.6 and the Alameda rate 743.6

2. The California Bureau of Criminal Statistics reported a series of data that can be utilized to develop an approximate measure of the complaint rejection rate. It is sufficient for purposes of comparison. Using data on the total felony complaints sought by the police each year and the estimate of total felony filings by the prosecutor in court (see note 4 below), the percentage of felony rejections by the prosecutor may be calculated. In 1973 on a sample basis and in 1974 for all cases in selected counties, including San Diego but not Alameda, the BCS has utilized a new system that gives a straightforward indication of complaint rejection.

San Diego	1966	1967	1968	1969	1970	1971	1972	1973	1974
Police Felony Complaints	2,251	3,061	4,372	6,079	7,954	8,277	N/A	N/A	13,423
DA Felony Issuances	2,148	2,820	3,951	6,058	7,200	7,468	8,376	7,234	N/A
Percent Issued	95.4	92.1	90.4	99.7	90.5	90.2	—	—	—

The new BCS system of data compilation ("offender-based transaction statistics"), obtained prior to publication, shows the following rejection rate in 1974:

Police Felony Arrests	19,908	
Released by Police	3,006	
Requested Felony	14,893	
D.A. Rejected	2,454	= 16.5% Rejection Rate
D.A. Granted	12,439	
Misdemeanor	6,775	
Felony	5,664	

In 1973 the BCS took only a sample of cases under the offender-based system in San Diego. In a personal communication, the BCS noted that the 1973 rejection rate was about 16% of the felony complaints requested, nearly the same as in 1974. Unfortunately, Alameda County was not selected for the offender-based transaction statistics sample that included San Diego. Hence the less precise and less direct method of assessing complaint rejections must be utilized.

Alameda	1966	1967	1968	1969	1970	1971	1972	1973	1974
Police Felony Complaints	3,419	4,441	5,860	8,660	10,345	9,871	N/A	N/A	11,511
DA Felony Issuances	2,658	3,081	4,109	6,115	6,868	6,507	5,698	4,620	N/A
Percent Issued	77.7	69.4	70.1	70.6	66.4	65.9	—	—	—

Figures on police felony complaints are not available for 1972 and 1973, but estimates can be projected from earlier experience. For those years, only the total numbers of police complaints brought in after felony arrests, including those brought in as misdemeanors, are available. If we determine from earlier years the proportion of the total brought in by the police as felonies, that proportion can be used to extrapolate police felony complaints estimates for the two missing years. The proportion is about 90%. Based on those estimates, the percent issued by the DA appears to have dropped even further in 1972 to slightly below 60%, and in 1973 to further below that level. One should regard these figures skeptically, but one can be confident in the overall rejection trend as it compares with San Diego (BCS, 1975b).

3. The California Bureau of Criminal Statistics (1975b) reported that of all felony cases the following percentages were disposed in lower rather than upper court:

	1966	1967	1968	1969	1970	1971	1972	1973
San Diego	14.7	19.5	28.1	28.5	48.0	50.7	61.0	50.5
(N:	2,018	2,673	3,462	5,538	7,033	7,623	8,404	7,389)
Alameda	39.8	47.3	48.6	53.6	64.5	61.1	53.8	59.6
(N:	2,567	2,990	3,667	6,201	6,614	6,437	5,961	4,557)

In only one year has San Diego shown a higher proportion of felony cases disposed of in lower court.

4. The California Bureau of Criminal Statistics reported the following numbers of felony complaints brought by police to the district attorney:

	1966	1967	1968	1969	1970	1971	1972	1973	1974
San Diego	2,251	3,061	4,372	6,079	7,954	8,277	N/A	N/A	13,423
Alameda	3,419	4,441	5,860	8,660	10,345	9,871	N/A	N/A	11,511

The following is an estimate of felony complaints filed by the DA in San Diego and Alameda courts:

	1966	1967	1968	1969	1970	1971	1972	1973
San Diego	2,148	2,820	3,951	6,058	7,200	7,468	8,376	7,234
Alameda	2,658	3,031	4,109	6,115	6,868	6,507	5,698	4,620

The estimate of total felony filing volume is calculated by combining lower court dispositions (felonies terminated in municipal court) and total filings in superior court, the two measures available from BCS data. This can only be an approximation of the true filing volume because the lower court figures refer to *dispositions* in any one year. The BCS counsels that dispositions tend to overestimate filings by between 10% and 15%. To estimate the actual felony filing totals for this study, the lower court disposition measure was reduced by 12% and combined with the upper court filings. The figures above, although not quotable as the precise filing volumes, are valid for purposes of comparison. Although 1973 shows a drop in filing volume for San Diego, the trend has been on the increase since 1966 at least; the increase resumed in 1974, according to district attorney figures (BCS, 1975b).

5. In the context of a growing caseload, the San Diego DA's Office showed no hesitation in assuming more trial work for itself. A statistical memorandum of August 6,1974, prepared by the office showed a 25% increase in jury trials from 1972-1973 to 1973-1974 (252 to 315). Court trials increased by 38% (154 to 213).

6. The study on which these accounts are based took place before penal tariffs and the distribution of sentencing authority were drastically revised in the "Uniform Determinate Sentencing Act of 1976," California Statutes, 1976, Chapter 1139.

7. See note 2 above. The California Bureau of Criminal Statistics (1975b) reported that police brought 7,954 felony complaints to the San Diego prosecutor in 1970, and 13,423 in 1974. Alameda, however, had 10,345 complaints brought in to the prosecutor in 1970 and only 11,511 in 1974. Similarly, San Diego had 15,757 felony arrests in 1973 and 19,908 in 1974. Alameda in contrast had 13,695 arrests in 1973 and 14,908 in 1974. Staffing levels (about 100 prosecutors in 1974) were virtually identical in the two offices.

8. Political cases connote automatic high visibility. News media or other audiences of the prosecutor (e.g., the police) keep a close watch on prosecutorial handling of the case from its initiation to its termination. As a result, the prosecutor is compelled to assume uncharacteristic postures, such as an unwillingness to negotiate, even though a case with similar facts and must lower visibility could well be disposed of by negotiation. A classic example of a political case in Alameda County was that of the arrest and trial of two members of the "Symbionese Liberation Army," the group that kidnaped Patricia Hearst.

9. It was also possible for felony pleas to be taken in the lower court and certified to the upper court for sentencing. This occurred in a small number of cases, sometimes very serious prison-type cases.

10. The California Bureau of Criminal Statistics (1975b) reported that in 1972 the crime rate per 100,000 population was 5,636.5 in San Francisco, compared with 4,223.7 in Alameda and 2,288.3 in San Diego County.

11. It may be necessary to develop new roles for the court in order to strengthen institutional controls of prosecutorial discretion. For more on that possibility, see Utz (1978) and Harvard Law Review (1976).

REFERENCES

ABRAMS, N. (1971). "Internal policy: Guiding the exercise of prosecutorial discretion." UCLA Law Review 19(1):1-59.

ALSCHULER, A. (1968). "The prosecutor's role in plea bargaining." University of Chicago Law Review 50(1):50-112.

_____(1975). "The defense attorney's role in plea bargaining." Yale Law Journal 84(6):1179-1314.

American Bar Association (1974). Standards Relating to the Administration of Criminal Justice. Chicago: American Bar Association.

BLUMBERG, A. (1967a). Criminal Justice. Chicago: Quadrangle Books.

_____(1967b). "The practice of law as a confidence game." Law and Society Review 1(2):15-39.

BREITEL, C. (1960). "Controls in criminal enforcement." University of Chicago Law Review 27(3):427-435.

California Bureau of Criminal Statistics (1975a). Criminal Justice Profile: Statewide. Sacramento, Calif.: Department of Justice.

_____(1975b). Criminal Justice Profiles: Alameda and San Diego Counties. Sacramento, Calif.: Department of Justice.

California District Attorneys' Association (1974). Uniform Crime Charging Standards. Los Angeles: California District Attorneys' Association.

California Law Review (1971). "Judicial supervision over California plea bargaining: Regulating the trade." 59(4):962-996.

CARTER, L. (1974). The Limits of Orders. Lexington, Mass.: Lexington Books.

CHAMBLISS, W. (1969). Crime and the Legal Process. New York: McGraw-Hill.

COLE, G. F. (1970). "The decision to prosecute." Law and Society Review 4(3):331-343.

CURTIS, C. P. (1954). It's Your Law. Cambridge, Mass.: Harvard University Press.

DAMASKA, M. (1973). "Evidentiary barriers to conviction and two models of criminal procedure: a comparative study." University of Pennsylvania Law Review 121(3):506-589.

DAVIS, K. C. (1969). Discretionary Justice. Baton Rouge: Louisiana State University Press.

EISENBERG, M. (1976). "Private ordering through negotiation: dispute settlement and rule making." Harvard Law Review 89(4):637-681.

FRANK, J. (1963). Courts on Trial. New York: Atheneum.

FRANKEL, M. (1975). "The search for truth: An umpireal view." University of Pennsylvania Law Review 123(5):1031-1059.

GALLAGHER, K. (1974). "Judicial participation in plea bargaining: A search for new standards." Harvard Civil Rights-Civil Liberties Law Review 9(1):29-51.

GOLDSTEIN, J. (1960). "Police discretion not to invoke the criminal process: Low-visibility decisions in the administration of justice." Yale Law Journal 69(4):543-594.

Harvard Law Review (1976). "Plea bargaining and the transformation of the criminal process." 90(3):564-595.

JOHNSON, P. (1970). "Multiple punishment and consecutive sentences: Reflections on the Neal Doctrine." California Law Review 58(2):357-390.

KADISH, S. (1962). "Legal norms and discretion in the police and sentencing process." Harvard Law Review 75(5):904-931.

KADISH, M., and S. KADISH (1971). "On justified rule departures by officials." California Law Review 59(4):905-960.

MATHER, L. (1974). "Some determinants of the method of case disposition: decision-making by public defenders in Los Angeles." Law and Society Review 8(2):187-216.

MILLER, F. (1969). Prosecution: The Decision to Charge a Suspect with a Crime. Boston: Little, Brown.

NAGEL, S. and M. NEEF (1974). "The adversary nature of the American legal system from a historical perspective." New York Law Forum 20(summer):123-164.

NEWMAN, D. J. (1956). "Pleading guilty for considerations: A study of bargain justice." Journal of Criminal Law, Criminology, and Police Science 46:780-790.

PACKER, H. (1964). "Two models of the criminal process." University of Pennsylvania Law Review 113(1):1-68.

REMINGTON, R. and V. ROSENBLUM (1960). "The criminal law and the legislative process." University of Illinois Law Forum, 1960 (winter):481-499.

ROSETT, A. (1967). "The negotiated guilty plea." Annals of the American Academy of Political Sociel Science 374(November):70-81.

SKOLNICK, J. (1967). "Social control in the adversary system." Journal of Conflict Resolution 11(1):52-70.

Southern California Law Review (1969). "Prosecutorial discretion in the initiation of criminal complaints." 42(3):519-545.

University of Pennsylvania Law Review (1964). "Guilty plea bargaining: compromises by prosecutors to secure guilty pleas." 112(6):865:908.

UTZ, P. (1978). Settling the Facts: Discretion and Negotiation in Criminal Court. Lexington, Mass.: Lexington Books.

WHITE, W. (1971). "A proposal for reform of the plea bargaining process," pp. 59-85 in Ninth Annual Defending Criminal Cases Law Forum. New York: Practicing Law Institute.

Chapter 5

HIGHLIGHTS OF PROMIS RESEARCH

WILLIAM A. HAMILTON

The manager has a specific tool: information. He does not "handle" people; he motivates, guides, organizes people to do their own work. His tool—his only tool—to do all this is the spoken or written word or the language of numbers. . . . Without ability to motivate by means of the written or spoken word or the telling number, a manager cannot be successful [Drucker, 1954:346].

If this view of management applies to courts and to prosecution agencies, we would not expect to find successful management in that sector very often. For it is clear that very few prosecutors, judges, or court administrators ever see telling numbers. Their recordkeeping systems are, in fact, usually incapable of yielding such numbers.

Courthouse folklore is commonly substituted for telling numbers in the formulation of public policy in the court and prosecution arena. The folklore, in turn, is based, in large part, on atypical, albeit interesting, cases that people find easy to remember. Frankfurter and Pound (1922) saw this problem over half a century ago when they collaborated in an empirical study of the criminal courts of Cleveland, Ohio: "The System is judged not by the occasional dramatic case, but by its normal, humdrum operations. In order to understand how law functions as a daily instrument of the community's life, a quantitative basis for judgement is essential."

The use of a new information management technology by prosecution and court agencies throughout the United States has underscored how

EDITOR'S NOTE: This is an edited version of a paper presented at a Colloquy on Criminal Justice Information Systems sponsored by the Council of Europe and Hosted by the Ministry of Justice of The Netherlands, October 23-25, 1978.

little we know about the normal, humdrum operations of the rule of law in our lives. More importantly, the use of this new technology suggests that prosecutors, judges, and court administrators can formulate much more rational policies and become much more successful managers when they have a quantitative basis for judgment.

The new technology is known as PROMIS. When it went into operation in January 1971 in the Washington D.C., prosecutor's office, PROMIS was an acronym that aptly described the function: Prosecutor's Management Information System. This is no longer true. In the ensuing seven years, PROMIS has evolved into a highly flexible case management information technology that can serve the needs of trial courts as well as prosecution agencies. Moreover, the latest version of the technology will soon be supporting civil as well as criminal case management needs and appellate court as well as trial court needs. Almost certainly, the PROMIS technology will also prove adaptable to regulatory and administrative law agencies in the future.

The Institute for Law and Social Research (INSLAW), a nonprofit research and development corporation in Washington, D.C., developed the PROMIS technology under funding from the United States Department of Justice, Law Enforcement Assistance Administration (LEAA).

With LEAA funding, PROMIS has been placed into operation in some twenty locations throughout the United States, including Los Angeles County, Manhattan, Detroit, Indianapolis, St. Louis, Milwaukee, New Orleans, Salt Lake City, Louisville, the state of Rhode Island, and, of course, Washington, D.C., where it originated. In recent months, LEAA has granted funds to install PROMIS in the other four boroughs of New York City (Brooklyn, Bronx, Queens, and Staten Island), in virtually every other major urban center of New York (state), in all of the superior courts of the state of Massachusetts, and in virtually every major urban center of the states of New Jersey and Michigan. In all, there are over 100 local or state prosecution and/or court agencies installing PROMIS in the United States. In addition, PROMIS is currently being installed within the federal legal system as a management tool of one of the major legal divisions of the U.S. Department of Justice: the Lands and Natural Resources Division.

PROMIS RESEARCH

PROMIS data is being placed in the public domain and will undoubtedly be a major source of criminal justice research in the future. Some of that research has already begun. In this chapter we review the highlights of several of the PROMIS-based studies which have been made at INSLAW.

Similar but Forgotten Problems
a Half Century Apart

The Frankfurter-Pound study of the Cleveland criminal courts in 1922 was followed by a number of other similar studies in the 1920s in St. Louis, Chicago, New York, and other cities. Most of what those studies found has been forgotten in the intervening half century. It is quite interesting that some of the insights from the PROMIS data in the 1970s for the first thirteen jurisdictions (Brosi, 1979) to become operational closely resemble what was found—and forgotten—in the ad hoc, hand-count studies of the 1920s. Some examples of these parallels are:

• The most common fate of an arrest for a serious crime is outright dismissal. Roughly 50% to 70% of felony arrests are either refused prosecution or dismissed before trial.

• One of the two principal reasons for this high case mortality is that police officers are not trained in how to collect evidence and lack incentives for making "quality" arrests, i.e., arrests that can stand up in court.

• The other major reason for case mortality is that lay witnesses and victims are not interviewed promptly and, lacking adequate communications, fail to show up when they are supposed to.

• There is a subset of defendants in the courts who are professional or career criminals, who are engaged in such crimes as robbery, burglary and larceny, and who appear before the same court 10 to 20 times in a decade for different crimes.

• Cases against "career criminals" are just as likely to be dismissed as cases against other defendants.

• As a medium for disposing of cases in court, trials are statistically insignificant. Except for outright dismissals, the most common medium of disposition is a plea bargain.

Cross-Jurisdictional Comparisons

Because the same information management technology is being used by agency after agency across the United States, we are beginning to get some clues about normal and abnormal volumes and proportions in our court systems. If studied, the exceptions to the norms may some day yield insights into court and prosecution management. For example, PROMIS data (Brosi, 1978) have revealed the following contrasts:

• Witness problems (i.e., the proportion of the case mortality attributed to problems with lay witnesses) are usually high in Detroit and unusually low in Indianapolis.

• In Detroit, plea settlements occur comparatively early in the court process and this, presumably, saves court time.

- New Orleans has a very low rate of rearrest while on conditional release (bail, probation, or parole).

- Indianapolis has a very high incarceration rate, and Detroit has a very low one.

- Los Angeles, New Orleans, and Indianapolis have short periods of time between arrests and final dispositions, while the State of Rhode Island experiences significantly long delays.

Criminal Justice Policy Studies

Under funding from LEAA, INSLAW has been conducting a series of indepth policy studies. These studies have utilized data from the Washington, D.C., prosecutor's office because that jurisdiction, as the first PROMIS user, had, at the time the studies began, the most extensive data base for research.

These studies have raised serious questions about the validity of many widely held opinions about how our court systems operate, particularly with regard to issues such as bail, speedy trial, plea bargaining, and sexual assault. This is consistent with what one would expect if, as believed, policymakers and opinion leaders have not had telling numbers available to them.

Most importantly, the connection between a quantitative basis for judgment and improved policymaking is apparent because the studies have prompted important new national criminal justice initiatives, such as the Career Criminal Program and the victim-witness assistance program, and appear likely to fuel other programs to improve the quality of police arrests, make bail decisions better focused on the issues of pretrial misconduct, utilize information technology in assuring speedy trials, and bring about greater consistency and evenhandedness in sentencing.

The following paragraphs provide examples of some of the PROMIS-based policy studies.

(1) The Career Criminal

The Career Criminal Program is a good example of the way in which PROMIS data can provide leads about the need for new criminal justice program initiatives.

Studies of the PROMIS data in the District of Columbia indicated that a small proportion of arrestees (7%) were responsible for a large proportion of the work load (24%) brought to the court system. These 7% were all arrested for felonies or serious misdemeanors (i.e., punishable by six months to a year in jail) on at least four separate occasions in the space of less than five years within the same city (Williams, 1978).

Moreover, PROMIS data indicated that many of these prolific offenders could be easily identified immediately after their arrest because they were already on bail, probation, or parole from other crimes. About 17% of the persons arrested had at least one other case pending in the same courthouse; 4% had at least two other pending cases. In addition, almost 9% of the persons arrested were on probation or parole at the time of their arrest (Williams, 1978a).

Another study attempted to measure the relative priority given to the cases involving the prolific, recidivistic offenders versus other felony cases. That study was unable to find any evidence that the seriousness of the defendant's prior criminal record was exerting much effect on the decisions of the assistant prosecutors (Institute for Law and Social Research, 1977a).

One other study, while not actually focused on the repeat offender problem, could be interpreted as supporting the idea that the crime control potential of the criminal justice system is insignificant *unless* there is a group of career criminals who are accounting for most of the crime. This study estimated that 4% of the robberies of commercial institutions, less than 1% of the burglaries of commercial institutions, and less than 2% of the felonious assaults result in even a single adult conviction and incarceration (Institute for Law and Social Research, 1977b). Unless some of those convicted and incarcerated also committed large numbers of the other robberies, burglaries, and assaults, the prospects of improving the ability of the criminal justice system to control crime are very discouraging.

These PROMIS data helped bring about LEAA funding for career criminal prosecution programs in major urban centers throughout the United States. Special cadres of experienced trial lawyers and investigators devote extra time and effort to the preparation and trial of cases involving serious, habitual offenders in an attempt to incapacitate them through conviction and incarceration.

Because PROMIS is an on-going system, researchers can continue to tap its data to evaluate the effectiveness of new program initiatives. PROMIS data are beginning to yield additional insights on how to structure career criminal programs:

- Focusing exclusively on the felony episodes of career criminals may not be the most effective approach. Over half (54%) of the felony defendants who recidivated within a two and one-half year period had at least one arrest for a serious misdemeanor within that ensuing two and one-half year period.

- Focusing on a single *crime type* may not be the most effective approach for incapacitating career criminals. Three out of four repeaters switched at least once in the space of two and one-half years between, for example, robbery and burglary (Williams, 1978a).

For programs seeking to take crime type into account, the most frequently chosen crime types of career criminals were, in descending order of frequency, burglary, robbery, larceny, and assault. These four crimes accounted for 61% of the episodes of career criminals over a two and one-half year period (Williams, 1978a).

Burglary and robbery also show up as frequently chosen crimes of repeat offenders who are rearrested while on conditional release (bail, probation, or parole). This is true for the District of Columbia and for every PROMIS jurisdiction for which such data have been available (Brosi, 1978). In the District of Columbia, for example, 32% of those charged with burglary and 31% of those charged with robbery were on conditional release at the time of their arrest (INSLAW, 1977b).

- In an adult prosecution system, if the purpose of the Career Criminal Program is to incapacitate those offenders most likely to continue committing large numbers of offenses in the coming years, it would be advisable to focus on teenage adults and adults in their early twenties (Williams, 1978a).

- Gun use, by itself, is an insufficient basis for singling out the most serious career criminals. There are career criminals who time and again cause injury to their victims whether armed with guns or not, and there are offenders who repeatedly use guns but do not injure their victims. The potential lethality of a gun may be a sufficient basis for according priority to crimes involving guns, but surely the highest priority should be reserved for cases in which the offender both uses a gun and has a history of injuring victims (Cook and Nagin, 1978).

(2) Improving Police Performance in the Collection of Evidence

In an attempt to look behind the common phenomenon of insufficient evidence collection by the police, researchers found a possible clue to reducing the problem in the future: a small subset of the arresting officers regularly bring in cases with sufficient evidence, both physical and testimonial. In fact 15% of the officers who made arrests in a recent year accounted for over half of all the convictions, whereas more than 30% of the arresting officers brought in no arrests that led to conviction. The officers in the 15% were found in every major geographic and specialized command. What distinguishes them from their peers were the following: (1) they routinely reach the crime scene quickly; (2) they frequently recover tangible evidence which in turn increases the convictability of the case; (3) they frequently locate and sustain the cooperation of larger numbers of lay witnesses (Forst et al., 1977).

As more is learned about this phenomenon—e.g., whether similar situations exist in other urban centers, and what motivates and explains the success of the minority of officers who do so well—it may be possible to launch experimental programs to help the other officers increase the number of arrests for serious crimes that survive in court.

In this regard, LEAA recently awarded a grant to INSLAW to analyze the problem in eight other PROMIS jurisdictions, and to conduct in-depth interviews with officers in two cities.

(3) Improving Witness Cooperation

In an attempt to probe the other most frequently cited reason for case mortality in the courts, namely the failure of witnesses to cooperate with the prosecution and court, in 1976 researchers Cannavale and Falcon drew a sample of witnesses' names and addresses from the PROMIS files and conducted household interviews with almost 1,000 of them. The sample was drawn to permit comparisons between cooperative and noncooperative witnesses.

The major difference found between the two groups was that those labeled as noncooperative were more likely to have failed to receive their notices to appear or to be confused about where or when they were supposed to appear or what they were supposed to do.

One out of four witnesses identified in police arrest reports could never be reached again because their names, addresses, or telephone numbers were incorrectly recorded. Imprecise directions about where to appear and the lack of information booths in the courthouse precluded others from appearing when scheduled.

This study helped to prompt LEAA to establish special funding for victim-witness assistance programs in selected district attorney's offices and courts throughout the county. These programs attempt to provide improved communications between the criminal justice system and the citizen witness.

In addition, PROMIS is proving to be an effective tool in improving communications. When witnesses call the court to find out where they are supposed to be, clerks can instantly retrieve the answer by entering the witness' name on to the PROMIS terminal. In the past, witnesses were expected to know the docket number, the defendant's name, or the police officer's name. Some jurisdictions are also using PROMIS to print automatically subpoenas for witnesses, telephone lists for follow-up notices, and letters informing witnesses of the final dispositions in their cases.

(4) Focusing Bail Decisions on
the Reduction of Pretrial Misconduct

Failure to appear and crime on bail are the two forms of pretrial misconduct which judges presumably try to minimize through their decisions on bail. Researchers found, however, that for the most part judges' decisions on bail were not effectively focused on either form of misconduct (Roth & Wice, 1978). The factors which appear through statistical analysis to be good clues to failure to appear, for example, do not seem to be influencing the bail decisions. The same is true with regard to factors which appear as good statistical clues to the likelihood of crime on bail.

With few exceptions, the factors upon which the judges appear to be relying in making their bail decisions are irrelevant to the issue of pretrial misconduct. For example, defendants who have a local residence are less likely to be subjected to financial conditions but neither more likely nor less likely to fail to appear or to be rearrested while on bail than defendants without a local residence. Homicide defendants are more likely to be subjected to financial conditions and yet they are neither more nor less likely to fail to appear or to be rearrested while awaiting trial.

Bail decision making may be an example of what Frankfurter and Pound had in mind when they said that policy judgments should not be based on the occasional dramatic case but, instead, on a quantitative assessment of the normal, humdrum operations of the court.

(5) Controlling Court Delay Through
Improved Scheduling Management

Researchers have also looked at the causes and consequences of delay. The court's continuance policy appeared to be the single most important cause of delay, more important than limitations in the number of judges or fluctuations in the volume of cases (Hausner and Seidel, 1978). Prosecutive policies also appeared to influence court delay. Over a two-year period in the study, prosecutors began filing charges and seeking and obtaining convictions in a larger proportion of police arrests, including cases of relatively less seriousness in terms of injury, property loss, or intimidation. This change in prosecution policy increased the volume of cases awaiting trial and, hence, the amount of delay.

As for the consequences of delay, courthouse folklore in the United States has it that delay reduces convictability. This may indeed be true for the occasional dramatic case, but it does not appear to be true for the normal, humdrum operations of the court. In the jurisdiction studied, there was very little difference in trial conviction rates for cases tried soon after indictment and cases tried long after indictment. The conviction rate was not being kept stable through some artificial device such as dismissing decaying cases or resorting to greater plea bargaining as time wore on.

Although many people believe that speedy trials are an effective tool for crime control, the researchers estimated that mere adoption of speedy trial limits would actually diminish crime control by reducing the volume of convictions. To avoid a loss of convictions, speedy trial limits should be accompanied by better management of continuances and improved case scheduling or by more judges and prosecutors.

PROMIS may prove to be a useful tool for controlling court delay through improved scheduling management. PROMIS records the reasons for each continuance in a case so judges can have a better basis for ruling on requests from lawyers.

Under funding from the National Science Foundation, INSLAW has added to the latest version of the PROMIS technology a separate module for computer-assisted scheduling. This module helps schedulers control appearances of attorneys and police officers to avoid conflicts among the former and consolidate hearings for the later. The new module allows schedulers to monitor the status of the calendar by constantly comparing resources required (as indicated by cases set) to resources available. The new module helps schedulers select cases for scheduling by identifying their progress and indicating whether they are backlogged. Finally, the new scheduling module produces reports for monitoring and evaluating schedule performance.

(6) Increasing the Fairness and Consistency of Sentencing Decisions

Researchers analyzing felony sentencing decisions found that a large proportion of the decisions (40%) were not explainable even after examining 200 factors in each case about the current crime and the prior criminal record of the defendant (Dungworth, 1978). Moreover some judges appeared twice as likely to impose incarceration as some of their colleagues even when looking at offenders similarly situated in regard to prior criminal record and current crime.

Contributing to the problem are laws which provide an extremely wide choice of penalties for a given crime but few standards on how to apply the laws. For example, there is very little discussion in the laws of the purposes of sentencing and how those various purposes (e.g., incapacitation, rehabilitation, just deserts) can be translated into consistent and fair decisions.

Also contributing to the problem is inadequate communications among the judges on what each deems as a suitable sentence for a given situation. PROMIS may be able to serve as a tool for improving communications among the judges and, thereby, raising the prospects for more consistent and evenhanded decisions. PROMIS could be programmed to produce for sentencing judges, in advance of their sentencing decision in a case, a statistical report which would summarize how the judges on that bench normally handle cases involving that kind of conviction and prior criminal record.

(7) Plea Bargaining: Who Gains? Who Loses?

The public debate about plea bargaining in the United States is fueled by the suspicion that it permits criminals to escape the kind of punishment they deserve, and would receive if we had more trials and fewer plea bargains.

A research study of plea bargaining that utilized PROMIS data on what actually happens in the courthouse found no support for the image of plea bargaining as a tool for leniency (Rhodes, 1978). Indeed, the study found evidence to the contrary. In general, plea bargaining appear to be a more effective instrument for crime control than trials.

The study examined the four highest volume serious crimes: robbery, burglary, larceny and assault. For the last three types of crime, defendants who pled guilty received substantially the same penalties that they probably would have received if convicted at trial. Moreover, statistical analyses suggest that a significant proportion of the plea-bargained cases would have resulted in acquittals had they gone to trial. Clearly, prosecutors are achieving more by plea bargaining than they could expect to achieve by going to trial.

Robbery was the one exception. Concessions were routinely awarded for robbery pleas, and these sentencing concessions were accompanied by higher rearrest rates for robbers who pled guilty compared with robbers who were found guilty. Statistical estimates, however, indicated that a large proportion of the robbery plea bargains would have resulted in acquittals if taken to trial. When this fact is taken into account, the concessions do not appear to be very significant. Rearrest rates for robbers who plea bargained were very close to the rates for all robbers who go to trial (including those who were convicted as well as those who were acquitted).

(8) Reforming the Handling of Sexual Assault Cases

There has been a public outcry in recent years about the way rape cases are handled in the courts. Reform programs focus on (1) improving the willingness of citizens to testify, on (2) eliminating the legal requirement for other evidence to corroborate the victim's testimony, and on (3) making male prosecutors, judges, and police more sensitive to the trauma of the female victims.

Research on sexual assault prosecutions raises doubts about whether these particular reforms will produce any improvements in the extremely low conviction rates for these types of crimes.

Using the PROMIS data that begin tracking crimes at the point of arrest, the study found that rape victims were already more determined to pursue their cases than the victims of other serious crimes, such as felonious assault, robbery, and burglary (Williams, 1978b). The problem was not the victim's willingness to cooperate but prosecutive doubts about the victim's credibility.

Removal of the requirement for corroborating evidence in the jurisdiction studied had not, as of the time of the study, resulted in any improvement in the conviction rate.

Finally, the study raises questions about whether the problem lies in part with male insensitivity to the plight of female victims. All types of sexual assault cases had very low conviction rates. This was true whether the victim was male or female, child or adult.

CONCLUSION

The day when research on prosecutorial decision making and the administration of criminal justice depended upon either ad hoc, manual collection of statistical data or the less precise methods of interviews and observations is past. A rich new base of criminal justice data is beginning to accumulate. It will soon include data from most major jurisdictions. Unlike the data bases assembled by the crime commissions of the 1920s it will not be limited to one time period. Instead it will be cumulative over time allowing for trend analysis. Moreover, it will also facilitate cross-jurisdictional comparisons. The value of this new data base both for providing a better understanding of how criminal justice is being administered and for helping to formulate national administrative policies is enormous. The early studies done on this data base and highlighted in this chapter have already begun to demonstrate these values.

Until now, research on the prosecutor's policies and decisions as well as on other components of the administration of justice was handicapped by the absence of relevant statistical data. In the future that will no longer be a problem. We are entering a new era of criminal justice research. Our ability to describe and explain the actions of the criminal justice system has been increased enormously. A powerful new tool has been developed. It remains for us to put it to use in the interests of understanding and improving the administration of criminal justice.

REFERENCES

BROSI, K. B. (1979). A Cross-City Comparison of Felony Case Processing. Washington, D.C.: Institute for Law and Social Research.

COOK, P. J. and D. NAGIN (1978). Does the Weapon Matter? Washington, D.C.: Institute for Law and Social Research.

DRUCKER, P. F. (1954). The Practice of Management. New York: Harper and Row.

DUNGWORTH, T. (1978). An Empirical Assessment of Sentencing Practices in the Superior Court of the District of Columbia. Washington, D.C.: Institute for Law and Social Research.

FORST, B., J. LUCIANOVIC, and S. J. COX (1977). What Happens After Arrest? A Court Perspective of Police Operations in the District of Columbia. Washington, D.C.: Institute for Law and Social Research.

FRANKFURTER, F. and R. POUND (1922). Criminal Justice in Cleveland. Cleveland: Cleveland Foundation.

HAUSNER, J. and M. A. SEIDEL (1978). An Analysis of Case Processing Time in the District of Columbia Superior Court. Washington, D.C.: Institute for Law and Social Research.

Institute for Law and Social Research [INSLAW] (1977a). Curbing the Repeat Offender: A Strategy for Prosecutors. Washington, D.C.: INSLAW.

———(1977b). Expanding the Perspective of Crime Data: Performance Implications for Policymakers. Washington, D.C.: INSLAW.

RHODES, W. M. (1978). Plea Bargaining: Who Gains? Who Loses? Washington, D.C.: Institute for Law and Social Research.

ROTH, J. A. and P. B. WICE (1978). Pretrial Release and Misconduct in the District of Columbia. Washington, D.C.: Institute for Law and Social Research.

WILLIAMS, K. M. (1978a). The Scope and Prediction of Recidivism. Washington, D.C.: Institute for Law and Social Research.

———(1978b). The Prosecution of Sexual Assaults. Washington, D.C.: Institute for Law and Social Research.

Chapter 6

FROM CRACKER BARREL TO SUPERMARKET: TAKING THE COUNTRY OUT OF PROSECUTION MANAGEMENT

WILLIAM F. WESSEL

Country prosecutors, like country general stores, account for their activities through the ever-present eye of the man who runs the shop. But when the general store owner suddenly finds himself at the junction of two highways that propel him into a truckstop business which must operate twenty-four hours a day, he suddenly realizes the need for changing his method of operation. He begins marking prices on his merchandise, installs a cash register, and establishes policies by which employees are expected to abide. He will probably also establish checkpoints to determine if he is being shortchanged by his employees or being victimized by shoplifting customers. He will begin to take inventory or set up inventory controls. He will establish quality control procedures to make sure the product being sold meets the standards he sets and is not subject to the varying standards of his employees.

The number of controls and checkpoints he establishes is going to be determined by three factors: (1) the remoteness that exists between his direct supervision and the operations; (2) the risk of loss sought to be controlled, discounted by the probability of its occurrence compared with the cost of the corrective remedy. For example, if inventory shortage through employee and customer pilfering costs only $1,000 a year, the store owner would not put in a security force costing $5,000; (3) the importance of the policy or objective in itself.

Similarly, when a prosecutor's office reaches a certain size, the chief prosecutor must establish controls and accountability in his shop. He cannot afford to run a cracker barrel operation in circumstances that call for supermarket techniques. The large urban or suburban prosecutor's office differs in important ways from the small country prosecutor's office. The country prosecutor has generally been in office longer, has smaller dockets, lower crime rates, and a working knowledge of most, if not all, cases on the docket. Frequently, he is a political kinsman of the judge(s) of the district. Thus, he can generally even any listing keel by a quick talk with the judge. If he has assistant prosecutors, they likewise have more experience (in terms of years) than their city counterparts. Moreover, they know the policies of the boss as well as they know the lay of the land. There is no need for written policies, or for gathering statistics or even bothering about points of decision making in the criminal process. The country prosecutor probably ran for office on no other platform than to maintain the status quo, and he probably worked on his predecessor's staff.

In contrast, the city prosecutor is not able to know all the cases on his docket. He usually has to deal with several judges whose political or ideological persuasions vary considerably. His assistants may not always know his policies because it is not possible for him to have direct, day-to-day personal contact with them. Neither can he afford to take the enormous amount of time necessary to set down all his policies in writing. This problem in communication is further aggravated by the fact that in the large office there is usually a high turnover among the assistant prosecutors. By the time an assistant has been around long enough to learn the policy preference of his chief, he leaves the office for a more lucrative job. The new assistants are typically fresh out of law school, inexperienced, and naive.

The chief prosecutor in the large jurisdiction must establish a game plan. He must recognize his managerial and policy-making responsibilities. He must realize he is an administrator of a large organization and must utilize all the managerial tools and techniques available to administrators of other large organizations. This means establishing specific, measurable goals; statistical and other accounting procedures for determining whether the goals are being met; mechanisms for enforcing office policy; and mechanisms for monitoring and altering policies.

Unfortunately, many prosecutors' offices have not recognized the need for establishing controls or gathering statistics. Prosecutors seem to have an occupational antipathy for anything that remotely involves statistics, efficiency, or accounting. Their attitude is always, "I'm a lawyer. I don't have to be quantified. I make my judgment, exercise my discretion in accordance with what my perception of the public needs are and whether I think they should be satisfied. My assistants are 'professionals.' " The trouble with such an approach is that each assistant prosecutor's insight, experience, and maturity are generally not in accord with the other prosecutors, and very often their perceptions of public needs have no more basis in reality than the *Alice in Wonderland* character, Humpty Dumpty, who chose his words to mean what he wanted them to mean.

Such an office, characterized by unchecked exercise of discretion directed toward no discernible goal, leads to knee-jerk reactions to daily problems, the solution of which is never predictable. This type of office can best be characterized as exemplifying management by crisis. In this office there exists very little paperwork; and what little there is, when it depends on a lawyer to complete it, is very nearly never done.

DISCRETION AND THE PROSECUTOR

The prosecutor has been given a wide berth in the exercise of his discretion in decision making. The U.S. Supreme Court recently recognized the history and importance of that discretion in Imbler v. Pachtman (1976) 424 U.S. 409, 96 S. Ct. 904 (cf. Butz v. Economou, _____ U.S. _____ (1978) 98 S. Ct. 2894 and Bivens v. Six Unknown Agents (1971) 403 U.S. 388, 91 S. Ct. 1999. [1] Recently, however, commentators have begun to question the latitude given to the prosecutor and have suggested ways and means of quantifying that discretion for the purpose of establishing criteria by which predictability can be measured (Davis, 1969; Jacoby, 1975).

There are two important aspects of the problem of discretion. One has to do with the setting of goals within law enforcement. The other has to do with ensuring the evenhanded treatment of similarly situated arrests, suspects, and defendants. The chief prosecutor is responsible for both of these aspects of discretion. Once he establishes his policies in law enforcement, he must assure that those accused of crime are treated consistently by all assistant prosecutors in his office.

Quality prosecution does not depend on the individual prosecutor. It depends rather on a complete system which provides mechanisms to assure that the goals set by the chief prosecutor are not undermined by those who carry them out, for it is in the frontlines that the real picture of the prosecutor's policies is painted.

My own experience in this problem area was obtained primarily as a defense lawyer in criminal cases and then as first assistant to District Attorney Harry Connick in New Orleans from early 1974 to mid-1977. Connick himself had been a long-time and successful defense attorney before becoming district attorney. He had the additional vantage point of having served as Assistant U.S. Attorney—Chief of the Criminal Division in the Eastern District of Louisiana.

Upon taking over the district attorney's office, we encountered the problem in New Orleans that occurs in virtually every office that is staffed by part-time assistant prosecutors, namely, lack of attention to the public's business, lack of carry through, high turnover, and few career prosecutors. This problem generally resulted in a staff of assistants who were short on experience. It also led to massive plea bargaining with no rhyme or reason behind it. It was wrongly assumed that the only way the docket could be moved was to bargain the case away. Pleas were bargained for in over 85% of the cases disposed of, and sentence bargaining was also going on. One would think that the docket would be very current, but it was not. With an average of 600 cases coming into the docket each month, there were over 7,000 cases awaiting to be tried by April 1, 1974. This meant that the case inventory was turning over on the average of about once a year.

Apparently the system in New Orleans was really no system at all. It worked haphazardly and always in favor of the defendant, never in favor of the public. The halls of justice were virtually empty by noon of any working day. There were few trials, a great number of plea bargains, and virtually no appeals (naturally, because there were few trials to appeal from). During four years before Connick took office there were over 202 persons arrested and charged for murder in New Orleans. During the same period there were only 22 trials for murder, in spite of the fact that the crime called for the death penalty and the defendant could not waive a jury. All of this in spite of a rising crime waive. Was this any way to run the public business? A private retailer would go broke in short order if his inventory turned over but once a year.

In addition, we both knew, as any defense lawyer knows, that the Sixth Amendment right to a speedy trial was a right that defendants really never wanted to exercise, especially if they were guilty; that time worked in favor of lost evidence, lost or disinterested witnesses and victims, and lack of interest by the police. We decided to co-opt the Sixth Amendment right to a speedy trial by means of adverse possession.

Knowing these things, the New Orleans office established the following goals for achievement:

(1) To eliminate frivolous plea bargaining, and assigning to plea bargaining a more fitting role as only one of many weapons in the prosecutor's arsenal;

(2) To reduce the average time for turnover of all cases to 60 days from time of arrest to disposition;

(3) To beef up the screening-intake division so that only those cases capable of withstanding the rigors of reasonable doubt would go on to the trial docket; and

(4) To concentrate on violent crime, particularly murder, rape, armed robbery, burglary and hard narcotics, with particular attention on the latter.

Later the office expanded on these policies by focusing on the individuals who were committing the crimes, which resulted in the formation of the Career Criminal Bureau and the Post Conviction Tracking Unit. From time to time certain areas of law enforcement required particular concentration and the office easily moved into those fields.

In order to achieve the overall goals of the office, the district attorney set up a system of accountability and control that ranked both seasoned lawyers and judges. The office's organizational structure was revamped so as to eliminate the select crime divisions of the capital crimes (murder and rape), armed robbery and narcotics. These select divisions were used previously as positions of prestige to be sought after by the aspiring successful assistant prosecutor. That part of the idea was not bad, but the experienced prosecutors in these units (except in the armed robbery unit) were not trying the less prestigous burglaries, thefts, simple robberies, and aggravated batteries. The expertise of the veteran prosecutors was not being shared with these less experienced assistants in the "pits" on a day-to-day basis. Furthermore, there were too many chiefs and not enough accountability.

As a result of our reorganization the former elite and specialized divisions were eliminated and two major divisions were set up, a screening division and a trial division, both of which reported directly to the first assistant.[2] The next step was to motivate the assistants for internal movement and to assure a high level of experience among the assistants in the screening division. Screening was given this priority because it was considered to be the backbone of the office. The greatest number and most significant decisions would be made by this division. These decisions would set the stage and tempo for all the subsequent decisions in each case. To encourage experienced assistants to go into screening, the best salaries were given. Since the job was essentially one devoted to paperwork, each assistant in screening was required to choose one case—any case—per month, but it was expected that the case be one that was likely to go to trial. So the screening division became the desirable place to be, offering high salaries, independence, supervisory control, and prestige.

In addition to the two major divisions, we established controls and methods of accounting to guarantee that office policies were carried out. Once a case was accepted by the screening division, no one could dismiss (nolle prosequi) it thereafter unless and until the screening assistant who had originally accepted it and the first assistant approved that action. If a case were to be nollied, the trial assistant had to fill out a request for dismissal. The request was submitted to the original screening assistant in the case. It contained the trial assistant's written reason for making the request. If the screening assistant approved the request, it went to the first assistant for the second approval. If the screening assistant disapproved, the case was kicked back to the trial assistant for trial. However, the latter could appeal the decision to the chief of the screening division.

Copies of all approved requests were kept in the First Assistant's office tabulated once a month using the following standardized reason codes:

(a) Witness-victim—no show or unwilling to prosecute
(b) Motion to supress evidence sustained
(c) Plea bargain
(d) Witness or victim credibility
(e) Lack of evidence
(f) Prescription (statute of limitations)
(g) Defendant turned informer
(h) Defendant prosecuted in other jurisdiction
(i) Other.

This monthly tabulation was cross-indexed by type of crime. The first assistant reviewed it with the division chief of screening, who in turn reviewed it with his assistants.

The usefulness of such a procedure is illustrated by an event in the New Orleans District Attorney's office which took place in 1976. A victim-witness division had been established one year earlier. One of its duties and responsibilities was to interview and follow up on all victim crimes. This meant that at the initial screening decision to accept a case involving a battery, theft, or robbery, the victim-witness counselors were called in. They would explain to the victim what to expect in terms of time lag, continuances, and so on. Subsequently, the counselors would follow up this meeting by phoning the victim in advance of trial, reminding him of trial dates and continuances. If there were any problems about getting off work or getting paid for time off to testify, the employer was likewise contacted by the unit.

The experience of the office before 1975 was that victims were all too willing to drop a case after the blood had cooled. This meant that there were high rates of nolle prosequi and reductions resulting from victims who were not willing to testify. Over 18% of all nolles in 1974 were due to witness-victim refusal to testify. When the victim-witness unit started operating at the screening level, the rate of nolles occurring by reason of victim refusals to testify dropped dramatically. By mid-1976 it was down to 10%.

But then in August and September 1976 the rate of nolles due to victim-witness refusals to testify began moving back to 17% of all nolles. When this trend was recognized at the end of November, the chief of screening was called in and asked whether the victim-witness unit was still picking up victims at screening. The answer was negative, and the chief of the victim-witness unit was called in to explain his lack of conformity to this office policy. Eventually, it was determined that the screening assistants had felt that no visible results were being achieved by the policy of picking up victims at screening. On their own initiative they stopped calling the victim-witness unit. The victim-witness unit, not being composed of lawyers, did not feel it was in a position to push the screening assistants. The policy had become inoperative by default. If the trial assistants had not had to account for their nolle requests, the change in policy would not have been detected. That in turn would have meant that any subsequent assessment of the policy and the efficiency of the victim-witness unit would have been based on erroneous data.

INITIAL SCREENING

The Achilles' heel of the elected prosecutor's office is the screening or intake division, with the greatest margin for error occurring in the area of refusals. It is therefore important that the prosecutor be able to respond intelligently to the critics of his charging policy. The prosecutor can do this only if he knows the reasons why he acted or refused to act and is able to point out the consistency of his action. The controls and procedures must be specifically designed to prevent a breakdown of the system at this strategic and sensitive point.

In New Orleans, to insure that cases were not rejected at screening for lack of temerity, the chief of screening was required to review and initial every refusal and the reason given for it. These forms were also tabulated, and the results were, on occasion, reviewed with the superintendent of police and his staff. Almost immediately the results of this organized program were felt; only 56% of all cases initiated by the police were accepted for prosecution.

The reaction to this phenomenon was rapid. The police complained that the district attorney was taking only sure bets. The defense bar hollered because it was no longer able to charge fees on cases that would ultimately end in nolle or reduction anyway. Defense attorneys previously could charge exorbitant fees and almost guarantee a successful conclusion to the defendant. The judges grew impatient and negative because the program prolonged their normal working day, and the prosecutors in the courtroom were acting too independently of the judicial power. They refused to reduce. One of the judges pulled this writer out of the grand jury room to personally request a reduction in a heroin case which was then in trial, which request was promptly refused. The court reporters were angry because there were more trials and more appeals and they weren't able to go to their private business in the afternoons or to their golf course or health spa. The assistant prosecutors did not like it because they were "professionals" and felt they should be able to use their discretion without any controls.

To offset the complaints and negativism on the part of the police, they were told in each case the reason for the refusal. If they were dissatisfied with the explanation, they could appeal to the chief of screening and ultimately to the first assistant. Most of the judges ultimately came around. Some were downright pleased to get out of so much plea bargaining and get down to the business of judging. A few judges, however, took a different tack, but that will be more fully explained later. The defense bar responded with an immediate surge of defendants that went to jury trial, from 124 in 1972 to a high of 764 in 1972. Jury trials ebbed later on under this program, but never sank to the low level of the pre-1974 years. Although rumblings of dissatisfaction from assistant prosecutors still can be heard sotto voce, most are happy with the system. They can always side-step a request for a nolle or reduction by a defense lawyer by blaming it on the front office.

CHECK POINTS OF CONTROL
IN TRIAL DIVISION

Given our rigorous initial screening program, it might seem that there would be little left for the trial division to do but try cases or accept pleas as charged. Not so. Even with tough screening, there continued to be some nolles and pleas to reduced charges. We described earlier how the nolles occurred. The reductions were accomplished by the approvals of both the senior assistant of the respective court section and the chief of the trial division. (There are ten court sections, each staffed by two prosecutors—one senior and one junior.) The signature of the chief of the trial division appears on both the approval and the reason for the reduction in the case folder. To secure the enforcement of this policy, one assistant was required to review all closed files to insure that a nolle form was properly filled out where a case was nollied, or that a reduction was approved where it occurred.

We established checkpoints not only for nollied and reduced cases but for the ones that went to trial as well. The chief of trials had the responsibility of reviewing with the trial assistants their trial briefs in each case that was lost at jury trial. The purpose of this was to insure that cases were not being lost for lack of preparation.

Another major area of concern for any large prosecutor's office is the problem of delay. In New Orleans, Connick established the goal of reducing delay from arrest to trial to sixty days. A three-part policy was established: (1) no continuance; (2) be prepared for trial; and (3) try your oldest cases first.[3]

The two checkpoints which were installed to insure evenhandedness in this matter of delay were the review of continuances asked for by the defense attorney, and the monthly inventory. Each month an inventory was taken by each senior assistant in the courts section. It was used to compare intake and dispositions. This report facilitated a determination of the caseload turnover rate. When compared with the daily reports of continuances, it also served to show the chief of the trial division if prosecutors were joining in requests for continuances. Later the office installed an embellished Prosecutor's Management Information System (PROMIS) which computerized the entire system in the office, giving speedier tabulations and responses and instantaneous retrieval of case information.

USES OF INFORMATION GATHERED

Unless the assistant prosecutors can be shown the value of information gathered, and unless the prosecutor-manager uses information to correct deviations from stated policy, it is pointless to gather it. Armed with such reports and statistics, the prosecutor can evaluate whether his goals are being achieved. For example, in New Orleans there was a community demand that the laws against obscenity be enforced vigorously against a sudden outpouring of dirty movies. Initially the police blamed the district attorney for not accepting the cases. A review of screening showed that none were being presented to the district attorney. The offenders were instead being booked in municipal court under a city ordinance. This was due to the policy of the previous district attorney who refused to prosecute dirty movie operators.

Subsequently, cases were being made by the police and charged by the district attorney. A review of the screening of these cases revealed that one or two prosecutors were applying not community standards but their own in determining which films were obscene. This was subsequently corrected.

The district attorney next forbade plea bargaining in obscenity cases. This resulted in waiver of jury trials by the defendants. They were tried by judges alone with the result that certain judges invariably found these defendants not guilty—not because the film was not obscene, but because of the judge's personal philosphy. The district attorney first tried to demonstrate to the judges involved the seriousness of the problems. There was not any positive reaction. The press and public then became aware of the problem. There was a turn-around in the judicial attitude, a reduction in jury waivers and an increase in guilty verdicts.

Another district attorney might have taken a different tack. He might have decided that, in the interest of economizing on judicial and prosecutorial time and effort, the goal might not be worth achieving if the bulk of defendants waived jury trials and were acquitted by the court.

A similar but much more striking problem occurred in New Orleans in the area of heroin prosecution. The district attorney established a policy of no plea bargaining in hard narcotics cases. No assistant was permitted to reduce or nolle such a charge without the written approval of the district attorney, or, in his absence, the first assistant. It was rare that an assistant asked for or obtained such approval. The checkpoint of control here was that each closed case folder was reviewed by a special assistant to determine if such an outcome occurred without that approval. Within one and a half years it was found that purity of heroin being sold on the streets dropped from 10-11% to less than 5%, and that heroin distribution was moving out of the city of New Orleans. In some months there were no arrests for heroin distribution in New Orleans. These facts suggested that the policy was having its intended effect.

Meanwhile, however, the district attorney learned through his in-house computer-assisted analysis of the results of jury and bench trials involving heroin cases that these defendants were waiving jury trials in distribution of heroin cases. The charge of distribution of herion carried a minimum sentence of life imprisonment upon conviction, but a few judges in New Orleans believed the life sentence was too stiff. When the defendant waived his jury trial, which he had the unbridled, unilateral right to do, those judges were returning lesser verdicts, which they had the unbridled, unilateral right to do. Plea bargaining was being moved out of the district attorney's office and into the judges' chambers.

The district attorney tried to discuss the issue with the judges involved, but the attempt proved useless. Finally, a media representative got wind of the problem and asked the district attorney to show his statistics. When the judges involved learned of the media investigation, a turn-around in the verdicts in bench trials became visible.

In the months before the investigative reporter's activities, juries were returning guilty-as-charged verdicts in 80% to 85% of the heroin distribution cases. In those sections of court where waivers of jury trial were going on, the judges were finding less than 50% guilty as charged and over 30% guilty of a lesser charge. The cases were reviewed to see if there were any inconsistencies in the charging standards. There were none. The only discernible difference was that in some of the cases where the waiver occurred, the history of deviant behavior was not as chronic. Otherwise the cases were virtually the same: sales of heroin to undercover agents. During the month that the reporter was quizzing the judges about the matter, guilty-as-charged verdicts on bench trials went to 80%; guilty of lesser, to 10%; not guilty to 10%.

The lesson to be learned is twofold. First, the fact that the prosecutor had set his policies and established checkpoints of control enabled him to evaluate his position in relation to other members of the system; and second, his office became the font, or source of information on the official activity of the criminal justice system.

The prosecutor with this kind of information available to him knows whether his policies are being followed and, if not, knows the points at which they are being subverted. It then is a simple matter to take the corrective measures. The above examples illustrate how prosecutors can check on whether policy is achieved, and show the only way that they can determine whether evenhandedness is being maintained.

The enlightened prosecutor who overcomes his aversion to management techniques and accounting procedures will quickly find that, in addition to being in the interest of the improved administration of justice, these techniques also serve extremely useful political functions. For one thing, with tight controls, he will reduce the possibility of cases being mishandled. For another, when he is called to account for the actions of his office, he will be able to give a concise and easily substantiated answer. For example, when the New Orleans police department objected that the district attorney's office was rejecting 70% of armed robbery cases during one or two months in early 1978, a computer print out of all rejections and the accompanying case reports showed that virtually all refusals were due to lack of evidence obtained by the police. The prosecutor who does not use these tools, acts intuitively and very often wrongly. He further leaves himself open to charges of favoritism and even suggestions of corruption.

In establishing checkpoints or auditing procedures, the manager-prosecutor must take care that he does not superimpose duplication of work effort or misuse of his limited resources. For example, the important aspect of reviewing trial briefs of only lost cases is that the chief of trials does not review every case that goes to trial. He is not acting as another lawyer on the case, and he is not placing himself in the position of second-guessing the trial assistant. He reviews only the cases that are lost. In most jurisdictions this would mean that less than 2% of all cases on the docket would be reviewed even if *all* jury losses were reviewed.

In similar fashion, the auditing control at screening is for the review of refused cases only. The chief of screening should review only those refused because (a) those are the ones that can hurt the prosecutor; and (b) review of accepted cases is automatically accounted for through the activity on the trial docket, i.e., nolle, reduction, win or loss at trial, and so on.

Other jurisdictions may decide that because of greater workload only target cases should be reviewed. For example, in the trial area, the chief of trials may review trial briefs in violent crimes only that are lost at trial. In screening, the chief may decide to review all refused violent crimes and review only at random all other refused crimes.

Checkpoints of control also serve the prosecutor by evaluating the impact of decisions made by other components in the criminal justice system as a by-product of tabulating the effects of his own. We have pointed out how philosophical differences between the judiciary and prosecutor may affect law enforcement policy. Likewise, other agencies, e.g., police, may have different outlooks and policies about the solution to crime problems. Although most cops are individual-oriented (i.e., bad dude), most police departments are crime-oriented (i.e., the sensational types of crimes like murder and rape).

In New Orleans in late 1977, the district attorney's office became acutely aware of the ever-increasing numbers and amounts of shoplifting going on. An analysis of screening activity showed that few if any charges of shoplifting were being presented by the police to the district attorney. Shoplifters were all being booked in municipal court. Further studies showed that only about 3% of all shoplifters were ever caught. Most received much less than the 10 days imprisonment allowed by the municipal code. A review of rap sheets on offenders showed that the shoplifter cut across crime lines; i.e., he had burglary robbery, or dope convictions in his background. Many were professional shoplifters.

Shoplifting of an item of less than $100 is ordinarily a misdemeanor in Louisiana, and most judges have been lenient on the charge. The chief investigator in the district attorney's office found a statute that made a repeat offender subject to a felony punishment. This statute could then be used with the Louisiana Habitual Offender Law to make some shoplifters subject to imprisonment at hard labor for as long as twenty years, for one shoplifting count. As a result, the district attorney set up his program for career shoplifters and got the police to book them in the felony (criminal district) court. He also met with the area merchants to promote the program and encourage arrests of shoplifters.

Although the success of the program has not been fully measured, there are many shoplifters sentenced to over six months in parish prison, and not a few sentenced to a period of years at the state penitentiary. The neighboring parish (county) has experienced a run of shoplifting while New Orleans merchants have reported satisfaction with the present reduced rate registered here. The prosecutor can and must obtain a handle on his activities and know the effect he makes on other agencies.

The advantages of installing controls at the points of decision-making are going to vary depending on the size of the office and experience of the assistant prosecutors. Similarly, the determination of whether to install them at all is going to be dependent on the same factors. It can be safely said, however, that the less experienced an office is, the more advantageous and even necessary is the need for controls and accounting. By experience is meant not necessarily the numbers of trials the assistants have had, but their maturity and experience in other branches of the law as well as the criminal law. An assistant prosecutor from a small community or rural district may go to trial perhaps once or twice a year. Yet, because he may have been in his position for five or ten years and also have a practice in civil law, his experience would probably be more valuable than his city counterpart who after two years in the district attorney's office has tried thirty to fifty major criminal trials, but has little other background in law and is short on maturity.

CONCLUSION

The prosecutor is not much different from the business man who runs a profit-making enterprise. He can and should be the manager of the criminal justice system, regardless of the size of his office. As manager, he has the choice of giving the store away, à la the shipshod country store operator, or of accounting for his action. With the prosecutor begins the formal process by which a man stands to lose his life, liberty, money, and honor. With him, also, may that process end. To the extent that he uses the power of his office fairly and wisely he will be judged favorably by his community. In a medium or large city, however, the evenhandedness of his administration can never be measured without setting policies, establishing checkpoints of control, and accounting for the decision making that affects the daily lives of his constituents.

NOTES

1. It is interesting to note when one considers the roles of the three major protagonists, police, prosecutor, and judiciary, that the prosecuor probably enjoys less discretion than the police yet more than the judiciary. The anomaly exists that as one moves up the ladder

of apparent professional education and expertise, discretion becomes more curtailed. The reason is perhaps that the system provides more opportunity for the review of the lower steps of the ladder. The prosecutor can review the exercise of police discretion and the courts review the prosecutors' actions. Little opportunity exists for review of judicial discretion. It may be that the opportunity for review and correction of errors at a later stage in the process makes the participants feel less of a need for present restraint.

2. Other divisions were also established, namely appeals and juvenile, child support, and victim witness.

3. Other prosecutors may try to solve their delay problems by engaging in plea bargaining. If they do, they must establish guidelines about the types of cases, circumstances, and the types of defendants in which a bargain will be made. If one assistant is reducing first-degree murder cases to manslaughter while another assistant is going down only to second degree, the office is left open to criticism; court-shopping or assistant-shopping will flourish; and the evenhandedness of justice will be diminished.

REFERENCES

DAVIS, K. C. (1969). Discretionary Justice. Champaign: University of Illinois Press.
JACOBY, J. (1975). "Case evaluation: Quantifying prosecutorial policy." Judicature 58:486-493.

Chapter 7

THE PROSECUTOR'S
PLEA BARGAINING DECISIONS

WILLIAM F. McDONALD
HENRY H. ROSSMAN
JAMES A. CRAMER

Studies of plea bargaining have identified many factors which are believed to influence plea bargaining decisions. However, because of the limitations of method or sample, these studies have raised but left unresolved a host of questions. Are certain factors relevant to all plea bargains? How much of an impact do specific factors have? Do their respective impacts vary under different conditions? Do prosecutors evaluate cases differently from defense counsel? How consistent is plea bargaining? This last question has several meanings, one of which refers to whether different attorneys (controlling for whether they are acting as prosecutors or defense counsel) would evaluate the same case the same way.

The research presented in this chapter is based on a method not previously applied to plea bargaining and on a sample which allows for comparisons not possible in previous work. It addresses those questions listed above regarding how the plea bargaining decision is determined. It

AUTHORS' NOTE: This research was supported by Grant Nos. 75-NI-99-0129 and 77-NI-99-0049 awarded by the National Institute of Law Enforcement and Criminal Justice, of the Law Enforcement Assistant Administration to the Institute of Criminal Law and Procedure, George-

focuses upon the evaluation of cases for plea bargaining, that is, the process of sorting and weighing information in order to decide whether to plea bargain and on what terms. A comparison is made to determine whether prosecutors do this differently from defense counsel. The importance of two factors, namely, the strength of the case and the seriousness of the criminal, are given special attention. They are analyzed in two ways: first, to determine consistency (i.e., do different attorneys evaluate these factors the same way); and secondly, to determine how much of a difference variations in these factors make in the evaluation of the case.

METHOD

Research on plea bargaining decision making has been based primarily on interviews and observations (Alschuler, 1968; Mather, 1974; Rosett and Cressey, 1976; Newman, 1956; Newman, 1966). A few studies have been based on statistical analyses of available records (Bernstein et al., 1977; Heuman, 1975; Rhodes, 1979). One study (Lagoy et al., 1976) used a decision simulation technique, but its sample was limited to 20 prosecutors from one state. The research presented in this chapter is based on several methods. In addition to interviews and observations with prosecutors, judges, defense counsel, and other criminal justice actors in 33 jurisdictions, a modified decision simulation technique was also used. The latter combined two techniques: the information processing analysis technique developed by Wilkins (1965) and applied to plea bargaining by Lagoy et al. (1976);[1] and a quasi-experimental design.

Sampling

Various kinds of samples were involved at different stages of the various components of this research project. Of the 33 jurisdictions chosen for site visits, 20 were chosen on a stratified random basis. They

town University Law Center under the Omnibus Crime Control and Safe Streets Act of 1968. We would like to thank the many prosecutors and defense counsel who cooperated in this study; and also the National College of Defense Attorneys and the National District Attorneys Association for providing access to their members; Herbert S. Miller for help in developing and administering the simulation; Marilyn Budish for processing the data; Mary Ann DeRosa for her tireless typing; Leslie Wilkins, Stephen Lagoy, and Al Biderman for their advice in designing the simulation; and Cheryl Martorana for her patient support of this project. Points of view and opinions stated in this document are the authors' and do not necessarily represent the official position or policies of the U.S. Department of Justice, Georgetown University, or any other organization, or person acknowledged above.

represent a 10% sample of all jurisdictions over 100,000 population. The sample is stratified to achieve a proportional representation of those jurisdictions from 100,000 to 500,000 and from 500,000 and over. The remaining 13 jurisdictions were chosen purposefully because of some feature which we deemed relevant to plea bargaining. Five of these jurisdictions were chosen for intensive analysis. These five where chosen to represent a continuum in the style of prosecutorial management in the jurisdiction. The continuum was from centralized to a decentralized style. Those jurisdictions are in order of decreasing centralization: New Orleans, Seattle, Tucson, Delaware County (Pennsylvania), and Norfolk (Virginia). The position of these jurisdictions in our continuum was determined on the basis of interviews and observations in each jurisdiction resulting in a judgment about the extent to which assistant prosecutors in a jurisdiction had their discretion guided, restricted, and reviewed by managerial policies and practices.

In the jurisdictions that were given short field visits, the selection of persons for interviews was made on both a purposeful and adventitious basis. Usually the chief officials of the court and the prosecutor's office and the public defender's agency and any other actors available were interviewed. In the five jurisdictions chosen for in-depth analysis, persons selected for interview were based on quotas of the different types of actors. Approximately ten prosecutors, ten judges, ten defense counsel, plus smaller numbers of other actors were interviewed in each of the five jurisdictions.

The decision simulation was administered to a total of 138 prosecutors and 105 defense attorneys, of which 46% were from the five cities studied in-depth. The others were obtained at national professional meetings and at jurisdictions convenient to the District of Columbia.

The process by which defense counsel and prosecutors evaluate a case for plea bargaining was examined both through interviews and the decision simulation. The interviews contained structured as well as unstructured questions. Respondents were asked the completely open-ended question "How do you 'evaluate' a case for plea bargaining? That is, what factors do you usually consider in determining the true value of the case and what the plea agreement should be?" They were subsequently asked more directed questions, such as how they evaluted their most recent cases; and how certain general factors, such as seriousness of the crime or the criminal or the strength of the case, influence their decisions.

The Simulation

The plea bargaining decision simulation was administered as follows. Respondents were asked to imagine that they were in a hypothetical jurisdiction with certain specific characteristics which were described to them (see Appendix A). It was explained that the use of a hypothetical jurisdiction was necessary because the study was being done nationally, and, therefore, jurisdictional differences had to be held constant. No respondent objected to this requirement or reported that it made the simulation less real. Virtually all the respondents who commented on the simulation reported that is was very realistic for them. This report was validated by our own observations that virtually all respondents took the simulation very seriously.

Respondents were further asked to imagine that a less experienced attorney came to them for advice about whether to plea bargain in a particular case and what the "bottom line" terms of the bargain should be. However, the only thing about the case that the senior attorney was told were the charge and the penalty for that charge in our hypothetical jurisdiction. The senior attorney (i.e., the respondent in the simulation) then had to seek as much additional information as he felt he needed in order to advise his less experienced colleague. The respondent was told that the answers to virtually all the questions which he might want to know about the case were contained on an "information board" or folder with which he was presented. The folder for the burglary case contained 39 items of information on separate cards included in plastic holders. The cards were fanned out so that only a half inch of the bottom of each card could be seen. On that half inch was written a short descriptive title of the information contained on the upper (hidden) portion of that card.

The respondent was instructed to take some time to familiarize himself with the labels on the cards and to think of things which he would want to know about the case in order to advise his junior colleague. He was then allowed to pick items of information he wanted to know and was instructed to stop as soon as he was ready to make a decision about what to do with the case. He was told that he could take as much time and consult as many items of information as he wanted but that he should try to act as close to what he would do in real life as possible.

The items of information chosen were recorded by the researcher in the order in which they were chosen. When the respondent was ready, he was asked to make several decisions. He could recommend that the case be dropped altogether from prosecution (this was only relevant when the game was played with prosecutors) or that it go to trial or that it be plea bargained. If the recommendation was to plea bargain, then the respondent was asked what the "bottom-line" (not the "opening offer") terms of the bargain should be. For prosecutors this meant how lenient an offer they would make before either insisting the case go to trial or dropping it. For defense counsel this meant the most severe terms he would accept before insisting the case go to trial.[2] Respondents choosing to plea bargain were asked to specify the bargain in terms of type and length of the sentence to be recommended to the court, and the estimated probability of conviction at trial assuming they were the attorney in the case and the case were tried in their local jurisdiction. Each respondent was given two cases to decide: one robbery and one burglary. Prosecutors and defense counsels were given the exact same sets of facts except that the words "prosecutor" or "defense counsel" were substituted at relevant places. A unique feature of our simulation is that two variables were manipulated, namely, case strength and seriousness of the offender. Case strength was varied by using two versions of the card entitled, "Evidence — Substance of Available." The seriousness of the defendant was varied by having two versions of the card entitled "Defendant's Prior Record and Police Reputation." (For a description of all items of information used in the simulation, see Appendix B.)

FACTORS IN PLEA BARGAINING: REVIEW AND INTERVIEW DATA

Numerous factors have been identified as being influential in plea bargaining. The review that follows discusses those factors reported by other researchers and substantiated by our own interview findings. A second analysis of the same factors based on our plea bargaining simulation will be presented in a subsequent section of this paper.

Caseload

One of the most common justifications for plea bargaining is the need to dispose of cases as rapidly as possible; otherwise, the court system would grind to a halt. Just how caseload pressures come to influence plea bargaining decisions, however, remains unclear. Alschuler (1968) believes these pressures are background factors which do not determine either which cases shall be plea bargained or on what terms. Rather, these pressures act at a distance and simply require that some portion of the caseload be plea bargained. Rhodes (1979) agrees. Mills (1971) describes caseload pressures as having a direct and distressing impact on plea bargaining. He reports how a New York public defender uses the backlog problem as a club to dictate the specific terms of the plea bargains he wants. If the terms are not met, he threatens to take all of his cases to trial. This practice is referred to as "court busting," but it appears to be more of a courthouse myth than a reality. We found virtually no cases in the jurisdictions we visited where "court busting" was an established practice. We heard of only two cases where a defense attorney threatened to take his caseload to trial if he did not get the deal he wanted in a particular case. In both cases the prosecutors were unperturbed by the threat and the situation backfired on the defense counsel. The defense attorneys went to trial with their caseloads but were quickly worn out by the heavy dose of trial work. The overwhelming majority of defense attorneys (50 out of 51) told us that they had never tried to court bust and had never heard of it happening. Most of them thought the idea of making such a threat was "ridiculous," "moronic," "very unwise," or "stupid."

Based on our interview data we would agree with the view that caseload pressures act as general determinates of the need to plea bargain but do not determine which specific cases will be bargained or what the terms of the bargains will be.

Seriousness of the Criminal and the Crime

Several researchers (Alschuler, 1968; Chambliss and Seidman, 1971; Lagoy et al., 1976; Neubauer, 1974; and Newman, 1966) and we, ourselves, have found that the seriousness of the criminal is indeed an influential factor in plea bargaining. But we have found that within and between jurisdictions there are substantial differences in how seriousness is defined in practice. Some judges will permit a record of prior convictions to be used only in sentencing discussions; and, this policy is carried over by prosecutors in their assessment of cases for plea bargaining. On the other hand, in other places prosecutors and judges readily consider arrest records and even well-articulated police suspicions of a defendant's involvement in criminal activities as the basis for determining the criminal's seriousness. Whatever definition is used, however, the result is reportedly the same. The more serious the criminal, the stiffer the terms of the plea bargain—all other things being equal. This is true, of course, only if the defendant decides to plea bargain. Previous research is contradictory on whether serious criminals (those having prior records) prefer to plea bargain or go to trial. Newman (1956) and Chambliss and Seidman (1971) suggest that such defendants are less likely than first offenders to go to trial because as recidivists they know the advantages of plea bargaining. Other researchers (Greenwood et al., 1973; Mather, 1974; Baldwin and McConville, 1977) have found that defendants with prior records are more likely to go to trial. In sum, then, research on the importance of a defendant's prior record is unclear with respect to the decision to plead guilty or to go to trial, but is in considerable agreement that if the defendant chooses to plead the prior record will affect the terms of the plea.

An interesting question that remains to be answered is, "How much does a unit increase in the severity of the seriousness of the criminal result in a unit increase in the severity of the terms of the plea bargain?" We are unable to answer this with any precision, but some of the serendipitious findings of our decision simulation shed some light on the matter. From conversations with respondents during the pretest as well as from spontaneous remarks during and after the actual administration of the simulation, we learned how specific items of information are translated by attorneys into increases or decreases in the lengths of time sought in plea bargaining. Occasionally a respondent would flip up one of the information cards in the simulation and groan, "There goes another year." We found that prosecutors and defense counsel engage in a very fine calculation of moral turpitude. Compared with the layperson's, the experienced criminal justice actor's analysis of moral turpitude is like the difference between measuring things in terms of pounds and ounces and measuring them in the finer units of grams, milligrams, and micrograms. There are subtle shades of differences and nuances which experienced attorneys appreciate but which are lost on the layperson.

For instance, in the pretesting of our hypothetical robbery with a knife case, prosecutors wanted to know such things as: Was the slashing completely unprovoked by the victim? Had the victim said anything at all or resisted in any way? Was the slashing necessary to accomplish the crime? Was it done out of nervousness or panic or out of simple meanness? When the robber presented the knife, how did he present it? Was there actual contact of the knife with the victim? While the layman may fail to appreciate the distinction between a knife that was used to threaten and a knife that actually struck a victim, criminal justice officials who are familiar with hundreds of such cases come to appreciate such distinctions and translate them into differences in time to be served. Prosecutors wanted to know not just whether there had been a slashing but how deep it was, whether there would be permanent injury or ugly scars in visible places such as on the face. This kind of information was used by prosecutors to assess not only how serious the crime had been but also how "mean" or "bad" the defendant was. There was no question that robbery with a slashing was a serious matter and had to be punished, but there was a question about the precise degree of punishment that this particular robbery deserved. While the layman may think that it is enough to know that a person is a "robber who slashes" in order to decide what sentence should be imposed, the experienced prosecutor has learned to make much finer distinctions. Some robbers who slash display a much greater disregard for the well-being of the victims than others; and since there is not unlimited capacity in the correctional system and since distinctions must be made, these differences are used as the basis for making them.[3]

Strength of the Case

A crucially important assumption behind much of the decision making in the criminal justice system is the belief that attorneys are able to evaluate case strength. That is, attorneys believe they are able to estimate the likelihood that if a case went to trial it would result in a conviction. Initial screening programs operate on the assumption that weak cases can be reliably identified and culled out early. The decision to plea bargain and the terms of the plea bargain are reported by virtually all researchers who address this issue (Alschuler, 1968; Mather, 1974; Neubauer, 1974; and Newman 1966) to be influenced by case strength. We have even had defense counsel tell us that the level of effort they put into a case not only at plea bargaining but also at trial depends on their estimate of the probability of conviction.

Despite the unanimous agreement on the crucial importance of this skill, there has been little effort to examine it systematically and determine whether lawyers can do what they claim to do and whether they do it evenhandedly. Alschuler (1968) concludes on the basis of anecdotal evidence that as cases get weaker plea bargains become more favorable to the defendant with the most favorable bargains offered when the prosecutor has "no case at all." In contrast, Mather (1974:286) quotes a prosecutor as saying that the weaker case is the more likely it is to be tried. We found that the vast majority of prosecutors give their most generous deals in their weakest cases. Of 24 prosecutors, 21 responded that this had been their practice. (That is, they answered "Yes" to the question: "Has your experience been that you generally offer the 'best' [from the defendant's perspective] deals in the weakest cases?")

Mather (1974) also analyzes the influence of case strength on the plea bargaining decision, relying upon interview data. However, in her analysis case strength is not examined by itself but rather in conjunction with the influence of case seriousness. Her concept of case seriousness combines the notion of seriousness of the crime and seriousness of the offender. It refers to the severity of the sentence that is likely to be imposed in a case. She dichotomizes case seriousness into "serious" and "light" cases; and she adopts the distinction used by public defenders between "deadbang" cases (strong chance of conviction) and "reasonable doubt" cases (weak chance of conviction). She says that deadbang, light cases were usually plea bargained; but it was not possible to predict whether reasonable doubt, light cases would be bargained or go to trial. For serious cases the decision to go to trial in either deadbang or reasonable doubt cases depended upon how good the prosecutor's plea offer was.

Evenhandedness

With regard to the matter of evenhandedness of plea bargaining, Mather's findings are unclear. She says that all public defenders agreed that both case strength and case seriousness should be considered in the plea bargaining decisions; but she also seems to say that there is not a high degree of agreement among attorneys about how to evaluate any particular case. Mather (1974:272) writes:

> Certainly, PD's varied in their judgments and their predictions, so that one attorney might evaluate his client's chances differently than another would have. Or, what is a 'good' bargain for one PD might not be to his colleague. But, in general there was a consensus on how to evaluate cases and choose the best method for disposition.

An informal study by the Institute for Law and Social Research provides some grounds to believe that under certain circumstances attorneys are unable to accurately assess case strength. One of the features in the early version of the PROMIS (Prosecutorial Management Information System) computer program was a case ranking system. The system prioritized the prosecutor's daily misdemeanor docket according to a formula that combined three criteria, one of which was the prosecutor's estimate of the probability of conviction. This criterion, however, was later found to be of little use. An in-house study determined that the prosecutors' judgments were no better than chance in their ability to predict conviction. It must be pointed out, however, that the prosecutors who were making these judgments were the least experienced prosecutors in the office. Perhaps the criterion would have been more useful if more experienced prosecutors had been involved.

Personal Attributes of Attorneys

Several researchers (Alschuler, 1975; Mather, 1974; Neubauer, 1974; and Newman, 1966) have pointed out and our own interview data confirm that certain attributes of attorneys (both prosecutors and defense counsel) can influence both the decision to plea and the terms of the bargain. One attribute is the attorney's reputation. A second is the personal relationship between the opposing attorneys.

An attorney's reputation is based on several things, including his honesty, his willingness to go to trial, and his ability at trial. Trying cases is hard work which both prosecutors and defense counsel try to minimize or avoid to some extent. Some attorneys are known for never going to trial. Alschuler (1975) refers to defense attorneys who never take a case to trial as the "plead them guilty bar." We found that it is equally true that some prosecutors prefer to negotiate cases rather than try them. It is believed that attorneys who never take cases to trial negotiate from a position of weakness, and, hence, either get less or give away more in their bargaining.

A second aspect of attorney reputation has to do with the trial skills of the attorney. Among attorneys who are willing to go to trial, there are various degrees of skill at trying cases. Again it is believed that this difference in skill affects bargaining. Supposedly, a skilled trial lawyer bargains from a stronger position than an inept one.

Alschuler (1975) points out, however, that an attorney can become so famous that he cannot get opposing attorneys to plea bargain with him. They would prefer to take him to trial and try to beat him in order to establish their own reputation. We never heard of this kind of situation in our interviews with attorneys. But we did occasionally hear of a related type of situation. Attorneys do develop personal animosities or "score cards" with each other. Some attorneys have told us that they believe certain other attorneys wanted to take them to trial to try to beat them because the last time they went to trial the opposing attorney had lost. It was never suggested, however, that this was the overriding consideration in the decision about whether to plea bargain or go to trial.

With regard to honesty, we heard in several jurisdictions that some attorneys have such a reputation for dishonesty that other attorneys refuse to negotiate with them (although they may make a flat, take-it-or-leave-it offer).

The Victim

There is little known about the victim's role in plea bargaining. After the initial stage of our national survey, we concluded (McDonald, 1977) that the victim's wishes were rarely considered in the plea bargaining decision making except for particularly notorious cases and in some jurisdictions regularly in cases of rape. The latter conclusion is supported by the findings of Lagoy et al. (1976).

Mitigating Attributes and Circumstances

Various attributes of the defendant or the victim or other special circumstances relating to the crime can be regarded as "mitigating" factors (see discussion below) and are believed to influence the decision to plea bargain and the terms of the deal. A list of potential special attributes and circumstances is lengthy. A partial listing of those identified by others (Alschuler, 1968; Lagoy et al., 1976; Mather, 1974; McDonald, 1976; Neubauer, 1974; Newman, 1966) and our interview findings is as follows:

(1) attributes of the defendant, such as his age, sex, race, marital status, social class, political or family connections, demeanor, history of employment, drug use, alcohol use, psychiatric problems, physical health problems, military service, and length of local residence;
(2) the defendant's relationship with the victim;
(3) attributes of the victim including things which could appear in the eyes of decision makers to make the victim "blameworthy" (in a more general sense than the legal notion of provocation) such as the victim's age, sex, race, social class, demeanor, prior record of criminal deviant behavior, and also the victim's willingness to testify and ability to establish a linkage between the defendant and the crime. (Of course, this latter item is usually considered in connection with evaluating case strength.)

Prosecutors and Defense Counsel Compared

There has been little effort to determine whether prosecutors and defense counsel differ in the way they evaluate cases for plea bargaining. Some studies (Mather, 1974; Neubauer, 1974) and our own interview data indicate that prosecutors and defense attorneys evaluate cases the same way—at least up to a point. They both agree on the importance of the big three factors: seriousness of the offense, seriousness of the offender, and the strength of the case. Beyond that, little is known about whether they continue to look at cases in the same way. On this point the literature contains only a few somewhat inconsistent hints. Three hypotheses can be identified.

Both Neubauer (1974) and Mather (1974) mention that defense counsel look for mitigating circumstances. But, they seem to differ on how this is done and hence whether this distinguishes defense counsel from prosecutors. Neubauer hints that the evaluation of mitigating circumstances is something which is done after and in addition to the basic assessment of the value of the case in terms of the big three factors. He describes defense counsel as making "particularistic appeals" in an attempt to persuade prosecutors that in this particular case for some special reason the terms of the bargain should be even less severe than the normal discount given to this type of case. The notion of a two-stage bargaining process is also hinted at by Alschuler's (1975) observation that defense attorneys try to improve upon standard or "normal" deals in a jurisdiction.

In contrast, Mather describes plea bargaining decision making as a one-stage phenomenon in which the defense counsel's assessment of mitigating circumstances is part and parcel of the calculation of the big three factors. Her description implies that there is no difference between prosecutors and defense counsel in their respective evaluations of a case (assuming they both consider the big three factors). A third view is implied by those researchers (e.g., Alschuler, 1968; Newman, 1966; Rosett and Cressey, 1976) who have reported that one of the functions prosecutors consciously perform at plea bargaining is to mitigate an undue harshness of the law (to tailor the punishment to the unique circumstances of the case and thereby assure that substantive justice is done). This view says nothing about whether there is a one-stage or a two-stage process in plea bargaining, but it strongly implies that prosecutors are as concerned as defense counsel about mitigating circumstances.

FINDINGS: DECISION SIMULATION

There is no concise way to convey the data regarding the items of information chosen in the plea bargaining simulation. The two tables presented below provide complementary, partial perspectives on the data. Both compare the decision making of prosecutors and defense counsel. Table 1 indicates for each item of information contained in the simulation the respective proportions of prosecutors and defense counsel who consulted the item at all before deciding what to do with the case. To highlight the comparison between the two types of attorneys, two additional calculations are provided. Column 3 indicates the differences in percentage points between the respective proportions of prosecutors and defense counsel consulting each item of information. Column 4 presents the difference between prosecutors and defense counsel in the form of a ratio of their respective proportions. The ratio was used to rank all items presented in the table in order of decreasing ratios of agreement between prosecutors and defense counsel. Neither measure adequately conveys the many-sided notion of "agreement" between attorneys. But taken together, these two measures give some perspective on the topic. For instance, 54% of both prosecutors and defense counsel consulted the card entitled "Defendant's Age." On the one hand, this means that there is no disagreement *between* prosecutors and defense counsel in the importance of this item of information; on the other hand, there is substantial disagreement *within* both of those categories of attorneys over the item of information.

Table 2 presents a portion of the same data arrayed differently. It shows what items of information were chosen by attorneys for each of their first twelve choices. Because of the length of this table, only the first twelve choices are presented and items chosen by very small proportions were combined into a miscellaneous category.

Case Strength

One notes in Table 1 that there is substantial agreement among all attorneys with regard to the big three factors. The concept of case strength cannot be reduced to any one card. But the two cards which are most obviously related to it are "Basic Facts of the Case" and "Evidence—Substance of Available." Ninety-one percent or more of each type of attorney consulted these two cards before making their decision. What is more, as indicated in Table 2, these two cards were usually the first cards chosen by both types of attorney. Another factor also related to case strength was "Effectiveness of Witnesses at Trial," which was chosen by two-thirds of each type of attorney and usually chosen early. Also consulted by the great majority of both types of attorneys was the "Defendant's Account of the Incident." The defendant may have an alibi or a defense or a plausible alternative version of what happened. Another factor is "Propriety of Police Conduct After Arrest." The police may have lost or weakened the case by making some constitutional error. The literature and our interviews have suggested that this last item is an important factor in plea bargaining. Supposedly, plea bargaining is the way prosecutors salvage cases in which the police have acted improperly. Thus, it is somewhat surprising that only 38% of the prosecutors and 35% of the defense counsel consulted this item. Perhaps this represents a vote of confidence in the lawfulness of the police in handling this type of crime. On the other hand, it may suggest that the local courts are not sympathetic to motions to suppress evidence because of blunders by the constable.

Still another factor related to case strength is whether or not there are codefendants. About 40% of both types of attorneys consulted this card. If a codefendant had been involved, it would have changed the nature of the case. The presence of a codefendant does not in itself make the case stronger or weaker, but it does make the case more complicated. Each defendant will have his own attorney and his own account of the incident. Multiple defendants provide the opportunity of bargaining one defendant against the other.

Still other factors less obviously related to case strength were consulted by some attorneys. Several items of information about the defendant are of this kind. If the defendant had been under the influence of alcohol or drugs, it may have been difficult to establish the requisite criminal intent. The case may have been not a burglary but the lesser crimes of unlawful entry plus larceny. Some of the prosecutors who consulted these cards later explained that they were concerned with the matter of intent. The fact that so few prosecutors (about one-third) checked these cards might be regarded as indirect evidence of the lack of prosecutorial concern for accurate charging. But, we feel that this

(text continued on p. 171)

Table 1: Comparison Between Prosecutors and Defense Counsel on Items of Information Selected In Burglary Plea Bargaining Simulation In Decreasing Order of Agreement*

Item	1 % of Prosecutors Choosing Item (N = 134)	2 % of Defense Counsel Choosing Item (N = 102)	3 Column 2 Minus Column 1	4 Column 2 Divided by Column 1
1 Defendant's Age	54	54	0	1.0
2 Defendant's Prior Record & Police Reputation	92	93	1	1.0
3 Evidence—Substance of Available	91	94	3	1.0
4 Ability of Defendant to Pay Restitution	13	13	0	1.0
5 Basic Facts of the Case	97	94	-3	0.9
6 Codefendants	39	43	4	1.1
7 Propriety of Police Conduct After Arrest	38	35	-3	0.9
8 Effectiveness of Witnesses at Trial	69	65	-4	1.1
9 Aggravating and Mitigating Circumstances	86	76	-10	0.9
10 Defendant's Aliases	15	13	-2	0.9
11 Detainers on Defendant	43	37	-6	0.9
12 Criminal History of Defendant's Family	8	10	2	1.2
13 Defendant's Account of Incident	73	87	14	1.2
14 Victim's Attitude Toward Bargain	41	30	-11	0.7
15 Pretrial Release, Probation/Parole Status at Time of Offense	39	54	15	1.4
16 Record of Alcohol Use by Defendant	26	37	11	1.4
17 Police Attitude Toward Proposed Bargain	38	23	-15	0.6
18 Defendant's Intelligence and Education	29	44	15	1.5
19 Defendant's Employment Status	43	63	20	1.5
20 Defendant's Psychological Problems	32	47	15	1.5

Table 1: (Cont'd.)

21	Record of Drug Use by Defendant	36	54	18	1.5
22	Length of Local Residence of Defendant	16	24	8	1.5
23	Defendant's Interests and Activities	10	15	5	1.5
24	Publicity/Community Sentiment	13	21	8	1.6
25	Length of Time Since Arrest in Instant Offense	22	35	13	1.6
26	Victim's Race, Age, Sex	10	17	7	1.7
27	Alternatives to Incarceration	22	45	23	2.0
28	Defendant's Pretrial Release Status for this Burglary	25	52	27	2.0
29	Defendant's Marital Status	16	39	23	2.4
30	Trial Judge's Reputation for Leniency	33	75	42	2.3
31	Reputation of Prosecutor or Defense Attorney	19	54	35	2.8
32	Defendant's Sex	12	36	24	3.0
33	Defendant's Military Record	9	27	18	3.0
34	Physical Health of Defendant	7	22	15	3.1
35	Backlog of Docket of Judge to Whom Case is Assigned	7	26	19	3.7
36	Defendant's Religious Affiliation	1	8	7	8.0
37	Defendant's Race/Ethnicity/Nationality	4	35	31	8.7
38	Relationship Between Prosecutor and Defense Attorney	5	45	40	9.0
39	Defendant's Sexual Orientation	1	9	8	9.0

*SOURCE: Georgetown Plea Bargaining Decision Simulation

Table 2: Rank Order of the First Twelve Items of Information Consulted Before Deciding Whether to Plea Bargain in Simulated Burglary Case by Type of Attorney

	(in percentages)		
	Rank Order of Item		
Prosecutors (N = 134)	% of Prosecutors/Defense Counsel Choosing Items		Defense Counsel (N = 102)
	Item Chosen First		
Basic Facts	79	73	Basic Facts
Evidence	7	9	Evidence
Prior Record	6	5	Judge's Reputation for Sentencing
Aggravating/Mitigating Circumstances	2	3	Prior Record
Misc. 6 items	6	10	Misc. 7 items
	100%	100%	
	Item Chosen Second		
Evidence	45	40	Evidence
Prior Record	19	23	Defendant's Account
Basic Facts	10	12	Basic Facts
Defendant's Account	5	3	Defendant's Race & Ethnicity
Effectiveness of Witnesses	4	22	Misc. 13 items
Aggravating/Mitigating Circumstances	4		
Misc. 11 items	13		
	100%	100%	
	Item Chosen Third		
Prior Record	17	29	Defendant's Account
Defendant's Account	16	17	Evidence
Aggravating/Mitigating Circumstances	14	14	Prior Record
Evidence	10	9	Defendant's Age
Effectiveness of Witnesses	10	5	Effectiveness of Witnesses
Defendant's Age	5	4	Aggravating/Mitigating Circumstances
Misc. 17 items	28	22	Misc. 14 items
	100%	100%	
	Item Chosen Fourth		
Defendant's Account	15	18	Prior Record
Prior Record	13	14	Defendant's Account
Aggravating/Mitigating Circumstances	11	9	Effectiveness of Witnesses
Effectiveness of Witnesses	10	7	Codefendants
Police Conduct	5	7	Aggravating/Mitigating Circumstances

Table 2: (Cont'd.)

(in percentages)		
Rank Order of Item		
Prosecutors (N = 134)	**% of Prosecutors/Defense Counsel Choosing Items**	**Defense Counsel** (N = 102)
None. Decision already made	4 5	Defendant's Age
Misc. 19 items	42 5	None. Decision already made
	4	Defendant's Sex
	31	Misc. 13 items
	100% 100%	

Item Chosen Fifth

Effectiveness of Witnesses	15 11	Prior Record
Aggravating/Mitigating Circumstances	13 11	Effectiveness of Witnesses
Prior Record	11 8	Pretrial Release Status at Time of Offense
Defendant's Account	20 8	Judge's Reputation for Leniency
Defendant's Age	9 6	Codefendants
Codefendants	6 6	Aggravating/Mitigating Circumstances
None. Decision already made	6 6	None. Decision already made
Misc. 20 items	30 4	Defendant's Age
	4	Defendant's Employment Record
	4	Pretrial Release Status for this Offense
	32	Misc. 19 items
	100% 100%	

Item Chosen Sixth

None. Decision already made	13 17	Prior Record
Aggravating/Mitigating Circumstances	10 9	None. Decision already made
Prior Record	9 8	Judge's Reputation for Leniency
Defendant's Age	7 8	Aggravating/Mitigating Circumstances
Defendant's Account	7 6	Defendant's Race & Ethnicity
Effectiveness of Witnesses	6 6	Effectiveness of Witnesses
Evidence	5 6	Pretrial Release Status at time of Offense
Detainers	4 4	Defendant's Age
Police Conduct	4 4	Defendant's Account
Victim's Attitude Toward Plea	4 4	Relationship Between Prosecutor & Defense Counsel

Table 2: (Cont'd.)

	(in percentages)		
	Rank Order of Item		
Prosecutors (N = 134)	**% of Prosecutors/Defense** **Counsel Choosing Items**		**Defense Counsel** (N = 102)
Misc. 16 items	31	28	Misc. 17 items
	100%	100%	

Item Chosen Seventh

None. Decision already made	18	12	None. Decision already made
Aggravating/Mitigating Circumstances	10	9	Defendant's Age
Defendant's Age	6	9	Aggravating/Mitigating Circumstances
Effectiveness of Witnesses	6	6	Prior Record
Prior Record	5	6	Pretrial Release Status for Instant Offense
Evidence	5	6	Pretrial Release Status at Time of Offense
Police Attitude Toward Plea	5	6	Detainers
Pretrial Release Status at Time of Offense	5	5	Judge's Reputation for Leniency
Pretrial Release Status for this Offense	4	4	Codefendants
Victim's Attitude Toward Plea	4	4	Reputation of Prosecutor as Trial Lawyers
Codefendants	4	33	Misc. 22 items
Detainers	4		
Misc. 17 items	24		
	100%	100%	

Item Chosen Eighth

None. Decision already made	26	16	None. Decision already made
Defendant's Age	4	7	Codefendants
Codefendants	4	6	Aggravating/Mitigating Circumstances
Victim's Attitude Toward Plea	4	6	Reputation of Prosecutor as Trial Lawyer
Pretrial Release Status at Time of Offense	4	5	Defendant's Sex
Police Conduct	4	5	Prior Record
Time Since Arrest for this Offense	4	5	Defendant's Account
Defendant's Drug History	4	5	Pretrial Release Status for this Offense

Table 2: (Cont'd.)

	(in percentages)		
	Rank Order of Item		
Prosecutors (N = 134)	% of Prosecutors/Defense Counsel Choosing Items		Defense Counsel (N = 102)
Aggravating/Mitigating Circumstances	4	4	Defendant's Employment History
Misc. 22 items	42	4	Police Conduct
		4	Pretrial Release Status at Time of this Offense
		33	Misc. 19 items
	100%	100%	

	Item Chosen Ninth		
None. Decision already made	30	20	None. Decision already made
Police Attitude Toward Plea	6	6	Defendant's Employment History
Defendant's Account	6	5	Defendant's Age
Prior Record	5	5	Police Conduct
Defendant's Age	4	5	Effectiveness of Witnesses
Defendant's Employment Record	4	5	Relationship Between Prosecutor & Defense Counsel
Defendant's Education	3	5	Pretrial Release Status for this Crime
Victim's Attitude Toward Plea	3	4	Defendant's Marital Status
Defendant's Alcoholic History	3	4	Judge's Reputation for Leniency
Detainers	3	3	Docket Backlog
Aggravating/Mitigating Circumstances	3	3	Defendant's Account
Misc. 21 items	30	3	Prior Record
		3	Detainers
		29	Misc. 20 items
	100%	100%	

	Item Chosen Tenth		
None. Decision already made	37	21	None. Decision already made
Pretrial Release Status at Time of Offense	7	9	Defendant's Employment History
Defendant's Drug History	5	7	Aggravating/Mitigating Circumstances
Defendant's Education	5	5	Reputation of Prosecutor as Trial Attorney
Defendant's Employment History	4	5	Defendant's Psychological History
Defendant's Psychological History	4	5	Defendant's Race & Ethnicity
Effectiveness of Witnesses	4	4	Defendant's Education
Police Conduct	3	4	Judge's Reputation for Leniency

Table 2: (Cont'd.)

(in percentages)

Rank Order of Item

Prosecutors (N = 134)	% of Prosecutors/Defense Counsel Choosing Items		Defense Counsel (N = 102)
Misc. 22 items	31	3	Defendant's Age
		3	Police Conduct
		3	Effectiveness of Witnesses
		31	Misc. 22 items
	100%	100%	

Item Chosen Eleventh

None. Decision already made	45	25	None. Decision already made
Defendant's Psychological History	6	5	Defendant's Age
Defendant's Age	4	5	Police Conduct
Judge's Reputation for Leniency	4	5	Reputation of Prosecutor as Trial Attorney
Detainers	4	4	Aggravating/Mitigating Circumstances
Aggravating/Mitigating Circumstances	3	4	Relationship Between Prosecutor & Defense Counsel
Local Residency	3	4	Defendant's Employment Record
Defendant's Alcoholic History	3	4	Defendant's Marital Status
Police Attitude Toward Plea	3	3	Defendant's Psychological History
Police Conduct	3	3	Judge's Reputation for Leniency
Misc. 21 items	22	3	Evidence
		3	Available Alternatives to Incarceration
		3	Victim's Attitude Toward Plea
		3	Pretrial Release Status for this Offense
		3	Pretrial Release Status at Time of this Offense
		3	Defendant's Drug History
		20	Misc. 10 items
	100%	100%	

Item Chosen Twelfth

None. Decision already made	50	28	None. Decision already made
Judge's Reputation for Leniency	4	7	Defendant's Sex
Defendant's Employment History	3	7	Defendant's Education
Defendant's Psychological History	3	7	Defendant's Employment History
Codefendants	3	5	Defendant's Psychological History
Pretrial Release Status for this Offense	3	4	Judge's Reputation for Leniency
Defendant's Alcoholic History	3	3	Victim's Attitude Toward Plea

Table 2: (Cont'd.)

(in percentages)		
	Rank Order of Item	
Prosecutors (N = 134)	% of Prosecutors/Defense Counsel Choosing Items	Defense Counsel (N = 102)
Misc. 21 items	31 3	Pretrial Release Status for this Offense
	3	Pretrial Release Status at Time of this Offense
	3	Defendant's Drug History
	30	Misc. 20 items
	100% 100%	

interpretation would be stretching the limitations of the simulation. Had these cards been labeled differently, more prosecutors might have consulted them. For instance, if the label had been "Defendant's State of Intoxication at Time of Offense," more prosecutors might have checked the card.

In addition to his records of drug and alcohol use, some attorneys checked other defendant attributes for the purpose of checking case strength. (Asking attorneys why they chose certain cards was not part of the original design of the research; but some attorneys volunteered explanations.) For instance, some prosecutors checked the defendant's race and then somewhat apologetically explained they were just making sure that he matched the description given by the witness. Some prosecutors checked the defendant's psychological history to make sure that the issue of an insanity defense would not come up.

Seriousness of the Criminal

There was almost unanimous agreement among both prosecutors and defense that the seriousness of the defendant (at least as indicated by the card "Defendant's Prior Record and Police Reputation") must be consulted before the plea bargaining decision could be made. More remarkable than this unanimity is the order in which this card was chosen. By the end of the third choice, 42% of the prosecutors and 18% of the defense counsel had consulted the item.

In addition, other cards relating to the defendant's seriousness were consulted by attorneys. The defendant's age, for instance, is relevant to his dangerousness because it establishes the rate of criminal activity over time and his progress in a criminal career. Other indicators of defendant's seriousness include such things as whether the defendant has outstanding detainers; whether he was on some form of release at the time of the instant offense; his military record; and whether he comes from a family which is involved in criminal behavior. Even the defendant's employment status represents in part a measure of his dangerousness. The defendant with a long history of unemployment readily fits the image of the criminal who will have to make a living through crime if he is on the street.

Seriousness of the Crime

The general level of seriousness of the crime is established by the nature of the charge—in this case, burglary. But there are considerable variations in the seriousness of different burglaries, depending upon the circumstances of the offense. The law, itself, captures these variations, but only crudely, with its distinctions between degrees of burglary. Experienced attorneys make even finer distinctions. The law sometimes distinguishes between day and night burglaries and between commercial and residential burglaries. Experienced attorneys add the distinctions of whether a residence is being lived in at the time, whether it was actually occupied at the time, and whether the trespasser was breaking in merely to get out of the cold or find a place to stay while intoxicated on drugs or alcohol or to steal or do violence. It is not surprising that the great majority (86% and 76%, respectively) of the prosecutors and defense counsel consulted the card "Aggravating and Mitigating Circumstances of the Offense," or that this card was usually consulted early in the decision making.

Caseload

Our earlier conclusion that caseload pressures act at a distance and are not a major factor in deciding what to do with individual cases is supported by the finding that only 7% of the prosecutors and 26% of the defense attorneys consulted the card entitled "Backlog of Docket of Judge to Whom Case is Assigned." Moreover, this card was not consulted by a substantial number of attorneys in the first 12 choices.

Differences in Information Processing
Between Prosecutors and Defense Counsel

The most noticeable difference in Table 1 between defense attorneys and prosecutors is that the defense attorneys consulted more information than prosecutors. In 29 out of the 39 items of information in the table, a greater proportion of defense attorneys than prosecutors consulted the item. For 22 of the items the proportion of defense attorneys was one and one-half times or more as great as that of the prosecutors. For only 8 items were prosecutors more likely than defense attorneys to consult the items; and for only 2 of these was the difference substantial. These 2 items are the attitudes of the victim and the police toward the plea bargain. The fact that 41% of the prosecutors were concerned for the victim's opinion of the plea bargain reveals a much higher degree of prosecutorial concern for this matter than was believed to have existed (McDonald, 1977). The fact that 38% of the prosecutors were concerned with the police attitude toward the plea bargain can be seen in two different ways. To hear the police complain about being ignored by prosecutors, one might regard this 38% as unexpectedly high. On the other hand, for police who complain they should be regularly consulted but are not, this figure would prove their case.

Also noteworthy about the prosecutor's concern for the police and the victim is the fact that concern appears earlier in the decision making among prosecutors than it does among defense counsel. These findings suggest that prosecutors have "clients" that they try to please that are not as much of a concern to defense counsel.

The distinctive approach of defense counsel to the evaluation of cases for plea bargaining can be further appreciated by reviewing those items of information which defense counsel consult substantially more often and/or substantially earlier than prosecutors. There are three broad classes of such items: defendant's attributes; personal matters relating to criminal justice actors; and all other things. Defense counsel are consistently more interested in personal attributes of the defendant including his sex, race and ethnicity, intelligence and education, employment and marital status, history of drug and alcohol use, and psychological problems, sexual orientation, physical health, and whether the instant crime was committed while on some form of release for another crime. The defense attorney's interest in these matters was unlike the prosecutor's concern that criminal intent might not be provable. Rather, we believe that the defense attorneys' higher rate of interest in these matters is a reflection of their special role in plea bargaining. That role was identified by an experienced public defender, quoted by Mather (1974:278) as follows:

> Let me put it to you this way: What is our job as a criminal lawyer in most instances? No. 1 is . . . no kidding, we know the man's done it, or we feel he's done it, he may deny it, but the question is, *Can they prove it?* The next thing is: *Can we mitigate it?* Of course you can always find something good to say about the guy—to mitigate it. Those are the two things that are important and that's what you do [emphasis in the original].

Assessing case strength is something both prosecutors and defense attorneys do. But, the job of "mitigating" the case seems to be the distinctive role of the defense counsel. The concept of mitigation can be construed in a narrow legal sense or in the broad sense used by this public defender. Both prosecutors and defense counsel are concerned with aggravating and mitigating circumstances in the narrow sense, such as whether a weapon was used, whether there was a provocation by the victim, or whether the victim was threatened. But the defense counsel's role of "mitigating" a case means much more than consulting the card "Aggravating and Mitigating Circumstances." It refers to the overall strategy and purpose of the defense counsel in plea bargaining. It means playing down the defendant's worst features and playing up his best. Thus, when it comes to the seriousness of the crime and the criminal, the defense counsel's job is to reinterpret reality so his client will appear in the best possible light. For instance, a defense attorney from Norfolk, Virginia, told us how he was able to get an "excellent" deal in a murder case by pointing out to the police and prosecutors that the victim was a well-known drug pusher whom everyone was delighted to be rid of. The attorney felt he could have gotten an even better deal but for the fact that his client "had shown bad form" in the killing. His client had confronted the victim over an alleged mistreatment of the client's sister. The victim had pleaded for mercy and then turned and ran. The client gave chase and shot the victim in the back. The defense attorney felt that if his client had shot the victim when they were face to face it would have been easier to portray him as simply an outraged brother. But the shooting in the back after the pleas for mercy could not be easily "mitigated." It conveyed the impression of a person who was heartless, hence, more dangerous, and, hence, deserving of a more severe plea bargain.

The job of mitigation begins with playing down the seriousness of the offense and the seriousness of the offender but does not end there. It involves looking "for something good to say about the guy." Neubauer (1974:219) seems to have been on the right tract in reporting that defense counsel evaluate cases the same as prosecutors as far as the big three factors are concerned but then go on to make "particularistic appeals." The idea of a two-stage model of plea bargaining, the first dealing with a general discount usually given to a class case and the second with improvements upon that discount, seems to be supported by our simulation data. It is this second aspect of plea bargaining where the defense counsel plays his unique role.[4] Here is where he looks for *any* reason that his client should get an additional break. We believe this accounts for the fact that defense attorneys so consistently consulted more information.

Several of them desperately flipped through the cards commenting, "Doesn't this guy have *anything* going for him?"

The second broad class of items which defense counsel consulted substantially more often and earlier than prosecutors involved personal characteristics of criminal justice actors. More specifically, defense counsel were more concerned than prosecutors with: (1) the trial judge's reputation for leniency (75% compared with 33%); (2) the reputation of the prosecutor (54% compared with 19%); and (3) the relationship between the prosecutor and the defense attorney (45% compared with 5%).

By the end of the ninth card, at least 30% of the defense attorneys (compared with 9% of the prosecutors) had consulted the "Judge's Reputation for Leniency" card. The major concern of the defense attorneys for the trial judge's sentencing practices indicate that the judge has a much more influential role in setting the limits of plea bargains than was evident before. Our interview findings were ambiguous on this point. On the one hand, it was clear with some judges that their sentencing practices established the upper limits of what a plea bargain would be. Prosecutors would either have to offer what everyone knew the judge would sentence anyhow or something better in order to get a defendant to plead. In several jurisdictions, we learned, judges would not tolerate prosecutors "embarrassing" them or "putting the heat on them" by recommending sentences more severe than the judge's usual standards. Moreover, it was not uncommon to hear that judges would reprimand prosecutors or call their supervisors and have them moved to a different courtroom if the prosecutor persisted in recommending higher sentences than what the judge cared to impose. (Thus, we are somewhat surprised to find in the decision simulation that relatively few prosecutors [33%] showed concern for the judge's sentencing practice.)

On the other hand, we also found that some judges seemed to follow what the prosecutor recommended. (Of course, these prosecutors might have been recommending what they knew the judges wanted to hear.) Other judges stated that they took the prosecutor's recommendation as the upper limit on the terms of any deal and then usually approved something less than that or split the difference between what the prosecutor and the defense wanted. In short, our interviews left us in a quandary about whether the judge's personal sentencing preferences played a decisive role in setting the limits of plea bargaining. Although the decision simulation does not fully resolve that quandary, it does suggest that in the minds of defense counsel the judge's preferences are decisive.

We return now to the other two "personal" items. Although the literature and our own interviews had indicated that the reputation of an attorney had a bearing in some plea bargains, there was nothing to indicate that these factors would be three to nine times, respectively, more important to defense counsel than to prosecutors. Nor was there anything to explain why defense counsel would go to these items much earlier than would prosecutors. If anything, Alschuler's critical description of the "plead them guilty bar" would lead one to suspect that prosecutors would be more concerned than defense attorneys with the reputation of the opposing counsel. We cannot offer any convincing retrospective explanations for why defense counsel attach much greater importance to these personal factors than do prosecutors.

Finally, we turn to the "all other" category. We cannot convincingly explain why defense counsel should be 3.7 times more interested in the state of the judge's docket. Perhaps it is because of the defense tactic of seeking continuances in order to delay a case in the hopes of weakening the case. Defense counsel's greater interest in "alternatives to incarceration" is for obvious reasons. The only surprising thing may be that only 45% of them consulted this card. As to why defense counsel should have a greater interest than prosecutors in the victim's age, sex, and race, we have no convincing explanation. In the basic facts of the case it was clear that the victim had not been personally confronted by the burglar. Also unclear is why defense counsel are more concerned than prosecutors with publicity. However, all of these differences might be explained as part of defense counsel's desperate search for any grounds for particularistic appeals.

Consistency of Estimates of Case Strength

The question of whether different attorneys presented with the same case would agree in their estimates of its chances of resulting in a conviction at trial is addressed by the data in Table 3. Two cases, a robbery and a burglary, each with a strong and weak version of case strength, were presented to attorneys. As Table 3 indicates, the attorneys were willing to give estimates of case strength in finer categories than the simple dichotomy of deadbang or reasonable doubt. They gave specific probabilities of conviction. Their answers have been grouped into seven categories to show the considerable disagreement that occurred in some cases. However, if one collapses these categories into three broader categories (namely, 40% probability of conviction or less, 41%-70%; and 71% or greater), then one can more easily see the degree of consistency with regard to these estimates. On the one hand, there is remarkably strong agreement among both prosecutors and defense attorneys in their conviction estimates for the strong versions of both cases. From 82% to 94% of these attorneys felt that these cases had a 71% or better chance of conviction. What is more, there is no statistically significant difference between prosecutors or defense counsel in their estimates in these strong cases. These findings are all the more remarkable when one recalls the terms of the simulation. That is, these attorneys had been instructed to give their estimates of the probability of conviction on the assumptions that (1) they would be the attorney at trial and (2) the trial would be before a jury like the ones with which they were familiar in their own respective jurisdictions. Given the pervasive courthouse folklore about the importance of differences in the trial ability of attorneys and differences in the preferences of local juries, one might have expected a much greater level of disagreement among attorneys in estimating the probability of conviction. Recall that our attorneys were from many different jurisdictions.

The fact there was so much agreement in the strong version of the two cases suggests that at least under certain circumstances the estimation of case strength can be done with a good deal of reliability. That is, when cases approach being "deadbang," and when the estimates of case strength are given in broad categories (such as "71% or better"), there will be considerable agreement among different attorneys about the probability of conviction, no matter who the attorney is and no matter what the vagaries of local juries may be.

On the other hand, looking at the two weak cases in Table 3, one notices considerably less agreement in the estimates of case strength. A striking disagreement occurs in the weak robbery case. Also noteworthy is that the same split occurs among both prosecutors and defense attorneys. The difference by type of attorney is not statistically significant.

In the weak burglary case, however, there is both a split among attorneys of the same type and between the two types of attorney. The latter split is statistically significant. More defense attorneys than prosecutors see this case as a very strong case (91% or stronger). But also, more defense attorneys than prosecutors (18% compared with 11.8%) see it as a weaker case (40% or less chance of conviction).

In sum, the findings suggest that when cases are strong different attorneys regardless of whether they are prosecutors or defense counsel will agree on the estimates of case strength. But, when cases are weak there will be moderate to substantial disagreement among attorneys and between attorneys of different types. Perhaps strong cases "try themselves" whereas the skills of an attorney and the vagaries of local juries make a greater difference in the weaker cases.

Table 3: Attorneys' Estimates of Probability of Conviction by Type of Attorney, Strength of Case, and Type of Crime*

Type of Crime	Strong Case		Weak Case	
Probability of Conviction	Prosecutors	Defense Attorneys	Prosecutors	Defense Attorneys
Estimated Probability of Conviction in Robbery Case Was:	(N = 69)	(N = 54)	(N = 69)	(N = 51)
Less than 20%	0.0	0.0	17.4	13.7
21-40%	0.0	1.9	8.7	11.8
41-60%	0.0	3.7	24.6	15.7
61-70%	5.8	5.6	5.8	3.9
71-80%	14.5	16.7	10.0	0.0
81-90%	29.0	22.2	0.0	0.0
91-100%	50.7	50.0	33.3	54.9
	100.0%	100.0%**	100.0%	100.0%
	$x^2 = 4.464$		$x^2 = 10.2431$	
	d.f. = 5		d.f. = 5	
	P = .49 n.s.		P = .07 n.s.	
Estimated Probability of Conviction in Burglary Case Was:	(N = 66)	(N = 52)	(N = 68)	(N = 50)
Less than 20%	0.0	0.0	4.4	4.0
21-40%	4.5	3.8	7.4	14.0
41-60%	7.6	1.9	19.1	6.0
61-70%	4.5	11.5	4.4	12.0
71-80%	22.7	11.5	22.1	4.0
81-90%	24.2	13.5	10.3	0.0
91-100%	36.4	57.7	32.4	60.0
	100.0%	100.0%	100.0%	100.0%
	$x^2 = 10.404$		$x^2 = 23.846$	
	d.f. = 6		d.f. = 6	
	P = .07 n.s.		P < .001	

*SOURCE: Georgetown Plea Bargaining Decision Simulation

**Percentages not summing to 100.0 are due to rounding errors.

The Prosecutor's Choice of Disposition

The question of what factors influence the prosecutor's decision to take a case to trial or dismiss it or plea bargain it was the subject of several analyses performed on the decision simulation data. Particular attention was given to the influence of prior record and case strength. Previous research and our own interview data gave us conflicting expectations about what relationships would occur between these two factors and this important choice of disposition route by the prosecutor.[5] Given the importance attached to prior record, we assumed that prosecutors would be less likely to dismiss the defendants with serious prior records. As to the effect of case strength, it was hard to know what to predict. There were some grounds to believe that each of the three options might be increased when a case is weak. Some prosecutors feel weak cases do not belong in the system. Hence, weak cases might be nollied more often. Alternatively, some prosecutors feel that weak cases are precisely the ones whose outcomes should be determined by the trial process. Hence, weak cases might be taken to trial more often. Finally, there is the "half-a-loaf" hypothesis first noted in the 1920s by Moley (1929) and reconfirmed by Alschuler (1968) and our own interview data. Some (or perhaps many) prosecutors feel it is their duty to try to get a conviction for something rather than dismiss a case or take the risk of losing it at trial. Hence the weaker the case the more likely the prosecutor is to plea bargain it.

Of the three hypotheses the half-a-loaf hypothesis is the one that most practitioners and researchers would probably expect to be supported by our simulation data. But, surprisingly, it was not. No matter how the data were analyzed (including an analysis of variance not presented here), the half-a-loaf hypothesis was consistently *not* supported by the data. Prosecutors were not more likely to plea bargain the weaker version of the cases. Prior record and strength of case did have a significant impact on the prosecutor's choice of disposition routes but not in a simple, straightforward way. Their greatest impact occurred when the two factors were taken together.

Table 4 illustrates this joint effect and also shows that the half-a-loaf hypothesis was not supported. The data indicate that when a defendant with a serious prior record is involved differences in case strength do not produce statistically significant differences in the prosecutor's choice between dropping the case, or taking it to trial or plea bargaining it. But, when a minor prior record is involved, then prosecutors are more likely to either go to trial or to drop the case than plea bargain it.

This finding suggests that prosecutors are more consistent and rational in their discretionary decision making than their critics believe. The data indicate that there is a logic to prosecutors' decision making. This fact alone should provide some comfort to those critics who fear that prosecutors exercise their discretion haphazardly. But whether or not the particular logic revealed by the data is regarded as desirable depends on one's perspective. There are two critical perspectives from which prosecutorial decision making is usually judged: (1) from the point of view of a person concerned with the safety of the community; and (2) from the point of view of a person concerned with the fairness and propriety of the procedures used in the administration of criminal justice. Both types of critics will find things to comfort and distress them in Table 4; but what is a comfort to one will be a distress to the other. Some of those persons concerned with the public's safety worry that prosecutors for reasons of laziness, ineptness, or political ambition prefer to get rid of (dismiss) weak cases and thereby put the community safety at risk. These people should be reassured by the finding that prosecutors are more likely to dismiss weak cases only if the defendant has a minor prior record. While this pattern makes sense from the point of view of community safety, it raises questions from the due process perspective. If cases are weak enough to dismiss, then it might be argued that prior record should not have an effect; that is, they should have been dismissed where the defendant had a serious prior record as well.[6]

On the other hand, one of the concerns of the due process critics is that plea bargaining is used by prosecutors to "get" serious defendants in weak cases that might be lost at trial. To these critics Table 4 should be of some comfort because it suggests that this is not the case. Among cases with a serious prior record there was no significant increase in plea bargaining among the weak compared with the strong version of the case. This same finding, however, may be distressing to the persons concerned with community safety. Being less troubled by the possible coerciveness of plea bargaining, these people may feel that the fact that prosecutors did not resort to plea bargaining significantly more often when serious criminals were involved represents a critical neglect of the public interest.

The Prosecutor's Sentencing Decision

In this analysis we present two sentencing decisions. The first is the prosecutor's choice between type of sentence, i.e., probation, jail time, or prison time; and the second has to do with the length of the sentence. The focus of our analyses is on the influence of prior record and case strength on these two decisions. In an analysis not presented here it was found that differences in the seriousness of prior record by itself did not significantly affect any of the four decisions analyzed here, i.e., the type of sentence and length of sentence decisions for the burglary and the robbery cases. As for the influence of case strength, it did by itself have a significant effect on the prosecutor's two sentencing decisions with respect to the burglary case (i.e., the type of sentence and the length of sentence) but not to the robbery case.

Table 4: Prosecutor's Disposition Decision by Strength of Case Controlling for Prior Record and Type of Crime*

Type of Crime Disposition Decision	Strong Case Serious Prior Record	Weak Case Serious Prior Record	Strong Case Minor Prior Record	Weak Case Minor Prior Record
(1) Robbery:	(N = 35)	(N= 38)	(N = 34)	(N = 29)
Nolle prosequi	0	5	3	21
Go to Trial	6	8	12	4
Plea Bargain	94	87	85	75
	100%	100%	100%	100%

$$x^2 = 1.9459 \qquad\qquad x^2 = 5.9730$$
$$\text{d.f.} = 2 \qquad\qquad\quad \text{d.f.} = 2$$
$$P(x^2) = .37 \ \text{n.s.} \qquad P(x^2) = .05$$
$$\text{gamma} = -.35$$

(2) Burglary:	(N = 29)	(N = 35)	(N = 35)	(N = 28)
Nolle prosequi	3	3	0	14
Go to Trial	10	6	11	11
Plea Bargain	87	91	97	75
	100%	100%	100%	100%

$$x^2 = .50155 \qquad\qquad x^2 = 7.3861$$
$$\text{d.f.} = 2 \qquad\qquad\quad \text{d.f.} = 2$$
$$P(x^2) = .66 \ \text{n.s.} \qquad P(x^2) = .02$$
$$\text{gamma} = -.84$$

*SOURCE: Georgetown University Plea Bargain Simulation

The analyses presented here in Tables 5, 6, 7, and 8 examine the influence of case strength and prior record when they are taken together. Five of the sixteen comparisons contained in these four tables were significant. That is, five combinations of case strength and prior record but not all combinations of case strength and prior record make a difference in the sentencing decisions of prosecutors. Table 6 shows that when one is looking just at cases involving minor prior records, then differences in case strength do have a significant impact on the prosecutor's decision about the type of sentence both in robbery and burglary. As one might expect (both logically and from what has been reported in the literature), prosecutors are more likely to seek a lenient type of sentence in a weak case.

Table 6 indicates that when dealing with just weak cases and only with burglaries (not robberies) a difference in the seriousness of the prior record has a significant impact on the type of sentence sought by the prosecutor. As one would expect (logically and because of the literature), prosecutors seek a more lenient type of sentence for the defendant with the minor prior record.

Table 7 indicates that only when one is dealing with cases that are burglaries and that involve minor prior records does the difference in the strength of the case make a significant difference in the length of sentence sought by the prosecutor in plea bargaining. Finally, Table 8 indicates that only in robbery cases that are weak does a difference in the seriousness of the prior record make a significant difference in the length of sentence sought by the prosecutor. As one would expect, the prosecutors seek a more lenient sentence for defendants with a minor prior record.

In summary, differences in case strength and seriousness of prior record do not by themselves or acting conjointly consistently influence the prosecutor's sentencing decisions. But when they do have significant impacts either alone or conjointly, the impacts are in the expected direction. That is, prosecutors are more likely to give more lenient deals in weaker cases and more lenient deals to defendants with minor prior records. Generally, it seems that the influence of these factors tends to be significant only in "marginal" circumstances, that is, in situations that present the greatest opportunity for dissensus over the appropriate disposition and sentence. No one thing identifies these situations; but, generally speaking, they can be thought of as the opposite of those cases that "try themselves." They are the cases that "do not dispose of themselves." They tend to be the ones with the less extreme circumstances, e.g., the crimes of medium seriousness; the cases that are neither terribly strong nor completely nonexistent; the ones involving defendants with some prior record but not a life of crime. The presence of one or more of these circumstances makes the calculation of what the just disposition and sentence should be much more difficult. Reasonable men are more likely to differ over these cases than over the cases with the more extreme circumstances. It is here apparently that differences in case strength and prior record can make the difference in what decisions are made about the case. This is not altogether surprising to us. We had chosen burglary because we regarded it as a "marginal" crime. In our early field work it seemed that the greatest amount of consensus among the various actors in the courthouse occurred in the more extreme cases. Burglary was one of those crimes that could go either way, depending upon differences in philosophy of the actors involved and differences in crime problem facing the jurisdiction. Some suburban jurisdictions regarded burglary as an extremely serious offense, whereas neighboring urban jurisdictions with

Table 5: Type of Sentence Sought By Prosecutor in Plea Bargaining by Case Strength Controlling for Prior Record and Type of Crime*

Type of Crime	Type of Sentence	Strong Case Serious Prior Record	Weak Case Serious Prior Record	Strong Case Minor Prior Record	Weak Case Minor Prior Record
Robbery:		(N = 26)	(N = 26)	(N = 21)	(N = 18)
Time in Prison		81	77	81	50
Time in Jail		11	15	19	28
Probation		8	8	0	22
		100%	100%	100%	100%
		$x^2 = .1672$		$x^2 = 6.3032$	
		d.f. = 2		d.f. = 2	
		$P(x^2) = .91$ n.s.		$P(x^2) = .04$	
				gamma = +.65	
Burglary:		(N = 17)	(N = 22)	(N = 22)	(N = 19)
Time in Prison		59	41	46	21
Time in Jail		29	18	27	5
Probation		12	41	27	74
		100%	100%	100%	100%
		$x^2 = 5.5864$		$x^2 = 9.1724$	
		d.f. = 2		d.f. = 2	
		$P(x^2) = .06$ n.s.		$P(x^2) = .01$	
				gamma = +.72	

*SOURCE: Georgetown University Plea Bargain Simulation

high burglary rates treated it as a less serious offense. Even within jurisdictions there was considerable variation between judges and other actors in their view of the seriousness of burglary, but it seemed there was greater consensus about robbery.

Similarily, there seemed to be greater consensus about what to do with strong cases than weak cases and with defendants with serious prior records than defendants with minor prior records. Thus, in retrospect we are not surprised to find that the influence of prior record and case strength appear to be significant only in those situations where agreement among actors in the system seems to be at its lowest.

Also, it is not surprising to find that when case strength did have an effect, it was in the direction of a more lenient sentence for weaker cases. This is part of what is implied by the half-a-loaf hypothesis. But, it is remarkable that the sentencing implications of the half-a-loaf hypothesis are borne out by the data when earlier we saw that the half-a-loaf hypothesis' implication regarding the prosecutor's choice of dispositions

Table 6: Types of Sentence Sought by Prosecutor in Plea Bargaining by Seriousness of
Prior Record Controlling for Strength of Case and Type of Crime*

Type of Crime	Type of Sentence	Serious Prior Record Strong Case	Minor Prior Record Strong Case	Serious Prior Record Weak Case	Minor Prior Record Weak Case
Robbery:		(N = 26)	(N − 21)	(N = 26)	(N = 18)
Time in Prison		81	81	77	50
Time in Jail		11	19	15	28
Probation		8	0	8	22
		100%	100%	100%	100%
		$x^2 = 2.0552$		$x^2 = 3.6151$	
		d.f. = 2		d.f. = 2	
		$P(x^2) = .36$ n.s.		$P(x^2) = .16$ n.s.	
Burglary:		(N = 17)	(N = 22)	(N = 22)	(N = 19)
Time in Prison		59	46	41	21
Time in Jail		29	27	18	5
Probation		12	27	41	74
		100%	100%	100%	100%
		$x^2 = 4.0437$		$x^2 = 7.6936$	
		d.f. = 2		d.f. = 2	
		$P(x^2) = .13$ n.s.		$P(x^2) = .02$	
				gamma = +.62	

*SOURCE: Georgetown University Plea Bargain Simulation

(i.e., that he would be more likely to plea bargain than to go to trial or
dismiss weak cases) was not supported by the data. Also remarkable is
the fact that prior record and case strength did not significantly affect the
sentencing decisions more often than they did. Our observation that they
seem to make significant differences only in marginal circumstances is an
ex post facto attempt to make some sense of the pattern that appeared in
the data. But, as an explanation of that pattern it is something less than
compelling. For us the data raise more questions than they answer.

Differences in Outcome Choices
Between Prosecutors and Defense Counsel

In addition to the question of whether prosecutors and defense
attorneys consult the same items of information there is the question of
whether they agree on what should be done with the case once they have
learned the facts. We noted earlier that in estimating the probability of
conviction there were no statistically significant differences between
prosecutors and defense attorneys in three of the four comparisons. It was

Table 7: Length of Sentence Sought by Prosecutor in Plea Bargaining by Strength of Case Controlling for Prior Record and Type of Crime*

Type of Crime Length of Sentence Sought	Strong Case Serious Prior Record	Weak Case Serious Prior Record	Strong Case Minor Prior Record	Weak Case Minor Prior Record
Robbery:	(N = 35)	(N = 38)	(N = 34)	(N = 31)
5 years or more	46	45	47	35
2-5 years	23	26	12	10
1-2 years	11	10	12	3
6 mos.-1 year	8	8	17	10
0-6 mos.	3	3	9	10
Probation	9	8	3	32
	100%	100%	100%	100%
	$x^2 = 1.6525$ d.f. = 5 $P(x^2) = .89$ n.s.		$x^2 = 1.5428$ d.f. = 5 $P(x^2) = .91$ n.s.	
Burglary:	(N = 31)	(N = 35)	(N = 35)	(N = 33)
5 years or more	29	29	14	24
2-5 years	23	14	11	6
1-2 years	5	11	11	3
6 mos.-1 year	13	6	11	12
0-6 mos.	23	11	34	9
Probation	5	29	17	45
	98%**	100%	98%**	99%**
	$x^2 = 7.6565$ d.f. = 5 $P(x^2) = .17$ n.s.		$x^2 = 12.3679$ d.f. = 5 $P(x^2) = .03$ gamma = +.14	

*SOURCE: Georgetown University Plea Bargain Simulation
**Due to rounding error.

only in the weak burglary case that the two groups differed.

We turn now to the three subsequent decisions analyzed in this chapter: the choice as to whether to plea bargain or go to trial;[7] the choice of type of sentence sought, i.e., prison time, jail tiem, or probation; and, finally, the choice as to length of sentence.

With regard to all three decisions we were uncertain about what, if any, differences we expected between prosecutors and defense counsel. The literature (Alschuler, 1975; Blumberg, 1967; Cole, 1975; Grossman, 1969; Skolnick, 1967) has emphasized that the adversary system exists in theory only. In practice, the informal social relationships which

Table 8: Length of Sentence Sought by Prosecutor in Plea Bargaining by Prior Record
Controlling for Strength of Case and Type of Crime*

Type of Crime Length of Sentence Sought	Serious Prior Record Strong Case	Minor Prior Record Strong Case	Serious Prior Record Weak Case	Minor Prior Record Weak Case
Robbery:	(N = 35)	(N = 34)	(N = 38)	(N = 31)
5 years or more	46	47	45	35
2-5 years	23	12	26	10
1-2 years	11	12	10	3
6 mos.-1 year	7	18	8	10
0-6 mos.	3	9	3	10
Probation	9	3	8	32
	99%**	101%**	100%	100%

$x^2 = 4.3197$ $x^2 = 11.0275$
d.f. = 5   d.f. = 5
$P(x^2) = .50$ n.s. $P(x^2) = .05$
     gamma = +.35

Burglary:	(N = 31)	(N = 35)	(N = 35)	(N = 33)
5 years or more	29	14	29	24
2-5 years	23	11	14	6
1-2 years	6	11	11	3
6 mos.-1 year	13	11	6	12
0-6 mos.	23	34	11	9
Probation	6	17	29	45
	100%	98%**	100%	99%**

$x^2 = 5.7220$ $x^2 = 5.630$
d.f. = 5   d.f. = 5
$P(x^2) = .33$ n.s. $P(x^2) = .34$ n.s.

*SOURCE: Georgetown University Plea Bargain Simulation
**Due to rounding error.

develop among defense attorneys, prosecutors, judges, and other courthouse actors compromise the adversarial nature of the relationship.
Defense attorneys have been described as having been co-opted, and as
being double-agents who sacrifice their clients' interests in the interest of
the smooth running of the court system, the maintaining of good relations
with judges and prosecutors, and the making of a faster buck. Plea
bargaining has been condemned as "an inherently irrational method of
administering justice" because, among other things, it "subjects defense
attorneys to serious temptations to disregard their clients' interest"
(Alschuler, 1975:1180).

Our interviews and observations confirmed that informal social relationships among courthouse actors do develop and in limited ways do influence their decisions and actions. It is undeniable that plea bargaining offers defense counsel numerous temptations to sacrifice their client's interest. But when we asked defense counsel, prosecutors, and judges how often defense counsel succumb to these temptations the answers were not all one way. Yes, a few defense attorneys are notoriously unethical. Yes, a few defense attorneys will do anything to avoid taking a case to trial. Yes, some defense attorneys reveal confidential information obtained from their clients to prosecutors in the course of plea bargaining. But, whether these and other tacts mean that the adversarial system is dead is another matter. We concluded that the existing literature had overstated the nonadversarial nature of plea negotiations. While it is true that defense attorneys act cooperatively with prosecutors in plea bargaining and do lean on their clients to plea bargain when the client would prefer to go to trial, it was not our impression that this was usually done with improper motives or that this usually involved a sacrifice of the client's interests. We do not feel that cooperation between defense attorneys and prosecutors precludes an adversarial relationship. It may just make the adversarial characteristics of the interaction more difficult to see.

Turning now to our first comparison, we have two alternative hypotheses about what the relationship might be between type of attorney and the decision to plea bargain or go to trial. Judging from the literature just reviewed, one might expect either that there would be no difference between defense attorneys and prosecutors (because defense attorneys have been co-opted and do not assume an adversarial posture when plea bargaining) or that if there were a difference it would be in the direction of more defense counsel deciding to plea bargain than to go to trial (because plea bargaining is easier, faster, and more convenient for defense attorneys). The results of our comparison are presented in Table 9. Once again the data are surprising. Neither of the two hypotheses deduced from the literature is supported by the data. There is a significant difference between prosecutors and defense counsel in whether they would plea bargain or go to trial. Second, and even more surprising, is the direction of the difference. Contrary to so much of what the literature would lead one to believe, it is the defense attorneys and not the prosecutors who are more likely to go to trial. This is true both in the robbery and the burglary case; and the relationship is quite strong in both cases.

When interpreting Table 9 and the other tables in this section, it is important to remember that all attorneys were clearly instructed to give

Table 9: Comparison Between Prosecutors and Defense Counsel in Their Decisions to
Go to Trial or Plea Bargain by Type of Crime*

	Prosecutors	Defense Counsel
Robbery:	(N = 127)	(N = 102)
Go to Trial	10	32
Plea Bargain	117	70
	$x^2 = 20.8559$	
	d.f. = 1	
	$P(x^2) < .0001$	
	gamma = -.80	
Burglary:	(N = 120)	(N = 98)
Go to Trial	8	21
Plea Bargain	112	77
	$x^2 = 10.1926$	
	d.f. = 1	
	$P(x^2) < .001$	
	gamma = -.58	

*SOURCE: Georgetown Plea Bargain Decision Simulation

their "bottom-line" recommendations, not their "opening offers." Thus, differences in their offers do not represent the distance between artificially inflated opening offers between two seasoned negotiators.[8] Defense counsel (in Table 9) who recommended that the case should go to trial were not engaging in a ploy to get a better plea bargain out of the prosecutor. Going to trial was their bottom-line decision.

Having excluded the possibility that the relationship described in Table 9 is due to negotiation tactics, it remains to explain what does account for the relationship. We are again forced to engage in a retrospective interpretation. Although we had felt that the literature had overstated the nonadversary nature of plea negotiations, we had not been prepared for the findings in Table 9. However, putting these findings together with those mentioned earlier in this analysis, it is possible to construct a rationale explaining why defense attorneys were more likely to go to trial. Earlier we noted that 75% of the defense counsel compared with only 33% of the prosecutors consulted the card entitled "Judge's Reputation for Leniency." The data presented earlier (Table 1) was only for the burglary case, but the same proportions were true of the robbery case as well. In both cases the description of the judge was the same. It read: "The trial judge is known to be lenient and considers probation in this type of case. He generally favors rehabilitative alternatives to incarceration."

Having read this card, it seems obvious why defense counsel should take the case to trial. They probably could not have gotten a better deal from a prosecutor than the maximum sentence they might get from this judge. Therefore, the logical thing to do was to take the case to trial and shoot for an acquittal. If they did lose, they would not "lose big." The judge makes plea bargaining with the prosecutor an irrelevant waste of time.[9]

Our second comparison between prosecutors and defense attorneys focuses on their choices of type of sentence and length of sentence. That is, the first choice is among prison time, jail time, or probation. The second choice is among different lengths of sentences. For both these comparisons we were uncertain about what to expect. Several alternative hypotheses could be constructed with equal plausibility. One line of reasoning would lead one to expect that the two types of attorneys would not differ in these two choices. It could be reasoned that assuming attorneys are able to evaluate cases, as they claim, then both types of attorneys should agree on the true value of the case, that is, the type of sentence and the length of sentence it deserves. Prosecutors and defense counsel might differ in their opening offers in plea bargaining, but the bottom line should be fairly close to agreement.

One could reach the same expectation from alternative starting points. For instance, the claim that defense counsel do not take an adversary posture in negotiations would also lead one to this expectation of no difference between types of attorneys. Alternatively, saying nothing about whether attorneys act in an adversarial posture, one could note the mere fact that in today's administration of justice 90% of the time prosecutors and defense counsel are able to reach agreements in plea negotiations. Hence, one would expect that there would be no difference between these types of attorneys in the bottom lines arrived at in our decision simulation.

On the other hand, given our earlier discussion about the defense attorney's special task of mitigating a case, i.e., trying to get a deal which is below the true market value of the case, one might expect that defense counsel's bottom line would always be lower (more lenient) than that of prosecutors. Or, one might reach this expectation from the belief that defense attorneys do take an adversarial posture in plea negotiations and consequently their demands will differ from those of prosecutors. Still other plausible hypotheses might be advanced. There is nothing in the existing literature to persuasively support one of these hypotheses over another.

We turn now to the data which are presented in Tables 10 and 11. In three of the four comparisons, there is no statistically significant difference between prosecutors and defense. Only in the robbery fact

Table 10: Comparison Between Prosecutors and Defense Counsel in Type of Sentence
Sought in Plea Bargaining by Type of Crime*

	Prosecutors	Defense Counsel
Robbery:	(N = 91)	(N = 62)
Prison Time	74	42
Jail Time	17	26
Probation	9	32
	100%	100%

$$x^2 = 18.381$$
$$\text{d.f.} = 2$$
$$P(x^2) < .001$$
$$\text{gamma} = +.57$$

Burglary:	(N = 80)	(N = 69)
Prison Time	41	27
Jail Time	20	27
Probation	39	45
	100%	99%**

$$x^2 = 3.2319$$
$$\text{d.f.} = 2$$
$$P(x^2) = .20 \text{ n.s.}$$

*SOURCE: Georgetown Plea Bargain Decision Simulation
**Due to rounding error.

situation in Table 10 is there a significant difference by type of attorney. However, contrary to what is indicated in Table 11, a separate analysis, not presented here, showed that there was also a significant difference between prosecutors and defense counsel in the choice of length of sentence for the robbery case. Thus, the data show that prosecutors and defense attorneys agree in the burglary case for both the type and the length of sentence, but they disagree in the robbery case for both decisions.

Although we were unable to predict these findings, we can offer some retrospective commentary on them. First, it should be remembered that these tables are based on the combination of all four versions (the high and low prior record as well as the strong and weak cases) of the two crimes used in the simulation. Therefore, the discrepancy in recommendations that appears in Table 10 and 11 should not be mistaken for an indication of a general inconsistency in sentencing. The disparity is an artifact of this particular analysis. Obviously, with the four different fact patterns presented, one would expect sentencing disparities *within* types

Table 11: Comparison Between Prosecutors and Defense Counsel in Length of Sentence Sought in Plea Bargaining by Type of Crime*

	Prosecutors	Defense Counsel
Robbery:	(N = 138)	(N = 105)
5 years or more	43	46
2-5 years	18	10
1-2 years	9	8
1-12 months	17	17
1-12 months	17	17
Probation	12	19
	99%	100%

$$x^2 = 4.4213$$
$$d.f. = 4$$
$$P(x^2) = .35 \text{ n.s.}$$

	Prosecutors	Defense Counsel
Burglary:	(N = 134)	(N = 102)
5 years or more	24	30
2-5 years	13	10
1-2 years	8	4
1-12 months	30	25
Probation	25	30
	100%	99%**

$$x^2 = 4.3413$$
$$d.f = 4$$
$$P(x^2) = .36 \text{ n.s.}$$

*SOURCE: Georgetown Plea Bargain Decision Simulation
**Due to rounding error.

of attorneys. The crucial question is whether one could expect these differences to exist between types of attorneys.

A second point worth recalling is that defense attorneys consulted far more information about the defendant's background as well as various other miscellaneous attributes of the case. Yet, even after consulting all this information, defense counsel still end up agreeing with prosecutors in the burglary case. This suggests that whatever else those items of information may be used for they do not automatically alter the estimates of the bottom-line value of the case. This does not mean that plea bargaining lacks an adversarial quality. In fact when these data are taken together with the findings in Table 1 and 2, the opposite conclusion is suggested. That is, even in the burglary case where the two types of attorney agree on the bottom line, the data suggests that there is an adversarial character to the plea negotiations. As indicated in Tables 1 and 2, prosecutors arrive at the bottom line after consulting a minimum of information. Defense counsel consult the same information and more. Even after consulting the additional information, however, they arrive at the same bottom line as the prosecutor. Therefore, one might ask why they bother to consult the additional items of information. We believe the answer is that even where the attorneys agree on the true value of the case the negotiations take on a subtle but real adversarial quality. While defense counsel may apear to be acting cooperatively, their special role is to interject information designed to conflict with the prosecutor's assessment of the case.

Of course, this may explain what is happening in the burglary case where the two types of attorneys agree, but it does not account for why the attorneys disagree in the robbery case. For that, we can only speculate that because robbery is regarded as a more serious crime, and the stakes are usually higher for all parties concerned, a stronger adversarial quality emerges in the attorneys. That is, we are suggesting that the adversarial nature of the negotiations changes with the seriousness of the crime. Perhaps when more is at stake each type of attorney feels the need to take a stronger position.

SUMMARY

- In evaluating cases for plea bargaining, prosecutors concern themselves with fewer items of information than defense counsel do.
- Prosecutors and defense counsel agree on the importance of case strength, seriousness of the offender, and seriousness of the offense. They also agree on the lack of importance of case load as a determinant of plea bargaining decisions in an individual case.
- Prosecutors are far more concerned than defense counsel with the attitudes of the police and the victim toward the plea bargain.
- Prosecutors are less concerned than defense counsel with a miscellany of attributes about the defendant and the case that do not bear directly on case strength, offender seriousness, or offense seriousness. They are also less concerned with the trial judge's reputation for leniency, the opposing counsel's reputation, or the nature of the personal relationship between the opposing counsel.
- Estimating the probability of conviction in a case is something which is done with a fair degree of reliability when the cases are strong, but not when the cases are weak. Prosecutors generally agree among themselves and with defense counsel in the estimates of the probability of conviction in strong cases. But prosecutors disagree among themselves and in one instance with defense counsel in the estimates of the probability of conviction in weak cases.

- The half-a-loaf hypothesis that prosecutors would be more likely to plea bargain in weak cases was contradicted by the data. Prosecutors were consistently more likely either to take weak cases to trial or dismiss them rather than to plea bargain them.

- However, the other implication of the half-a-loaf hypothesis, namely, that the weaker the case the more lenient the plea offer will be, was partially (but not consistently) confirmed. Differences in case strength did significantly affect the prosecutor's choices as to type and length of sentence but only under certain conditions (i.e., when the crime was less serious and/or when a prior record was involved). Even when one or both of these conditions were present, case strength did not always significantly affect the prosecutor's plea offer.

- Differences in the seriousness of prior record did not by themselves have a significant effect on the prosecutor's two sentencing decisions. But, among weak cases, differences in the seriousness of the prior record do have a significant impact on these decisions. As one would expect, the less serious prior record is given the more lenient sentence.

- Prior record and case strength seem to exert significant influences only in "marginal" situations, that is, those fact situations where there is likely to be the greatest lack of consensus among criminal justice actors about what the appropriate disposition and sentence should be, e.g., in "medium" serious crimes, when cases are weak, or when they involve a minor prior record.

- Contrary to what the literature would lead one to expect, defense counsel were more likely than prosecutors to take a case to trial. However, this may be true only if the trial judge has a reputation for leniency.

- In the robbery case prosecutors and defense counsel disagree in both of the sentencing decisions. But, in the burglary case they did not significantly differ in either of these decisions.

- "Court busting" appears to be a myth. Virtually all defense counsel said they never have threatened and never would threaten to take all their cases to trial as a tactic to get a better deal in a particular case.

CONCLUSION

Most of what is known about the plea bargaining decision-making process has been based on interview and observational data. The findings of the present study, based primarily on a decision simulation with a quasi-experiment, strengthen and refine some previous findings but contradict others and raise several new questions. Contrary to popular belief, prosecutors and defense counsel are not concerned with the question of the court's backlog or caseload when they are attempting to evaluate what to do with individual cases. Contrary to courthouse folklore, defense attorneys do not use the threat of taking their cases to trial (i.e., to "courtbust") in order to obtain more favorable terms in plea bargaining. As previously reported, the three big factors of case strength, seriousness of the defendant, and seriousness of the offense are regarded by both prosecutors and defense counsel as important in the evaluation of cases for plea bargaining. Not well understood in the past was whether and how prosecutors and defense counsel differ in their evaluations of cases for plea bargaining, whether the big three factors had the impact on plea bargaining decisions which they were alleged to have, and whether attorneys presented with the same set of facts would arrive at the same estimates of probability of conviction.

This study indicates that prosecutors and defense attorneys evaluate cases the same way up to a point. After the three big factors are evaluated, defense counsel go on to look for anything that might be said on behalf of their clients in order to improve upon the normal plea bargaining discount arrived at on the basis of the big three factors. In addition, defense counsel are far more interested than prosecutors in information about the personal characteristics of the criminal justice actors. These two differences suggest that defense counsel do play a unique role in plea bargaining. That role seems to consist of three different tasks. First, defense counsel try to assure that the big three factors have been properly evaluated and that the usual discount for the particular type of case has been established. Secondly, defense counsel look for tactical advantages in order to advise their client about which route to take. If the judge is notoriously lenient, then there would be a tactical advantage to go to trial and try to win an acquittal. Even if the defendant is convicted, he will not "lose big," given that the judge is lenient. On the other hand if the judge were more severe, then bargaining with the prosecutor may be the better tactic. The third task is that of "mitigating the case." The job here is to find any reason why the defendant should be given more than the usual discount in the case. This seems to be done by introducing information which is designed to contradict the prosecutor's judgment about what the basic value of the case should be.

Contrary to those analyses which have stressed the nonadversarial nature of plea bargaining, our findings suggest that there is an adversarial component. However, that component is of such a latent quality that it can easily be overlooked. Although it is true that cooperative relationships do develop between criminal justice actors, our analysis of the way in which they process information in connection with reaching their plea bargaining decisions suggests that there is a difference between prosecutors and defense counsel both in the amount and type of information they consult and in the decisions they make on the basis of that information.

The nature of the adversary relationship that does exist in plea negotiations lies in the difference in information processing more than in the difference in the outcomes of that decision process.

With regard to the evenhandedness of certain aspects of plea bargaining, we conclude that it is more likely to occur under some conditions than under others. With regard to that crucially important skill known as the ability to estimate the probability of conviction, we found that when cases are strong both prosecutors and defense counsel can agree in estimating the probability of conviction. But when the cases are weak, there is far less agreement. Similarly, with regard to the impact of differences in case strength and differences in seriousness of prior record, we found that these factors have a significant influence on the prosecutor's sentencing decision only under certain conditions. Once again, those conditions are either where cases are weak or where there is a minor prior record or the crime is a less serious crime. Why this should be true is not readily apparent.

The results of our simulation do not answer the policy question of whether plea bargaining should be eliminated or allowed to continue. However, they do show that some of the arguments in that policy debate are either entirely inaccurate or subject to important modifications. The plea bargaining decision-making process is not as haphazard as it may appear. Our nonrandom sample of prosecutors drawn from across the country revealed that there is a logic to prosecutorial decision making and that it is distinct from that of defense attorneys. Whether one agrees with that rationale depends on one's policy preferences. Our research will not settle the debate on plea bargaining, because that is ultimately a debate over policy choices. However, in clarifying and refining some of the factual bases on which that debate rests, we have altered the terms of the debate.

NOTES

1. Although we used the same technique as Lagoy, there are major differences in the content of the simulation, the variables used, the nature of the samples involved, and the inclusion of a quasi-experimental component.

2. Technically speaking, defense counsels do not accept or reject plea bargains. Their clients do. However, in actual practice, we found that defendants rely heavily on the advice of attorneys and although some attorneys go to great lengths to avoid making a decision for the defendant most are willing to express their opinion about what the best deal is. Therefore, in reporting our findings here, we shall speak as if the decision were made by the defense counsel.

3. The belief that such distinctions can and should be made is often the basis for objections to sentencing reform proposals that would eliminate or drastically reduce the freedom of criminal justice officials who make these fine adjustments. On the other hand, the belief that these adjustments are not being made evenhandedly has been given as the main argument in favor of such sentencing reforms.

4. Although we have described plea bargaining as a "two-stage model," we don't mean to imply that defense counsel consciously divide their thinking into two parts. We are making such division only for analytic purposes.

5. American defendants today are not required by law to go to trial. They may plead guilty. Thus, when we speak of prosecutors "choosing" to go to trial, we only mean they are refusing to offer a plea bargain. The defendants might still plead guilty as charged.

6. It is not our purpose to try to answer these policy questions here; rather we only intend to show the data that give rise to them. However, for some discussion of the issues involved, see McDonald, Chapter 1, this volume and also the final report of the Georgetown Plea Bargaining Study (forthcoming).

7. We have deleted the option of nolle prosequi from this part of the analysis because it is only relevant to prosecutors.

8. Of course, it is possible that the attorneys may have ignored our instructions and given bottom lines which were really closer to opening offers. However, we feel this would have to have been done on a less conscious level, because our instructions were clear and unambiguous.

9. We regret that we did not describe one of the judges as a severe sentencer to see if this would have altered the results in this particular comparison.

REFERENCES

ALSCHULER, A. W. (1975). "The defense attorney's role in plea bargaining. Yale Law Journal 84:1179-1314.

_____(1968). "The prosecutor's role in plea bargaining." University of Chicago Law Review 36:50-112.

BALDWIN, J. and M. McCONVILLE (1977). Negotiated Justice: Pressures to Plead Guilty. London: Martin Robertson.

BERNSTEIN, I. N., E. KICK, J. T. LEUNG, and B. SCHULZ (1977). "Charge reduction: An intermediary stage in the process of labeling criminal defendants." Social Forces 56:362-384.

BLUMBERG, A. (1967). Criminal Justice. Chicago: Quadrangle Books.

CHAMBLISS, W. J., and R. D. SEIDMAN (1971). Law, Order, and Power. Reading, Mass.: Addison-Wesley.

COLE, G. F. (1975). The American System of Criminal Justice. North Scituate, Mass.: Duxbury Press.

GREENWOOD, P. W., S. WILDHORN, E. C. POGGIO, M. J. STRUMWASSER, and P. DeLEON (1973). Prosecution of Adult Felony Defendants in Los Angeles County: A Policy Perspective. Santa Monica, Calif.: Rand.

GROSSMAN, B. A. (1969). The Prosecutor. Toronto: University of Toronto Press.

HEUMAN, M. (1975). "A note on plea bargaining and case pressure." Law and Society Review 9:515.

LAGOY, S. P., J. J. SENNA, and L. J. SIEGEL (1976). "An empirical study of information usage for prosecutorial decision making in plea negotiations." American Criminal Law Review 13:435-472.

MATHER, L. M. (1974). "The outsider in the courtroom: An alternative role for the defense," pp. 263-289 in H. Jacob (ed.), The Potential for Reform of Criminal Justice. Beverly Hills, Calif.: Sage.

_____(1976). "Criminal justice and the victim: An introduction," pp. 17-55 in W. F. McDonald (ed.), Criminal Justice and the Victim. Beverly Hills, Calif.: Sage.

McDONALD, W. F. (1977). "The role of the victim in America," pp. 295-307 in R. E. Barnett and J. Hagel (eds.), Assessing the Criminal: Restitution, Retribution, and the Legal Process. Cambridge, Mass.: Ballinger

MILLS, J. (1971). "I have nothing to do with justice." Life (March 12):56.

MOLEY R. (1929). Politics and Criminal Prosecution. New York: Minton, Balch.

NEUBAUER, D. W. (1974). Criminal Justice in Middle America." Morristown, N.J.: General Learning Press.

NEWMAN, D. J. (1966). Conviction: The Determination of Guilt or Innocence Without Trial. Boston: Little, Brown.

_____(1956). "Plea guilty for considerations: A study of bargain justice." Journal of Criminal Law, Criminology and Police Science 46:780.

RHODES, W. M. (1979). "Plea bargaining, crime control and due process: A quantative analysis," in W. F. McDonald and J. A. Cramer (eds.), Perspectives on Plea Bargaining. Lexington, Mass.: Lexington Books.

ROSETT, A. and D. R. CRESSEY (1976). Justice by Consent. Philadelphia: J. B. Lippincott.

SKOLNICK, J. (1967). "Social control in the adversary system." Journal of Conflict Resolution 11:52-70.

WILKINS, L. T. (1965). Social Deviance. Englewood Cliffs, N.J.: Prentice-Hall.

APPENDIX A

CHARACTERISTICS OF SIMULATED JURISDICTION
(A copy of this may be handed to Respondent in the Plea Bargaining Simulation)
In this jurisdiction the following conditions prevail:

(1) Prosecutors are permitted to present to the court plea agreements involving charge reductions and dismissals and sentence recommendations.
(2) These agreements are generally followed by the judges.
(3) Time served in pretrial custody is always deducted from sentences imposed.
(4) There are no mandatory sentences for repeat or habitual offenders.
(5) Any motions in a case are heard immediately prior to trial.
(6) No offenses are impeachable convictions.
(7) There is an individual (vs. a master calendar) system of case docketing. Every judge gets an equal share of the caseload and is responsible for disposing of it himself.
(8) There is a 90-day speed trial rule.
(9) There is no youth corrections act.

APPENDIX B
ROBBERY CASE INFORMATION

Description Title	*Unit Of Information*
Introductory Statement	A. You are a senior defense attorney when a junior defense attorney has come for advice about a plea negotiation in which he is involved. The defendant is charged with armed robbery. The defendant is willing to plead guilty for a consideration. Assume that the law in this hypothetical jurisdiction provides the following penalties: armed robbery is up to 30 years.

———

Introductory Statement	B. You are a senior prosecutor when a junior prosecutor has come for advice....
Defendant's Race/Ethnic/ Nationality	1. White, American, U.S.
Defendant's Age	2. 25 years old.
Defendant's Sex	3. Male
Basic Facts of the Case	4. At 2:30 P.M. on a Saturday in a mixed residential/commerical area the defendant accosted a male age 19 with a knife and demanded money. The victim gave him his wallet which contained one ten dollar bill, his student identification card and two credit cards. Minutes later a passing police patrol car was summoned by the victim who gave a description of the defendant. Approximately 15 minutes after the offense the defendant was arrested several blocks from the scene of the crime. The victim identified the defendant as the robber.
Length of Time Since Arrest In Instant Case	40. Defendant was arrested 2½ months ago.
Defendant's Intelligence & Education	7. Normal intelligence. High school graduate. No college. School record is unremarkable, no record of disciplinary problems.
Defendant's Employment Status	8. Defendant is currently employed as a machinery operator for local ceramic manufacturing plan. Defendant has held this position for 6 months. Defendant's record shows 10 jobs as machine operator in light to heavy industry over last 5 years, interspersed with periods of unemployment. Usually defendant leaves rather than being fired.

199

Descriptive Title		*Unit of Information*
Defendant's Psychiatric Problems	9.	None
Criminal History of Defendant's Family	10.	None
Codefendants	11.	None
Trial Judge's Reputation for Leniency	12.	The trial judge is known to be lenient and considers probation in this type of case. He generally favors rehabilitative alternatives to incarceration.
Public and Community Sentiment	13.	Community sentiment against robbery is pretty strong. However, this case has received no publicity or press coverage.
Propriety of Police Conduct After Arrest	14.	Not an issue.
Evidence—Substance of Available (Strong Version)	15.	Police arrested defendant 15 minutes after and 7 blocks from scene of offense based on the following description: "White male, 19-25 yrs. of age, green checked pants." The defendant matched that description.
		The victim made an identification of the defendant at the scene of the crime (approx. 3:00 P.M., one-half hour after offense). He said he remembered a small (½ inch) scar on the defendant's right cheek as well as the general contours and shape of the defendant's face.
		Victim's I.D. and credit cards were found 5 feet from defendant at scene of arrest and the defendant did have $16.00 in cash on him, including one ten dollar bill. It was not fingerprinted. Victim's wallet was not recovered.
		No weapons were found. There are no other witnesses to the crime.
Evidence—Substance of Available (Weak Version)	42.	Police arrested defendent 15 minutes after and 7 blocks from scene of offense, based on the following description provided by victim: "White male 19-25 yrs. of age." The defendant matched that description. The prosecutor conducted a follow-up interview with the victim. He was only able to add to the description that the defendant was the right weight and height.
		At scene of crime (approx. 3:00 P.M., one-half hour after offense), the victim said he was "sure that was the guy." But at an interview

Descriptive Title	*Unit of Information*
	last week he said that the crime "happened so fast" that the victim couldn't be absolutely sure. It was ascertained that the victim was not contacted or pressured by defense counsel or the defendant.
	The defendant did have $16.00 in cash on him, including one ten dollar bill. It was not fingerprinted. Victim's wallet was not recovered. No weapons were found. There are no other witnesses to the crime.
Date of Trial in Instant Offense and Probability of Continuance	16. The case is scheduled for trial in 7 days. It is unlikely the judge will grant a continuance.
Backlog of Docket of Judge	17. This judge is an efficient administrator and is always current on the calendar. There is no backlog.
Available Alternatives to Incarceration	18. 1. Probation; 2. Work-Release; 3. Vocational Rehabilitation Programs; 4. Military Service; 5. Psychiatric/Family Counseling; 6. Diversion; 7. Restitution.
Pretrial Release Status for this Robbery	19. Defendant is presently released on his own recognizance.
Police Attitude Toward Proposed Bargain	20. Police are generally opposed to plea bargaining. They are particularly concerned with street crime. Beyond this, the arresting police officers have no attitudes specifically related to this case.
Defendant's Account of Incident	21. Defendant claims he is innocent; that it is a case of mistaken identity. He said he was out walking for pleasure and was not at the scene of the crime.
Effectiveness of Witnesses at Trial	22. A. The victim is an art major specializing in sculpture and photography of the human body and face. He has never testified at a trial before and is a little uncomfortable about taking the stand.
	B. The arresting police officer is a five-year veteran with much experience as a witness and comes across well on the stand.
Defense Counsel Reputation	23. A recent law school graduate who has been defending criminal cases for seven months. She is extremely aggressive, however, several of your fellow prosecutors have found that a reasonable plea negotiation can be accomplished. Her preparation is generally excellent and her courtroom presentation is generally adequate.

Descriptive Title	*Unit of Information*

Reputation of Prosecutor
23. A recent law school graduate who has been prosecuting criminal cases for seven months. She is extremely aggressive, however, several of your fellow defense counsel have found that a reasonable negotiation can be accomplished. Her preparation is generally excellent and her courtroom presentation is generally adequate.

Defendant's Prior Record & Reputation
(Nonserious Version)

41. *Arrests*   *Dispositions*

(1) One juvenile contact at age 14 for malicious mischief — Disposition unknown

(2) One arrest at age 18 for disorderly conduct — Dismissed
Reputation: Police do not know defendant

Defendant's Prior Record
(Serious Version)

5. *Arrests*   *Dispositions*

(1) Three juvenile contacts*, one at age 14 for assault two at age 16 both for unlawful entry — Disposition unknown

(2) Arrest for burglary, age 18 — Probation, 1 year

(3) Arrest for robbery, age 19 — Dismissed

(4) Arrest for attempted rape, age 21 — Dismissed

(5) Arrest for robbery, age 24 — Dismissed

* In this jurisdiction defendants under age 18 are treated as juvenile.
Reputation: Police believe, through a reliable informant, but cannot prove, that defendant is responsible for several robberies in the area.

Ability of Defendant to Pay Restitution
25. Defendant could pay restitution.

Victim's Attitude Toward Bargain
26. Victim is concerned with street crime in general, and is angry at the defendant in particular for accosting him. However, the victim believes that his case has been well handled to this point by the criminal justice system officials and is willing to leave all decisions in the hands of the prosecutor.

Victim's Account of Incident 27. Victim was walking down street to visit his girlfriend for a date later that evening. He was

Descriptive Title		*Unit of Information*
		accosted by the defendant, a complete stranger, who demanded money. He was terrified and immediately complied. After handing over his wallet the defendant slashed him and knocked him down for no reason. The whole incident was over "very quickly."
Victim Characteristics	28.	White male (age 19), college student, no record, no prior victimizations.
Pretrial Release, Probation/ Parole Status at Time of Offense	29.	Defendant at liberty, no restrictions. Not on probation, parole, or pretrial release or other supervision at time of instant offense.
Aliases	30.	None
Physical Health	31.	Excellent
Alcohol Use	32.	Moderate social drinker, no evidence of intoxication at time of arrest.
Aggravating & Mitigating Circumstances of the Offense	43.	The victim's arm was slashed by the robber without provocation and he was pushed to the ground. The victim was later taken to the hospital and received five stitches for the laceration he received.
Sexual Orientation	34.	Heterosexual
Military Record	35.	None, defendant eligible for draft, but was not called.
Religion	36.	None
Detainers	37.	None
Length of Local Residence	38.	Local resident for five years.
Defendant's Interests & Activities	39.	Unknown
Drug Use	33.	None.

APPENDIX C
BURGLARY CASE INFORMATION

Descriptive Title	*Unit of Information*
Descriptive Title	Unit of Information
Introductory Statement	A. You are a senior defense attorney and a junior defense attorney comes to you for advice about a plea negotiation he is involved with. The defendant is charged with burglary at night and is willing to plead for consideration. Assume that the law in your jurisdiction provides that the penalty for burglary at night is up to a 10-year maximum. Any sentence less than 10 years, including probation, is legally permissible. The indictment/information has been filed. No motions have been filed. The case is scheduled for trial within two weeks.
Introductory Statement	B. You are a senior prosecutor and a junior prosecutor comes to you for advice. . . .
Defendant's Race/ Ethnic/ Nationality	1. White, American, U.S.
Defendant's Age	2. 22 years old.
Defendant's Sex	3. Male
Basic Facts of the Case	4. At 11:30 P.M. police respond to a radio dispatch about an individual seen exiting the window of a house. The police apprehend the defendant one block from the house. Resident of the house reported that money and jewelry were taken. At the time of the apprehension the defendant had $207.50 in his pocket. Also jewelry was found in a bush three feet away from him. Entry to the house had been gained through an unlocked but closed window. A neighbor called in the prowler report.
Defendant's Interests & Activities	38. Defendant reports family-centered activities and participation in local sports. He is a member of a local league softball team.
Defendant's Marital Status	6. Defendant is married with one child, age 3
Defendant's Intelligence & Education	7. Normal intelligence, high school graduate, one year junior college, not currently in school.

Descriptive Title	*Unit of Information*
Defendant's Employment Status	8. Defendant is an emloyee of a local fast food restaurant. Has held this position for six months. Has had several prior positions since leaving school three years previously, none longer than six months.
Defendant's Psychological Problems	9. None
Criminal History of Defendant's Family	10. None
Codefendants	11. None
Trial Judge's Reputation for Leniency	12. Judge has reputation for severity in burglary of residence cases. He can be persuaded to go along with the sentence recommendation of the prosecutor.
Publicity/Community Sentiment	13. Community sentiment against burglary is strong. However, this case has received no publicity or press coverage.
Propriety of Police Conduct After Arrest	14. Not an issue.
Evidence—Substance of Available (Weak Version)	40. The police officers responding to the radio dispatch stopped the defendant because he matched the general description on the radio dispatch, (namely, a "white male") and because he was one block from the scene of the burglary. Jewelry which was later positively identified by the victim as his was found in a bush three feet away from the place where the defendant was stopped by the police. The neighbor who reported the prowler could not be located in order to give an identification. The victim's house was checked for fingerprints but none matching the defendant's were found. The jewelry could not be subjected to fingerprint analysis. The victim was unsure of the amount of money stolen.
Evidence—Substance of Available (Strong Version)	15. The police officers responding to the radio dispatch saw the defendant who matched the description given of a young white male with red plaid trousers. He was a block away from the scene of the burglary. When he saw the police he made a motion. It appeared to the police that he was throwing something into a nearby bush. When the bush was checked the police found jewelry which was later positively identified as belonging to the burglary victim.

Descriptive Title	*Unit of Information*
	Also, the victim indicates that two hundred dollars (ten $10's, and 20 $5's) were stolen. The defendant was carrying $207.50 (ten $10's, 21 $5's, and some change) at the time of arrest. No fingerprints were found at the victim's home. The neighbor reporting the prowler was not identified.
Backlog of Docket of Judge to Whom Case Was Assigned	16. This judge has a hard time keeping up with his docket. He is already over 50 cases behind and his docket is growing.
Length of Time Since Arrest in Instant Offense	17. Defendant was arrested in this case 28 days ago.
Alternatives to Incarceration	18. 1. Probation; 2. Work-Release; 3. Vocational Rehabilitation Programs; 4. Military Service; 5. Psychiatric/Family Counseling; 6. Diversion; 7. Restitution.
Police Attitudes Toward Proposed Bargain	19. Police are generally opposed to plea bargaining. The arresting officer thinks the defendant should get some time.
Defendant's Account of the Incident	20. Defendant said he was walking on his way home and that someone ran past him and threw something into a nearby bush. He says he won the money he had on him in a crap game with people he cannot identify.
Effectiveness of Witnesses at Trial	21. (1) Police Officer A has been on force for four months. He is the one who saw the defendant first and who conducted the search. He has not yet testified in any case at trial. (2) Police Officer B has been on the force over seven years and has testified in numerous cases. (3) The burglary victim is a middle-aged white male who has never testified at trial before. He has no hesitancy about testifying and he can positively identify the jewelry. (4) The neighbor who called in the prowler report refused to identify himself and could not be found for use as a witness.
Reputation of Prosecutor	22. The prosecutor is generally regarded as a good trial lawyer.
Defense Counsel Reputation	22. The defense attorney is generally regarded as a good trial lawyer.
Relationship Between Prosecutor and Defense Attorney	23. The junior prosecutor has had no prior contact with this attorney.
Relationship Between Prosecutor and Defense Attorney	23. The junior defense attorney has no prior contact with this prosecutor.

Descriptive Title	*Unit of Information*
Ability of Defendant to pay Restitution	24. Defendant could pay restitution.
Victim's Attitude Toward Bargain	25. Victim is upset and feels the defendant should be "behind bars."
Victim's Race, Sex, Age, etc.	26. White male, 40, respected businessman, no record, no prior victimizations.

Defendant's Prior Record and Police Reputation (Nonserious Version)

39.

	Arrests	*Dispositions*
(1)	1 juvenile contact, 7 years earlier	No adjudication
(2)	1 juvenile contact, 5 years earlier	Adjudicated "Not involved"
(3)	Shoplifting, 25 days before instant offense	(No entry on rap sheet)

Reputation: Arresting police officers in instant offense say defendant "hangs around with the wrong kind of people."

Defendant's Prior Record and Reputation (Serious Version)

5.

	Arrests	*Dispositions*
(1)	1 juvenile contact, 5 years earlier	Adjudciated "involved"
(2)	1 juvenile contact, 3 years earlier	Adjudciated "not involved"
(3)	Burglary, 2½ years earlier	Dismissed
(4)	Burglary, 9 months earlier	Dismissed
(5)	Burglary, 8 months earlier	(No entry on rap sheet)

Reputation: Police believe, through a reliable informant, he is responsible for several other burglaries. They know he was in the neighborhood but can't prove he aided them.

Descriptive Title	*Unit of Information*
Pretrial Release, Probation/ Parole at Time of Offense	28. He was on release on his own recognizance for a pending shoplifting case which has since been dropped.
Defendant's Aliases	29. None
Physical Health of Defendant	30. Good
Record of Alcohol Use by Defendant	31. Moderate social drinker. There was no evidence of being under the influence of alcohol at the time of arrest.
Record of Drug Use by Defendant	32. Defendant denies drug use but arresting officers say the crowd the defendant hangs around with is "into hard drugs." Defendant was not on drugs at time of arrest.
Defendant's Sexual Orientation	33. Heterosexual
Defendant's Military Record	34. None

Descriptive Title		*Unit of Information*
Religious Affiliation of Defendant	35.	Protestant—Baptist
Detainers on Defendant	36.	None
Aggravating or Mitigating Circumstances of the Offense	43.	The victim was in the house and asleep at the time of the crime. No contact was made between the burglar and anyone in the house. There was no property damage to the house or its contents.
Defendant's Pretrial Release Status for this Burglary	27.	Released on own recognizance
Length of Local Residence of Defendant	37.	Lifelong resident of local community

Chapter 8

THE PROSECUTORIAL FUNCTION AND ITS RELATION TO DETERMINATE SENTENCING STRUCTURES

STEPHEN P. LAGOY
FREDERICK A. HUSSEY
JOHN H. KRAMER

Although many of the activities, processes, and policies of criminal justice agencies are relatively idiosyncratic, criminal sentencing is a most observable arena in which we find a coalescing of interest. Although not concerned directly with length of sentence, the police are concerned that arrest results in conviction (LaFave, 1965:514-517); prosecutors are concerned with convictions as well, but must also attend closely to the "production function"[1] of efficiently processing offenders through the court (Duffee, Hussey, and Kramer, 1978:361-364); defense attorneys are concerned with getting the best possible outcome for their clients which involves cooperating with judges and prosecutors to a certain degree (American Bar Association, 1971; but see also Alschuler, 1975); judges must make adjudicative as well as dispositional decisions[2] which are in the best interests of society and the offender—interests that may seem in conflict (Remington et al., 1969:711-720); correctional agencies, including probation, must accept clientele and perform whatever change processes they can (see generally Mangrum, 1975); and parole boards may play a central role in deciding the actual duration of sentence (Stanley, 1976:47-81; Amos and Newman, 1975:76-129).

With the exception of the prosecutor, the role that each agency will play in the sentencing decision has been described extensively in the literature and is generally well understood. Essentially, the judge must set a minimum and maximum term for each offender within the limits of the penal sanction established by the legislature, and the parole board must determine the appropriate moment within the court-imposed term at which the offender should be released to parole supervision in the community (see generally Dawson, 1969). This interactive process involving decisions of the legislature, judicial, and executive branches of government[3], has traditionally held its manifest goal to be the rehabilitation of offenders through an individualized, therapeutic correctional process. However, pursuit of that goal is tempered to some extent by administrative concerns common to all complex organizations. In the criminal justice system, one such concern is that offenders be processed as efficiently as possible (Remington et al., 1969:35-38).

Irrespective of organizational unit, the production function demands that the organization's resources be organized in such a way that the goal of efficiency can be optimized. For example, the police discretionarily select for arrest those offenders who are perceived as providing the most probable return on investment of time and expense (LaFave, 1965:83-143). Similarly, prosecutors select "role ready" defendants to insure a high conviction rate and rapid turnover of cases (Duffee and Fitch, 1976:48-55). The production subsystem is generally referred to as the "primary subsystem" because the organization "evolves about the task or problem that is represented in production" (Duffee, Hussey, and Kramer, 1978:286). Regardless of the criminological goal to which the system ostensibly adheres, of primary concern to each organizational unit is the processing of criminal offenders. This fact dictates that there be a practical operating equilibrium within the system achieved through integration among the policies and practices of the several criminal justice agencies (Remington et al., 1969:37-38; Ohlin and Remington, 1958:496). It is in this context that the nature of the sentencing power of the prosecutor can be most clearly understood.

PROSECUTORIAL POWER IN SENTENCING

In contrast to the voluminous literature on the sentencing power of legislatures, courts, and parole boards, little has been written concerning the prosecutorial role in the sentencing process. Nevertheless, some scholars suggest (see, for example, Alschuler, 1978:68-70) that the office of the prosecutor has a greater impact on sentencing than any of the other agencies noted above. The prosecutor's power in sentencing derives primarily from two aspects of the prosecutorial function. The first is the prosecutorial responsibility to formulate criminal charges. For example, if the prosecutor decides to charge a lesser crime than the facts support (or not to charge at all), the judge is precluded from imposing the legislatively prescribed sanction for the specific conduct actually committed (See Miller, 1970:151-178; Dawson, 1969:188-192). The second source of power derives from the ability to provide (or withhold) information and recommendations bearing on the terms of sentence prior to the actual imposition of sentence by the judiciary. To the extent that judges entertain and acquiesce in prosecutorial sentence recommendations and, conversely, to the extent that prosecutors withhold influential information from judges, the prosecutor has a direct impact on the terms of sentences actually imposed (American Bar Association, 1971:131-134; Eisenstein and Jacob, 1977:268).[4] Moreover, in the exercise of this discretionary power, the prosecutor is invisible and invulnerable to externally imposed structure or control to an extent unknown in other sentencing agencies (Bubany and Skillern, 1976:473-495 and sources cited therein).

Whether or not prosecutorial power is exercised in a discretionary manner depends, in part, on systemic pressure for efficient and economical processing of criminal offenders (i.e., production; but see Rosett and Cressey, 1976:104-115; Heuman, 1975; Lagoy, Senna, and Siegel, 1976:458). To achieve maximum efficiency in the adjudicatory process, the criminal justice system relies on the guilty plea which is, by far, the prevalent form of criminal adjudication (Newman, 1966:8; President's Commission on Law Enforcement and Administration of Justice, 1967: 134). Compared with the complexities of a criminal trial, the guilty plea is a model of adjudicative efficiency. However, the system's encouragement of guilty pleas (and, hence, the maximization of efficiency) implies that the criminal defendant must be convinced that it is in his best interests to waive several significant constitutional protections (e.g., right to a jury trial, freedom from self-incrimination).[5] To induce the desired cooperation, agencies draw on their extensive discretionary decision-making power.

Under traditional sentencing structures, inducements have been of two primary types—the common judicial practice of imposing more lenient sentences for defendants convicted by plea than by trial ("implicit" bargains; Newman, 1966:60-66; American Bar Association, 1968a:36-37; but see United States v. Wiley [1960] 278 F. 2d 500), and negotiated prosecutorial concessions (charge adjustments or sentence recommendations) in return for defendants' guilty pleas (plea bargains; Newman, 1966:76-130). The power of the judge to elicit a guilty plea depends heavily on a sentencing structure which allows great judicial latitude in the sentencing of persons convicted of similar offenses (Dawson,

1969:174-188). Indeterminate sentencing structures wherein the judge specifies a minimum, which may be relatively low, and a maximum, which may be relatively high, make it possible for a judge to portray to a defendant that he does have great sentencing latitude. However, the ideal of determinate sentencing does not permit a court to convey an image of wide latitude. Indeed, a principal objective cited by determinate sentencing reformers is the narrowing of judges' discretionary power in sentencing. Absent a judge's ability to sentence those pleading guilty more favorably, defendants will have little to gain by facilitating the administrative tasks of the production subsystem through their guilty pleas. In contrast, the prosecutor's power to grant concessions is not so easily curtailed by alterations in sentence structure (Dawson, 1969:188-192). It is this insulation from the effects of sentencing reform which makes the prosecutor the key figure in the inducement-based subsystem of criminal courts.[6] But prosecutorial independence is a two-edged sword. While insuring maximum caseflow at minimum expense, prosecutorial autonomy can be an impediment to the realization of the broader ideological goals of the justice system. The centrality of the prosecutor's production function implies that a primary concern of the prosecutor in sentence reform would be to maintain efficiency in processing. Larger goals (such as uniformity, proportionality, and fairness), which are the primary foci of sentence reform, are likely to be of secondary importance to the prosecutor's administrative concerns and are likely to be an issue to him only to the extent that they are compatible with the production function.[7]

ISSUES IN SENTENCING REFORM

The situation described above—the ability of the prosecutor to influence judge and client alike, and of the prosecutor and judge to offer inducements for guilty pleas—is presently found in the familiar context of indeterminate sentencing structures. However, indeterminate sentencing and the rehabilitative ideal which it operationalized have been under intense and growing attack in the last ten years. Much concern has been expressed over the efficacy of institutional treatment as well as the justice of parole board decisions. The questions expressed over the failure of treat-lead various scholars and professionals to conclude that the indeterminate sentence is an anachronism and must be replaced. Discussion about reforms in sentencing are not new to the criminal justice system, but not until recently has there been a total shift away from the basic indeterminate sentencing structure. Assertions about the inequities in

indeterminate sentencing have contributed to decisions in four states—
Maine, California, Indiana, and Illinois—to abandon the ideals of
individualized treatment and to adopt "determinate sentencing." An
essential element of determinate sentencing is that on the day of
sentencing an offender knows with reasonable certainty when he will be
released from prison. The date of release is well known to the offender
generally because parole board release decision making has been
eliminated, and in Maine all vestiges of parole have been abolished.
Many critical issues have been thrust to the fore in the controversy
surrounding sentencing reform. By and large, these concerns may be
grouped onto one of two categories—Ideological or crime responsive.
The ideological issues arise primarily from the growing disenchantment
with "therapeutic" justice. Under the tenets of indeterminate sentencing
and the rehabilitative ideal, it was appropriate, indeed even necessary, to
subject each offender to close scrutiny in order to discover any unique and
fundamental problems of which the commission of a crime was only
symptomatic. The fervent commitment of the criminal justice system to
the medical model, within the aegis of indeterminate sentencing, can be
seen in the following:

> The commission of an offense must, by its anti-social nature, indicate some
> overpowering breakdown, or a remission of that facility which human
> beings have, or are expected to have, to maintain their status as law-abiding
> citizens. In a sense, then, an offense may be seen as symptomatic of an inner
> conflict which the ego is not able to deal with effectively [Russell and
> Whiskin, 1970:10].

The renunciation of the ideals of rehabilitative justice has led to the
adoption of a wholly different collection of ideological concerns—
principally the issues of discretion, disparity, certainty, fairness, and
proportionality. Although each of these issues presents a distinct
criterion for the evaluation of a determinate sentence structure, indeterminate sentencing receives poor marks on all counts in much of the
current professional literature. In a somewhat confusing proliferation of
treatises on sentence reform (see, for example, Dershowitz, 1976; Fogel,
1975; Frankel, 1972; O'Donnell, Churgin, and Curtis, 1977; von
Hirsch, 1976), the indeterminate sentence has been assailed as unfair,
arbitrary, and capricious; as supportive of unprincipled discretion; and as
productive of criminal sentences that are unjustifiably disparate with
reference to each other and disproportionate to the severity of the crime
committed.

In sharp contrast to the ideological aspects of this debate are the issues
we have identified as crime responsive. These issues are seen in the often
articulated public concern that we, as a society, are losing the war against

crime—a war formally declared by our chief executive more than a decade ago.[8] From this perspective, the primary shortcoming of indeterminate sentencing, individualized treatment, and the rehabilitative ideal is their failure to reduce crime. In short, it is held that our traditional sentence structure has resulted in a response to crime that is slow, timid, uneven, and overly lenient. While of relative low visibility in the professional literature, these crime-responsive issues potentially have a greater impact on the actual substance of sentence reform than the ideological concerns mentioned above because it is around crime-responsive issues that public opinion, and thus political pressure, is most easily mobilized (see Gettinger, 1977:18-20).[9] Furthermore, the recent empirical evidence which has eroded the ideological foundation of indeterminacy (i.e., the failure of rehabilitative efforts; See Robinson and Smith, 1971; Bailey, 1966; Martinson, 1974) appears at the same time to have provided a catalyst for such mobilization.

Despite the divergence between these two lines of thought, determinate sentencing provides a common, though not neutral, ground for those with crime-responsive concerns and for those with ideological interests. It has become a cause which can be advocated with equal vigor from both ends of the political spectrum.[10] Those who advocate determinate sentence structures for ideological reasons point out that they will be more fair, more honest, more humane, and, ultimately, more effective than the status quo. Concommitantly, those primarily concerned with reducing crime through revised sentencing structures view determinate sentencing as a more appropriate societal response to crime. By adjusting sentence structure so that criminal sentences will be swifter, more certainly applied, and free from modification (reduction) once imposed, it is argued that the deterrence value of the penal sanction will be significantly enhanced. Given the widespread appeal of these arguments, it is little wonder that legislative activity in the direction of determinate sentencing of criminals has been so frenetic of late.[11] But this widespread appeal raises a fundamental question: Can alteration of sentence structure alone result in the range and magnitude of benefits ascribed to it by proponents? Stated in another way, can the ideological discrepancies between the due process and the crime control models of the criminal justice system be reconciled by tinkering with one "cog" in the justice machine (see Clear, Hewitt, and Regoli, 1977:1-2; Zalman, 1977:266-275)?[12] The obvious concern expressed in these questions is heightened by the speed and intensity with which legislatures seem to be answering them in the affirmative.

SENTENCING REFORM AND
ORGANIZATIONAL REALITY

While the participants in the current sentencing debate appear to be highly motivated, enthusiastic people of integrity, it is these very qualities that convey an impression of system naivete. Specifically, there seems to be a relatively consistent failure to acknowledge or defer to the fact that the criminal justice system is exceedingly complex organizationally. Furthermore, statutory enactments or proposals for code reform seem equally naive; although many agencies or programs receive attention in them, it is neither systematic nor systemic. Both proponents and reform proposals must recognize more fully that the plethora of agencies comprising the system are inextricably intertwined in the performance of the system's primary tasks. And although a detailed discussion of organizational theory is not necessary at this point, it is important to remember that, as a conglomeration of complex organizations, the criminal justice system requires "a simultaneous functioning of all components to accomplish one task, and . . . without all parts working together, the task will be left undone" (Duffee, Hussey, and Kramer, 1978:285). This fact of organizational life has serious implications for proponents of reform in the sentencing process. As in the case of any alteration of the system's structure, success or failure in reaching the objectives of sentencing revision is largely dependent on effective interrelationships between various subsystem components in the performance of primary system functions (for example, production).[13] Current literature attention to the nature of the impact of determinate sentencing on criminal justice system subcomponents frequently refers to the probation, parole, and institutional components. We, however, will examine the unique role of the prosecutor, focusing on how that role is affected by code reforms, and, in turn, on how the prosecutor can affect the implementation of revised codes.

The lofty and far-reaching objectives which sentencing reformers ascribe to radical changes in sentence structure may well be undercut by "various kinds of accommodative responses [by criminal justice agencies] . . . so that they may continue to perform their customary tasks . . . with the usual expenditure of time, effort and money" (Ohlin and Remington, 1958:496). It is far easier to accept the truth of this statement in a general sense than it is to estimate the precise impact of the prosecutor on the several determinate sentencing structures now in existence. For although rehabilitation has fallen from favor, there is no consensus about which sentencing objective, or objectives, should take its place paradigmatically. It is hardly surprising, then, that discrepant sentencing structures have evolved from attempts to blend the conceptions of punishment, rehabilitation, deterrence, and incapacitation with fairness, certainty, and other motives of sentencing. Despite the impression projected in the popular literature (see, for example, Time Magazine, 1977:98-99) that determinate sentencing reforms are highly homogeneous phenomena, Maine, Indiana, California, and Illinois—the first four states to have operationalized "determinacy"—have done so according to highly divergent legislative patterns.

PROSECUTORIAL POWER
AND SENTENCING REFORM

An assessment of how prosecutorial power will interact with determinate sentencing reforms would be facilitated by the development of a predictive typology which takes into account the variations among sentence structures. Given the recent emergence of determinate sentencing, there is little empirical evidence upon which such a typology could be based. However, there have been efforts to typologize alternative indeterminate sentence structures, one of which (Ohlin and Remington, 1958) is particularly germane to our analysis of prosecutorial sentencing power. Although that work predates the determinate sentencing movement and most modern organizational theory, it is of timeless utility in the analysis of the relationship between sentence structure and the administrative functions of the criminal justice system.

In their analysis, the authors predicted the comparative effects of legislatively fixed versus judicially fixed minimum and maximum terms on indeterminate sentence structures.[14] Their focus was the nature and extent of the accommodative responses by administrative agencies to structural variations. Much of their discussion dealt with the role of the prosecutor (and prosecutorial concessions) in maintaining administrative efficiency through a steady flow of guilty plea adjudications. The importance of this role, it was said, is enhanced to the extent that changes in sentence structure threaten systemic efficiency by, for example, limiting judicial ability to reward cooperative defendants. Thus, to the extent that the legislature curtails judicial discretion, there will most likely be a concommitant increase in the prosecutor's share of effective discretionary power (Ohlin and Remington, 1958:503-507). Regardless where the locus of discretion happens to be, however, Ohlin and Remington (1958:506-507) point out that plea inducements (judicial or prosecutorial) are effective only to the degree that they can give the criminal offender a real bargain (implicit or explicit).

The foregoing analysis suggests that two factors are of primary importance in the development of a typology according to which we might project the extent of prosecutorial sentencing power under determinate sentencing structures. The first dimension (*share*) is based on the degree to which judicial discretion is curtailed or narrowly defined by reform. The second dimension is provided by the potential severity of the fixed term (*stake*). The courts, in general, will be invested with greater discretionary power as parole boards and other correctional components are stripped of power. It appears likely that the prosecutor's power will increase directly as judicial influence is more narrowly defined or controlled; and it will vary directly with the risk (stake) faced by a defendant when confronted with full prosecution for a crime.[15] The nature of prosecutorial power resulting from these two dimensions is illustrated in Figure 1.

		STAKES (potential sentence severity)	
		Low	High
SHARE (of discretion)	Low	weak	moderate
	High	moderate	strong

Figure 1: Prosecutorial Power as a Function of Sentence Structure

This typology suggests that the prosecutorial impact on sentencing will be greatest under sentencing structures typified by drastic curtailment of judicial discretion and severe sentences (e.g., high mandatory sentences). Conversely, the prosecutorial impact will be least under structures marked by wide judicial discretion and lenient sentences (e.g., civil penalties for possession of marijuana). Between these two extremes, prosecutorial power will vary according to the degree to which these two factors are present in the sentencing structure within which the prosecutor functions.

Of course, we realize that this typology is a vast oversimplification of the dynamics of criminal prosecution and sentencing and that many influential factors have not been included in our analysis.[16] Nevertheless, from the perspective that the primary function of the criminal justice system is production (i.e., criminal processing), this typology is a useful starting point for analysis of the relationship between the prosecutorial function and determinate sentencing structures. Before attempting to characterize prosecutorial sentencing power according to this typology in the four determinate sentencing states, a review of the salient features of each sentencing statute would be helpful.

THE STATUTORY FRAMEWORK OF DETERMINACY[17]

As indicated earlier, the operationalization of determinacy has proceeded along widely divergent paths in the four "pioneer" states. One is hard pressed to identify characteristics common to all four statutes other than the fact that the offender, at the time sentence is imposed, can predict his release date with some certainty. However, the manner in which discretionary power is allocated in the fixing of that date varies greatly among the four states. Similarly, there is considerable divergence in the severity of criminal penalties permitted for specific conduct under the four sentence structures.

Maine

Maine became the first jurisdiction to abandon the indeterminate sentence and parole when its comprehensive criminal code revision went into effect on June 18, 1976. Although the legislation was characterized as a harbinger of a new era in criminal sentencing, Maine's "definite" or "flat" sentence approach differs considerably from those that have since appeared.

Aside from its total abolition of parole (decision making *and* supervision), perhaps the most noteworthy characteristic of the sentencing scheme established by Maine's code revision is the centrality of the judiciary in sentence determination. In jurisdictions with indeterminate sentences, judges typically have great discretion in imposing punishments, but actual time served is controlled to a considerable degree by administrative agencies such as the parole board. In contrast, most states that have enacted or proposed determinate sentencing schemes subsequent to the Maine revision have focused generally on a more legislatively oriented model in which specific sentences or sentence ranges are prescribed for each offense. Maine is unique in that its judges are empowered to impose fixed sentences limited only by statutory maxima with no routine external review. Specifically, the Maine code establishes six categories of crime and, with the exception of the offense of murder (for which the code presently allows imprisonment for any term of years or life and establishes a minimum term of 25 years), prescribes only the upper limit of the criminal sanction for each category (Title 17-A Maine Revised Statutes Annotated, section 1252). Within these limits, the trial court is allowed to impose imprisonment for any definite term. The ranges of potential punishment established by the code and summarized in Table 1 are not inconsiderable by any means. However, the apparent severity of these sanctions is mitigated by the absence of statutory provisions allowing for substantial enhancement or enlargement of "normal" sentence ranges. Such enhancements are common to the codes of the states discussed below and are based on the presence of variety of offense-related (for example, bodily injury to victims) or offender-related (for example, prior record) variables.[18]

Table 1: Crime Categories and Sentencing Ranges in Maine

CLASS	SENTENCE RANGES
Murder	Life or any term of years not less than 25
Class A	0-20 years
Class B	0-10 years
Class C	0-5 years
Class D	0-1 year
Class E	0-6 months

Perhaps more important in the mitigation of actual sentence severity is the absence of minimum terms under the Maine code. This fact enables judges to adjust sentences downward from the maximum in virtually every crime category to accommodate perceived differences in offenders or offenses that are technically equivalent according to statute. Thus, in cases where judges feel that incarceration is the proper disposition, they are spared having to impose an excessive minimum. The absence of flat minimums makes it possible for the judge to incarcerate when he has crossed the threshold of the "in/out"[19] decision and would otherwise have probation as the only viable, but too lenient, alternative. In essence, absence of minima allows judges to fill definitional and dispositional gaps in criminal codes through sentencing adjustment. (See American Bar Association, 1968b:148-149; Alschuler, 1978:72). Nevertheless, when a judge deems probation the appropriate disposition, the Maine code allows him virtually unfettered discretion. Unlike the three other states under consideration, Maine's statute does not specify a large category of nonprobationable offenses. Probation is a judicial sentencing alternative for virtually all offenses under the Maine code, with murder and second-offense burglary (sections 1201 [A] and 1156) the exceptions to the rule.

It is clear from the foregoing discussion and from our illustration in Table 1 that sentences may vary widely for similar offenses under Maine's criminal code. Thus, the sentence structure is "determinate" only in the sense that once imposed by the court, terms of imprisonment are relatively free from further change.

California

The language of California's revised sentence structure asserts that the purpose of sentencing is punishment alone and that the goals of the sentencing system should be the elimination of sentence disparity and promotion of sentence uniformity (California Penal Code Section 1170 [a] [1]). In its manifest intent, then, the California code is consistent with the ideological perspectives of the more prominent proponents of sentencing reform. However, the realization of sentencing objectives in California, as elsewhere, will depend on the interaction between sentence structure and agencies, such as the prosecutor, involved in criminal justice administration.

California's sentence structure encompasses a system of determinate sentences in which parole discretion is abolished and judicial discretion is narrowly defined. Specifically, the California legislature established a presumptive sentencing scheme which limits prison terms to a very narrow range of possibilities. Although not specifically categorized by class, every felony offense falls into one of four categories for purposes of sentencing. For each such category, three possible incarcerative terms are specified (section 1170 [a] [2]). The middle term, or "presumptive" sentence, must be imposed by courts unless aggravating or mitigating circumstances are presented and proven during a sentencing hearing (section 1170 [b]). In such cases, the court is limited to the higher term (that is, in cases of aggravating circumstances) or the lower term (that is, in cases of mitigating circumstances) specifically prescribed by the legislature. However, if the court chooses to impose the higher or lower term, the judge's factual findings and the reasons for the sentence must be stated for the record (section 1170 [b]). A summary of this structure, provided in Table 2, reveals sentence ranges that must be characterized, initially at least, as lenient when compared with those of the other states under consideration. This characterization may not turn out to be wholly consistent with sentencing practices, however, for several aspects of the code either increase the likelihood of incarceration or provide for enlargement of the presumptive term. Furthermore, the code fixes

Table 2: Felony Categories and Range of Penalties in California

Presumptive Sentence	Range in Aggravation	Range in Mitigation
2 years	+ 1 year	− 8 months
3 years	+ 1 year	− 1 year
4 years	+ 1 year	− 1 year
6 years	+ 1 year	− 1 year

minimum terms for each class below which judges cannot sentence. Confronted with an offender for whom both probation (overly lenient) and the minimum prison term (overly severe) seem inappropriate, a judge is likely to feel compelled to impose the prescribed prison term where, absent minima, he might simply adjust the term downward. Moreover, if a California judge feels that probation is the proper disposition, he may be precluded from ordering it by provisions which prohibit probation or restrict its use in a variety of situations (sections 1203 [d] and 1203.6). Additionally, the California code prescribes a rather elaborate scheme for the enlargement of the presumptive term. In addition to permitting an increased base term upon a finding of aggravated circumstances, the code specifies enhancements to that term for a variety of situations, including offenses involving use of a firearm, offenses resulting in great pecuniary loss, offenders with prior imprisonment records, and consecutive sentences for multiple offenses (sections 1170.1, 667.5, 12022, 12022.5-12022.7). Finally, capital punishment and life imprisonment terms are possible for certain specified offenses (sections 190, 209).[20]

Under the California code revision, the parole release decision power of the Adult Authority has been eliminated. In its place, a Community Release Board administers supervision of offenders released on parole at the expiration of their sentence, reduced by good-time credit (sections 3000, 5075-5077). The maximum parole period for all determinately sentenced offenders under the code is one year, and although parole may be revoked for a technical violation, the maximum term on return is six months. However, in no event can the total period of parole exceed one year (section 3057). Thus, unlike Maine which completely eliminated the parole function, the California statute has retained parole in a narrowly defined supervisory capacity but has effectively eliminated any vestiges of the traditional sentencing authority of parole-type agencies.

Indiana

The sentencing provisions of the Indiana code are perhaps best described as a hybrid approach to determinate sentencing. While adopting the mechanics of presumptive sentencing (specified penalties, aggravating/mitigating factors, limited parole function) the code grants considerable judicial discretion in the determination of sentence lengths. Thus, in terms of its apportionment of sentencing authority, the code is neither "judicial" (as in Maine) nor "legislative" (as in California) in its approach.

The Indiana code classifies all crime into ten categories (five classes of felonies, two classes of misdemeanors and, three classes of infractions), prescribes the appropriate range of sentences for each category, and requires the trial court to impose a fixed term at the time of sentencing. It specifies a presumptive sentence of incarceration for all felonies while allowing substantial deviations from that sentence in cases where the trial court finds aggravating or mitigating circumstances. As can be seen in Table 3, Indiana's presumptive terms are relatively high, its sentencing ranges are extremely wide, and the severity of maximum sentences is substantial. Moreover, far from softening the harshness of this basic sentence structure, the remaining sections of the Indiana code appear to enhance the potential severity of punishment.

Table 3: Felony Categories and Sentencing Ranges in Indiana

Class	FELONIES		
	Presumptive Sentence	Range in Aggravation	Range in Mitigation
Murder*	40 years	+ 20 years	− 10 years
Class A	30 years	+ 20 years	− 10 years
Class B	10 years	+ 10 years	− 4 years
Class C	5 years	+ 3 years	− 3 years
Class D**	2 years	+ 2 years	0

*The death sentence may be imposed in instances where the state proves the existence of a statutorily defined aggravating circumstance (IC 35-50-2-9).

**Judge has discretion to treat such offenses as Class A Misdemeanors (IC 35-50-2-7).

For example, in addition to instituting rather substantial minimum prison terms for each felony category, the Indiana code further restricts judicial leniency by creating a sizable list of nonprobationable offenses.

This list includes all defendants with a prior felony conviction, a variety of offenses involving weapon use or serious bodily injury, serious drug dealing, and murder (section 35-50-2-2 [a]). A murder conviction may also result in capital punishment when the state proves the existence of at least one statutorily defined aggravating circumstance (section 35-50-2-9). Additionally, the code permits the state to petition the court to sentence a convicted felon who has two prior unrelated felony convictions as an "habitual offender." Persons in this category receive a *mandatory* thirty-year term *in addition* to the term imposed for the current offense (section 35-50-2-8). Finally, in the case of conviction for multiple offenses, the trial court is given the discretionary power in most instances to order that the sentences be served either concurrently or consecutively (section 35-50-1-2 [a]).

Consistent with the shift to determinacy, the decision-making authority of the Indiana Parole Board has been altered considerably. Under the revised code, imprisoned felons are released at the expiration of a fixed term, less good time (section 35-50-6-1 [a]). However, every person released prior to the expiration of the term imposed by the court is placed on parole for the remainder of that term (section 35-50-6-1 [b]). The parolee must be discharged if parole is not revoked within one year from the date of release; if parole is revoked, the parolee is imprisoned for the remainder of his original sentence less good time earned after revocation (sections 35-50-6-1 [b] and [c]). In such cases, the Indiana Parole Board retains decision-making authority reminiscent of its precode function—it may (or may not) reinstate the inmate on parole at any time prior to the new release date. In this limited sense, then, the Indiana Parole Board retains some small measure of sentencing authority. This differs markedly from Maine and California, which effectively removed parole-type agencies from sentence decision making in their code reforms.

Illinois

Illinois has wrestled with determinate sentencing reform since 1975 when David Fogel's "justice model" for sentencing was first considered by the Illinois legislature (see Fogel, 1975:249-260). Several years and numerous political skirmishes later, a determinate sentencing structure, reminiscent of Fogel's model but significantly different in many respects, has emerged. This most recent attempt at determinacy is quite unlike the other statutes discussed above, but in terms of apportionment of discretion, its basic sentence structure is most similar to the Maine code.

Specifically, the Illinois revision has revamped the traditional parole decision-making function and has vested the judiciary with primary responsibility for setting the length of determinate prison sentences. As in

Maine, there are no presumptive or suggested terms with which incarcerative decisions must be in accordance. Under the Illinois statute, when a judge chooses to imprison an offender, he may select any term within limits set by the legislature for each class of felony. However, unlike Maine, these limits include a legislatively fixed minimum as well as maximum term (Illinois Annotated Statutes, Chapter 38, section 1005-8-1).

In addition to the regular sentence ranges, the statute is unique among the four states in that it provides an entirely separate schedule of "extended terms" for repeat felony offenders and in cases of offenses accompanied by "exceptionally brutal or heinous behavior indicative of wanton cruelty" (sections 1005-8-2 and 1005-5-3.2). The enhanced schedule is similar in form to the regular sentence structure described above—upper and lower limits are specified for each class of felony, and judges are allowed to impose any definite term within those boundaries. However, the length of enhanced terms is considerably greater—the upper limits of the regular schedule equal the minima, and the enhanced maxima equals twice the enhanced minima. When the two schedules are viewed simultaneously (see Table 5), it is apparent that the range of permissible sentences as well as the potential severity of sentences are great under the Illinois statute. However, the range and severity of sentences actually imposed are likely to be affected by several related statutory provisions.

Table 4: Crime Categories and Sentencing Ranges in Illinois

Class	Regular Terms	Extended Terms
Murder	Life or 20-40 years	Life or 40-80 years
Habitual criminal*	Mandatory Life	
Class X	6-30 years	30-60 years
Class 1	4-15 years	15-30 years
Class 2	3-7 years	7-14 years
Class 3	2-5 years	5-10 years
Class 4	1-3 years	3-6 years

*Persons convicted of "forcible offenses" (treason, murder, rape, deviate sexual assault, armed robbery, aggravated arson, aggravated kidnapping for ransom) with two or more prior forcible offenses convictions (38 I.A.S. section 33B-1).

First, while allowing a considerable range within the sentence schedules, the statute calls for the establishment of a Criminal Sentencing Commission which, among other duties, is to promote uniformity, certainty, and fairness through "standardized sentencing guidelines" and other unspecified "recommendations (section 1005-10-2)." The statute is silent about the nature, extent, and applicability of the commission's guidelines and recommendations, but it is clear that the commission is provided with the means by which the present level of judicial discretion (and the effective range of prison terms) might be curtailed. The state supreme court is given a similar mandate to adopt rules which will promote "uniformity and parity of sentences" within state trial courts (section 1005-5-4.2). Second, although the statute establishes rather severe terms of imprisonment, it specifies that probation and conditional discharge are the preferred forms of sentence and must be imposed absent a threat to the public or a deprecation of the seriousness of the offense resulting from the offender's release (section 1005-6-1). In making the "in/out" decision, the judge is required to consider specified factors in mitigation and aggravation and to state on the record the reasons for the sentence imposed (sections 1005-5-3.1, 1005-5-3.2, and 1005-4-1). Yet, despite the preference for probationary sentences, the Illinois statute creates a significant class of offenses (for example, murder, class X felonies) and offenders (class 1 and 2 felony repeaters) for whom probation is not allowed (section 1005-5-3 [c] [2]). One final factor which should be mentioned relative to sentence severity is the effect of minimum incarcerative terms. As discussed in our analyses of the Maine, California, and Indiana statutes, such terms create gaps in the range of sanctions available to judges and require that a choice be made between substantial imprisonment and community supervision when neither appears uniquely appropriate.

As mentioned above, the Illinois statue has altered the traditional decision-making function of the Parole and Pardon Board. Inmates are still subject to postincarceration supervision, but release to that status is no longer a discretionary matter. At the time a sentence of imprisonment is imposed, the "mandatory supervised release term" is specified (section 1005-8-1 [d]). The length of the term (one, two, or three years) is based on the class of the offense, and the term begins at the expiration of the sentence less good time (one day of credit for each day served) (sections 1005-8-1 and 1003-6-3). Responsibility for determining the conditions of release, for imposing sanctions for violations, and for revoking the release status lies with the Prisoner Review Board (section 1003-3-1 [a] [5]). Despite the elimination of "parole" discretion in the initial release decision, the Prisoner Release Board may, in its supervisory function, affect the actual time served. For example, upon revocation, the board is empowered not only to recommit the offender for the uncompleted portion of the mandatory supervised release term, but may also order the prisoner to serve up to one year of his *original sentence* which was not served because of the accumulation of good time credit (section 1003-3-9 [a]). Moreover, persons who have been recommitted may, at the board's discretion, be rereleased to the *full* mandatory supervised release term—this despite the fact that part of that term was completed prior to revocation and recommittment (section 1003-3-10). Conversely, the board may release and discharge offenders from supervision at any time *prior* to the completion of the mandatory supervised release term if it determines that the person "is likely to remain at liberty without committing another offense" (section 1003-3-8 [b]). Thus, in the revocation, recommittment, rerelease, and early discharge decisions, the Prisoner Review Board retains a measure of control over actual sentence lengths (this is particularly so if one conceptualizes actual sentence length as the period during which the offender is "at risk").[21] In this respect, the Illinois statute is somewhat similar to the Indiana code.

In addition to the basic features of the four statutes discussed above, each permits some modification of the terms of sentence after imposition. For example, each state allows for the reduction of time served through the accumulation of "good time" credit (17-A Maine Revised Statutes Annotated, section 1253; California Penal Code, section 2931; Indiana Code, 35-50-6-3; 38 Illinois Annotated Statutes, section 1003-6-3). Although the precise rate at which credit may be earned varies among the states, good time is generally seen as a necessary disciplinary strategy (particularly with the demise of traditional parole release), the use of which is controlled by procedural safeguards. Each of the states also allows for sentence modification through resentencing by the trial court (17-A Maine Revised Statutes Annotated section 1154; California Penal Code section 1170; Indiana Code 35-4.1-4-18; 38 Illinois Annotated Statutes section 1005-8-1 [c]). However, in all but Maine, such adjustment is possible only for a limited time after the initial imposition of sentence.[22]

PROSECUTORIAL POWER IN
THE FOUR PIONEER STATES

Maine: Low Prosecutorial Power

It is clear from the foregoing discussion that there is considerable variation in the basic sentencing structures of the first four determinate sentencing states, both in terms of allocation of discretionary power (share) and potential sentence severity (stakes). This observation is significant, for although these factors are not solely determinative of prosecutorial power, they are likely to have great influence on it. Returning to our predictive typology discussed above, it is possible to characterize the relative power of the prosecutor in the several states along these two dimensions (see Figure 2).

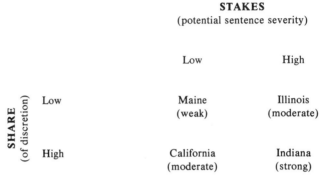

STAKES
(potential sentence severity)

		Low	High
SHARE (of discretion)	Low	Maine (weak)	Illinois (moderate)
	High	California (moderate)	Indiana (strong)

Figure 2: Prosecutorial Power as a Function of Determinate Sentencing Structures in Four States

For example, under the Maine Criminal Code, the apportionment of discretion weighs heavily in favor of the judge, both in terms of the "in/out" decision and the sentence length decision once incarceration has been chosen. Virtually the only limitation on judicial discretion in Maine is at the top end of potential incarcerative terms—that is, legislatively fixed maxima. As a result of this sentencing structure, potential penalties for the various offense categories overlap considerably. Consequently, charge reductions by prosecutors do not necessarily result in sentences that are less severe. For this reason, charge bargaining is not likely to be an effective means for encouraging defendant cooperation because defendants are not guaranteed more favorable treatment in return for guilty pleas. The remaining alternative available to the prosecutor is bargaining for sentence recommendations, and the effectiveness of this plea inducement strategy is directly dependent on judicial willingness to cooperate. Clearly, then, under Maine's sentencing scheme, the share of discretion which the prosecutor controls is relatively small.

Turning our attention to potential sentence severity, the Maine sentencing scheme must be considered only moderately severe, in light of the length of maximum terms (especially when compared with Indiana and Illinois) and the absence of both minimum terms and sentence enhancements. Thus, in Maine, both the prosecutor's discretionary share and the potential stakes of conviction are comparatively small. Prosecutorial influence is therefore likely to be more limited under the Maine Criminal Code than in that of any of the other states discussed.

Indiana: High Prosecutorial Power

If we posit Maine as representing one end of the prosecutor influence spectrum, the other end is anchored by the sentence structure of the Indiana code which has been described by many (Clear, Hewitt, and Regoli, 1977:1) as a "prosecutor's law." The statute combines limitations on judicial discretion (e.g., presumptive terms, nonprobationable sentences for certain violent felonies and all repeat felony offenders, and a mandatory thirty-year prison term for third-time felons) with potentially severe sanctions. Assuming that a reduction in judicial discretion results in an increase in prosecutor discretion, as Ohlin and Remington (1958) contend, this combination of high prosecutorial share and high stakes of conviction creates a situation in which the prosecutor is most likely to become the dominant force in the criminal process. And although empirical support for this prediction is lacking, there is considerable speculation in Indiana (Clear, Hewitt, and Regoli, 1977:11-13) that prosecutors will be under increasing pressure to utilize the many discretionary alternatives which the statute provides. For example, the aforementioned statutory proscription of suspended sentences and probation have the potential for being rendered impotent by prosecutorial charging practices. Clear, Hewitt, and Regoli (1977:11-12) point to the criminal "attempt"[23] and "lesser included offense" provisions of the code as negotiable items available to the prosecutor at the charging stage, the effect of which is the avoidance of nonprobationable convictions and thus an increase in prosecutorial power. Similarly, charge reduction to the class D felony level (which may be sentence either as a felony or misdemeanor) in combination with a prosecutorial sentence recommendation can circumvent the stringent statutory penalties for repeat felony offenders.

At the sentencing stage, the Indiana prosecutor finds himself in an equally powerful position. He may, in addition to specific sentence recommendations, present or withhold from the court information as to the existence of "aggravating" or "mitigating" factors. Because these factors serve as justification for judicial deviation (which may be substantial) from the presumptive term,[24] the prosecutorial role at sentencing adds to the cadre of plea inducements at the prosecutor's disposal under the Indiana code. These attributes of determinate sentencing in Indiana lead us to characterize the power of the prosecutor in that state as the most influential among the four.

California: Moderate Prosecutorial Power

Perhaps more than any other attribute, the basic sentence structure of the California Penal Code is marked by the strict definition of judicial discretion. Not only are presumptive terms of incarceration specified for the various felony categories, but the range of those terms is severely limited. The "in/out" decision is also controlled by provisions making certain types of offenses nonprobationable, although not to the extent found in the Indiana code. Nevertheless, it is clear that the prosecutor in California has the greatest share of available discretion among the prosecutors of the four states. However, the enlargement of prosecutorial power which one might associate with such an apportionment of discretion is offset considerably by the comparative leniency of potential criminal sanctions under California law. As stated by Alschuler (1978: 73), "A prosecutor who can threaten only a penalty of three years following a defendant's conviction at trial plainly has less bargaining power than a prosecutor who can threaten a sentence of 25 years." Not only must one characterize the regularly prescribed (presumptive) terms as lenient, but permissible adjustments to those terms are comparatively quite small. Thus, power deriving from the prosecutor's ability to present or withhold information bearing on sentence modification (for example, aggravating or mitigating circumstances) is not nearly so influential in California as it would be in a state which provided for substantial judicial modification of the presumptive term.[25] The California Penal Code embodies, therefore, a sentencing scheme in which the prosecutorial share of discretion is high but the stakes of criminal conviction are low. That being so, the power of the prosecutor under California's determinate sentencing system can be characterised as only moderately influential.

Illinois: Moderate Prosecutorial Power

Prosecutorial power under the Illinois statute is characterized similarly (moderately influential) for dissimilar reasons. As was the case with Maine's code, the Illinois law does not attempt to restrict judicial discretion through the specification of presumptive terms. Under the law as presently written,[26] the judiciary has a fairly free hand in the imposition of prison terms within the statutorily set minimum and maximum limits. Moreover, in cases where grounds exist for the imposition of an extended term, the judge may or may not choose to impose it. The net effect of these provisions is that judges have an extraordinarily wide range of possible prison terms from which to choose, particularly in cases of extended term defendants.[27] In addition, probation is an available, although somewhat restricted, sentence alternative. Thus, while the Illinois revision imposes some constraints on judicial choice in sentencing (for example minimum terms and nonprobationable offenses), the judicial share of discretion clearly outweighs that of the prosecutor. Given the range of potential penalties and the resultant overlap among the offense categories, charge reduction, of itself, will be an ineffective plea inducement in Illinois. Prosecutors will be dependant on judicial cooperation in sentence bargaining to guarantee the rapid caseflow which the production function demands.

However, offsetting the small prosecutorial share of discretion, the Illinois statute creates what are perhaps the highest stakes of conviction (i.e., potential sentence severity) among the four states. Thus, while they may bear little resemblance to actual judicial sentencing practices, maximum penalties may be an effective prosecutorial threat to noncooperative defendants. This threat of what von Hirsh (1976:105) calls "exemplary severity"[28] is possible only under statutes (like that of Illinois) which permit penalties greatly in excess of the norm. The offsetting effects of the comparatively small prosecutorial share of discretion and the high stakes of conviction lead us to characterize prosecutorial power under the Illinois statute as moderately influential.

SUMMARY

As we have pointed out, treatises extolling the virtues of determinate sentencing, as well as documents which have established determinate sentencing structures in the four states, have largely ignored organizational implications. It would appear that reformers have moved linearly ahead with the objectives of increasing the equity and certainty in punishment without carefully considering potential threats to the certainty of achieving these goals. Although the literature on sentencing is not replete with references to organizational concerns, the admonitions of Ohlin and Remington (1958) seem as relevant today as when first written.

Essentially, Ohlin and Remington alert us to the fact that when changes are made in the sentencing system, accommodative responses are likely to occur which act to undermine the intent of the changes. Organizational perspectives which have been elaborated since the development of the Ohlin/Remington "accommodative response" hypothesis allow us to see more clearly both the specialization of system personnel in the pursuit of the production function *and* the resistance to organizational change emanating from an organization's maintenance subsystem, a subsystem complementary to production and one which acts to maintain stability and predictability in an organization. When confronted with a reform as significant and massive as the implementation of determinate sentencing, any function, such as prosecution, of the criminal justice system will be caught in competing forces as it seeks to reestablish equilibrium, if indeed the old equilibrium has been upset. Thus, even though we emphasized the production function in this article, the maintenance dynamic will act to sustain the status quo. In all probability, however, the maintenance function will relinquish control if it is clear that production will be enhanced with no loss in stability.

The implementation of determinate sentencing will have direct impact on the courts and corrections, but it appears, initially at least, that the courts are in much more control of the change than is the corrections component. Prosecutors, in particular, who are very close to the defendant-processing scene are perhaps most directly affected by the implementation of determinate sentencing, and from our analysis it appears that they generally have gained greater control of discretion with few, if any, losses.

CONCLUSION

In general, it would seem that prosecutorial discretion is enhanced in several instances when compared with previous indeterminate sentencing in these states. While Maine has not apparently enhanced prosecutorial discretion, neither has it curtailed it. On the other hand, in all likelihood, the other three states have considerably enhanced the prosecutor's role in sentencing compared with what it was under the indeterminate system. In California, under indeterminacy, the prosecutor had minimal control over the length of imprisonment; however, under the state's new sentencing format the prosecutor can have extensive influence on the sentence through charge bargaining.

Prosecutorial power, while often alluded to, has been infrequently studied. It will be of great importance to examine closely, in the states moving to some form of determinacy, the use and changes in case processing by prosecutors. We offer our typology of prosecutorial power to those who will be examining systemic response to determinate sentencing.

NOTES

1. The production function or subsystem is concerned with the organization of the agency's work force, or the human resources of an organization, into units to get the organization's work done. The tendency in organizations is to specialize so that the organizational goal of efficiency can be optimized.

2. Given the overwhelming predominance of guilty plea convictions (Newman, 1966), sentencing is the major judicial decision in most cases.

3. Zalman (1977) has characterized this process as "diffusion" of sentencing power, a primary source of problems in sentencing. By diffusion is meant "that sentencing power is polycentric, divided among several agencies and among numerous decision makers" (269-270).

4. There is little empirical evidence about the extent of this impact. However, one survey of prosecutors (Teitelbaum, 1972) suggests that prosecutorial influence on the judiciary may be substantial in the determination of sentence. In response to the question "If your office does make sentence recommendations to the court, do you believe they are followed?" 50% of the prosecutors answered "all the time" or "almost all the time." An additional 42% answered "more than half the time" (94-95). The study was limited to sentence recommendations in cases of defendants convicted at trial and excluded recommendations made as part of a plea bargain. It is conceivable that the correlation between recommendation and disposition would have been perceived as greater if plea bargains had been included.

5. In return for waiving constitutional safeguards, defendants typically receive more favorable treatment from the system than do defendants who invoke those safeguards. Uncooperative defendants (i.e., those who exercise constitutional rights) are thus effectively penalized when they receive less favorable treatment upon conviction than those convicted by plea. This aspect of the system's "encouragement" of guilty pleas has been seen by some (National Advisory Commission on Criminal Justice Standards and Goals, 1973:43; Alschuler, 1968) as inherently coercive and by others (Harvard Law Review, 1970) as simply unconstitutional.

6. As a general rule, when legislatures have restricted judicial latitude in sentencing (for example, mandatory sentences, nonprobationable offense categories, and habitual offender statutes) "pressures that would otherwise be directed to the trial judge to reward defendant cooperation do not cease; rather, they are directed to other officials, principally the prosecuting attorney" (Dawson, 1969:188).

7. For an analysis of the administrative function of the prosecutor and that function's relation to other prosecutorial responsibilities, see Alschuler (1968).

8. The existence of a state of war is clear in the following excerpt from Lyndon Johnson's message to the Congress on March 9, 1966.

> The problems of crime bring us together. Even as we join in common action, we know there can be no instant victory. Ancient evils do not yield easily to conquest. We cannot limit our efforts to enemies we can see. We must, with equal resolve, seek out new knowledge, new techniques, and new understanding.

9. An excellent illustration of political response to crime control issues is California's sentencing revision. Gettinger (1977:18-19) reported the following turn of events:
Many observers point to recent events in California as an example of how the political process can warp what started as a reform effort. The original California law sailed through the legislature with a minimum of opposition. A coalition representing the entire spectrum of the criminal justice community—police, district attorneys, public defenders, prisoners—actively supported the bill. When he signed the bill last September, Governor Jerry Brown hailed it as "the most far-reaching criminal justice reform of the last 50 years."
But in January Los Angeles Police Chief Edward Davis denounced the bill as "the great California prison break." He called it "a gift from the antagonists of criminal justice in Sacramento to the inhabitants of Troy—a huge wooden horse filled with murderers, robbers, rapists and burglars which will be released upon our communities and towns."

Suddenly politicians who had previously voted for the bill found major defects, and they tripped over each other to propose stringent amendments. Cleanup legislation had been expected to be necessary to clear up procedural problems before the law went into effect. But instead the cleanup amendments became a vehicle for many of these strict provisions. Liberals denounced the amendments, which by this time had the backing of Governor Brown, as a violation of the spirit of the original bill. Soon, however, even they were begging the legislature to settle for the Brown-backed revisions.

In one wild day of legislative fervor, a senate committee adopted so many amendments to the cleanup legislation—all of them proposed by various law enforcement groups—that even the following week no one knew exactly what had been adopted. Somewhat sheepishly, the committee rescinded most of its actions. But the coalition that had brought about "the most importance piece of reform in criminal justice in the last 50 years" had fallen utterly apart.

"It's hard to overstate how badly we were screwed," remarked a rueful Jim Smith, a lawyer for the Prisoners' Union who had been an important part of the original negotiations. Mike Salerno, a young legislative aide who co-authored the sentencing legislation, said, "I'm shocked. I didn't think the legislature would fold like this."

10. The broad-based appeal of determinate sentencing is nowhere more clearly illustrated than in the U.S. Senate's adoption of Bill 1437 and in the political divergence of its sponsors (Senators McClellan and Kennedy).

11. In addition to Maine, California, Indiana, and Illinois, many state legislatures are currently considering determinate sentencing structures.

12. This problem is well stated by observers of the Indiana Code reform:

Living in a state that has debated and adopted fixed sentencing, we can certify that broad expectations emerge almost with a life of their own. In the eyes of one interest group or another the new Indiana Penal Code is variously expected to increase deterrence, increase humaneness, increase prison populations, decrease discretion, make penalties more appropriate to the offense, equalize penalties, reduce arbitrariness, increase public protection, increase system efficiency, reduce harshness and reduce leniency. Someone is bound to be disappointed [Clear, Hewitt, and Regoli, 1977:2].

13. For example, consider the following description of the production subsystem of criminal courts.

The court productive process has been divided into a number of key roles by which the throughput task is achieved. The driving force in the production line is the prosecutor, whose job it is to demonstrate that each unit of input has reached a certain level of acceptability in the court system. His task is structured by the judge, who has the job of enforcing production standards. Defense counsel acts as a quality control device, providing continuing feedback during the throughput phase. The court clerk, the judge, or the court manager schedules the throughput progression by manipulation of the court calendar, announcing the time at which various demonstrations of acceptability will be made. The probation staff, at least in cases of major production units (felons), files a report of final output measure, by which the judge makes conclusions about most likely export or output agencies (Duffee, Hussey, and Kramer, 1978:363).

14. In the current determinate sentencing debate, the comparative advantages of legislative and judicial sentencing authority are, likewise, a basic issue.

15. As noted by von Hirsch (1976),

The prosecutor's bargaining power comes from the defendant's knowledge that if he does not agree to plead quilty to a reduced charge, the prosecution may have sufficient evidence to convict on the more severely punishable original charge. . . [T] he existing system gives the prosecutor undue added bargaining leverage through the threat of exemplary severity if the defendant refuses to plead guilty. The defendant who goes to trial not only risks conviction on the more serious original charge but incurs the extra risk that, if convicted, he will be made to suffer a punishment that is uncharacteristically severe for that charge (104-105) (see also Alschuler, 1978:73).

16. For example, Eisenstein and Jacob (1977:267-268) stress the importance of courtroom "workgroups" in the ultimate sentencing decision: "The organizational structure of the courtroom establishes other, severe constraints on the sentencing decision. Contrary to the protestations of many prosecutors and judges, sentences are collective decisions in which all participants have some influence."

17. The following discussion of determinate sentencing statutes is drawn, in part, from Lagoy, Hussey, and Kramer (1976).

18. California Penal Code sections 1203 (d) and 1203.06; Indiana Code section 35-50-2-2(a); Illinois Annotated Statutes, chapter 38, section 1005-5-3(c) (2).

19. Wilkins et al. (1978:1) describe the sentencing decision as a bifurcated process. "The first decision to be made is whether or not to incarcerate an individual. After that comes a determination of time to be served: i.e. how long a sentence should be imposed?" The first of these decisions is referred to as the "in/out" decision.

20. First degree murder and kidnapping for robbery or ransom.

21. While vesting the board with a limited amount of sentencing power, Illinois law limits the "at risk" period to the original term imposed by the court plus the statutorily prescribed mandatory supervised release period (section 1003-3-10).

22. Maine's code provides that sentences in excess of one year are deemed "tentative" and that the court may resentence an inmate upon a petition by the Department of Mental Health and Corrections based on its evaluation of the inmate's "progress toward a noncriminal way of life" (17-A M.R.S.A. section 1154). Some (e.g., Zalman, 1977:272) have speculated that the statute forms the basis of a quasi-parole release process to be administered by the corrections department and the judge (see, also, Zarr, 1976:143-147). However, there are serious questions concerning the statute's constitutionality under Maine law. For example, two recent decisions of the Maine Superior (trial) Court held that resentencing under the statute would constitute an unconstitutional usurpation of the executive pardoning power (State v. Abbott [1978]. York County Criminal Action, Docket Numbers 67-564 through 67-567; State v. Green (1978). York County Criminal Action, Docket Numbers 76-545, 76-573, 76-574). As of this writing, no inmate has been resentenced.

23. According to Clear, Hewitt, and Regoli (1977:11),

The Indiana Code has been described by many insiders as a "prosecutor's" law. Much of the increased prosecutorial discretion is based in the substantive law. For example, a number of offenses are nonsuspendable. But the new penal code provides that any offense which can be charged may also be charged as an "attempted" offense, which carries the same penalty (except in the case of murder). The primary distinction is that all "attempted" offenses are suspendable. The new "attempt" clause has the dual effect of giving the prosecutor flexibility to bargain while silently providing added pressure on the defendant to bargain, since attempt is an offense whose elements of proof are generally much less rigorous than the regular criminal statutes.

24. Although loosely defined under the Indiana code, aggravating and/or mitigating circumstances must be found by the court before a presumptive term may be enhanced or decreased. The judge is also required to state on record his reasons (presumably including a finding that aggravating and/or mitigating factors exist) for the sentence imposed. Given that defendants may appeal from sentencing decisions, judges may be somewhat hesitant to stray from the presumptive term. This could work to further narrow the *effective* range of judicial discretion—the apparent range of sentences is quite wide—thereby expanding the range of prosecutorial power (but see Clear, Hewitt, and Regoli, 1977:13-14).

25. See note 21, note 23, and the accompanying text. On the other hand, as judicial latitude in sentencing is statutorily curtailed in determinate sentencing systems, the prosecutorial charging decision, should conviction follow, becomes, effectively, the sentencing decision.

26. As discussed earlier, the Illinois Criminal Sentencing Commission has been given authority to promote "uniformity, certainty, and fairness" through "standardized sentencing guidelines." We cannot predict what form these guidelines will assume nor what effect they may have on judicial sentencing discretion. Under current proposals (Wilkins et al., 1978; Zalman, 1977), sentencing guidelines are not perceived as binding on the sentencing court but merely as a point of reference for the sentencing decision.

27. An extended term defendant is one "convicted of any felony, after having been previously convicted in Illinois of the same or greater class of felony, within 10 years," or one who commits any felony accompanied by "exceptionally brutal or heinous behavior indicative of wanton cruelty" (Illinois Annotated Statutes, chapter 38, section 1005-5-3.2 [b]).

28. See note 15 and the accompanying text.

REFERENCES

ALSCHULER, A. W. (1978). "Sentencing reform and prosecutorial power: A critique of recent proposals for 'fixed' and 'presumptive' sentencing," in Determinate Sentencing. Washington D.C.: U.S. Government Printing Office.

_____(1975). "The defense attorney's role in plea bargaining." Yale Law Journal 84:1179.

_____(1968). "The prosecutor's role in plea bargaining." University of Chicago Law Review 36:50-112.

American Bar Association Project on Standards for Criminal Justice (1971). Standards Relating to the Prosecution Function and the Defense Function. Approved Draft. New York: Institute of Judicial Administration.

_____(1968a). Standards Relating to Pleas of Guilty. Approved Draft. New York: Institute of Judicial Administration.

_____(1968b). Standards Relating to Sentencing Alternatives and Procedures. Approved Draft. New York: Institute of Judicial Administration.

AMOS, W. E. and C. L. NEWMAN (1975). Parole. New York: Federal Legal Publications.

BAILEY, W. (1966). "Correctional outcomes: An evaluation of 100 reports." Journal of Criminal Law, Criminology and Police Science 57 (June):153-160.

BUBANY, C. P. and F. F. SKILLERN (1976). "Taming the Dragon: An administrative law for prosecutorial decision making." American Criminal Law Review 13:473-505.

CLEAR, T. R., J. D. HEWITT, and R. M. REGOLI (1977). "Discretion and the determinate sentence: Its distribution, control and effect on time served." Presented at the American Society of Criminology Annual Meetings, Atlanta, Georgia, November 16-20.

DAWSON, R. O. (1969). Sentencing: the Decision as to Type, Length, and Conditions of Sentence. Boston: Little, Brown.

DERSHOWITZ, A. M. (1976). Fair and Certain Punishment. New York: McGraw-Hill.

DUFFEE, D. and R. FITCH (1976). An Introduction to Corrections: A Policy and Systems Approach. Pacific Palisades, Calif.: Goodyear.

DUFFEE, D., F. A. HUSSEY, J. H. KRAMER (1978). Criminal Justice: Organization, Structure, and Analysis. Englewood Cliffs, N.J.: Prentice-Hall.

EISENSTEIN, J. and H. JACOB (1977). Felony Justice: An Organizational Analysis of Criminal Courts. Boston: Little, Brown.

FOGEL, D. (1975). We Are the Living Proof: The Justice Model for Corrections. Cincinnati: W. H. Anderson.

FRANKEL, M. E. (1972). Criminal Sentences: Law Without Order. New York: Hill and Wang.

GETTINGER, S. (1977). "Three states adopt flat time; others wary." Corrections Magazine 3(September):16-36.

Harvard Law Review (1970). "The unconstitutionality of plea bargaining." 83:1387-1411.

HEUMANN, M. (1975). "A note on plea bargaining and case pressure." Law and Society Review 9:515.

LaFAVE, W. R. (1965). Arrest: The Decision to Take a Suspect into Custody. Boston: Little, Brown.

LAGOY, S. P., F. A. HUSSEY, and J. H. KRAMER (forthcoming). "A comparative assessment of determinate sentencing in the four pioneer states." Crime and Delinquency.

LAGOY, S. P., J. J. SENNA, and L. J. SIEGEL (1976). "An empirical study on information usage for prosecutorial decision making in plea negotiations." American Criminal Law Review 13:453-471.

MANGRUM, C. T. (1975). The Professional Practitioner in Probation. Springfield, Ill.: Charles C. Thomas.

MARTINSON, R. (1974). "What works?—Questions and answers about prison reform." Public Interest 35(Spring):22-54.

MILLER, F. W. (1970). Prosecution: The Decision to Charge a Suspect with a Crime. Boston: Little, Brown.

National Advisory Commission on Criminal Justice Standards and Goals (1973). Courts. Washington, D.C.: U.S. Government Printing Office.

NEWMAN, D. J. (1966). Conviction: The Determination of Guilt or Innocence Without Trial. Boston: Little, Brown.

O'DONNEL, P., M. J. CHURGIN, and D. E. CURTIS (1977). Toward a Just and Effective Sentencing System. New York: Praeger.

OHLIN, L. E. and F. J. REMINGTON (1958). "Sentencing structure: Its effect upon systems for the administration of criminal justice." Law and Contemporary Problems 23:495-507.

President's Commission on Law Enforcement and Administration of Justice (1967). The Challenge of Crime in a Free Society. Washington, D.C.: U.S. Government Printing Office.

REMINGTON, F. J., D. M. NEWMAN, E. L. KIMBALL, M. MELLI, and H. GOLDSTEIN (1969). Criminal Justice Administration: Materials and Cases. Indianapolis: Bobbs-Merrill.

ROBINSON, J. and G. SMITH (1971). "The effectiveness of correctional programs." Crime and Delinquency 17:67-80.

ROSETT, A. and D. R. CRESSEY (1976). Justice by Consent: Plea Bargains in the American Courthouse. Philadelphia: J. B. Lippincott.

RUSSELL, D. H. and R. E. WHISKIN (1970). The Massachusetts Court Clinics Offender Therapy Series. APTO Monographs No. 1. International Journal of Offender Therapy.

STANLEY, D. T. (1976). Prisoners Among Us: The Problem of Parole. Washington, D.C.: Brookings Institution.

TEITELBAUM, W. J. (1972). "The prosecutor's role in the sentencing process: A national survey." American Journal of Criminal Law 1(1):75-95.

Time Magazine (1977). "Fixed sentences gain favor." December 12:98-99.

von HIRSCH, A. (1976). Doing Justice: The Choice of Punishments. New York: Hill and Wang.

WILKINS, L. T., J. M. KRESS, D. M. GOTTFREDSON, J. C. CALPIN, and GELMAN, A. M. (1978). Sentencing Guidelines: Structuring Judicial Discretion. Monograph. Washington, D.C.: U.S. Government Printing Office.

ZALMAN, M. (1977). "A commission model of sentencing." Notre Dame Lawyer 53:266-290.

ZARR, M. (1976). "Sentencing." Maine Law Review 28:117-148.

Chapter 9

THE SOCIAL AND OCCUPATIONAL MOBILITY
OF PROSECUTORS: NEW YORK CITY

JAMES J. FISHMAN

Analyses of the professions and their place in society have tended to look at professions organically by gauging the prestige of the profession itself. They have missed an important variable, namely the great degree of internal stratification within the profession (Lynn, 1963; Vanneman, 1977). The legal profession, like other occupations, is rigidly stratified. Entry into the profession, mobility within it, and the status level in the profession which a lawyer eventually achieves are all strongly influenced by class origins, education, and job experience. This system of stratification has numerous implications for a theoretically open society. Among other things, it shapes the occupational screening process that determines the nature and quality of the lawyers who will administer that society's criminal justice system. Thus, to better understand the administration of justice, the legal profession, and their respective roles in society, one must understand this screening process. This chapter attempts to do that by focusing on the office of the prosecutor.

It is based on research done in 1971 and 1978 on the New York City prosecutors' offices in Kings and Bronx Counties. First, it examines those characteristics which are associated with entry into the job of assistant prosecutor; then it examines the career line or work history (i.e., the job sequences common to a particular portion of the labor force) of assistant district attorneys (hereinafter, ADAs). It also addresses the matter of the prosecutors' standing within the legal profession and the mobility that position affords (Spilerman, 1977). Finally, it reports the decline in the community ties of the assistant prosecutors and other significant changes that occurred with the effort to make the office more professional and less subject to political patronage.[1]

An Overview of the New York Bar:
Social Background and Professional Hierarchy

There are an estimated 40,000 lawyers in New York City alone (Goldstein, 1977). The New York Bar has traditionally represented the largest corporate and financial clients, and until recently has retained a monopoly on the international practice of law. At the peak of the New York Bar's stratification system are the large Wall Street and Park Avenue law firms. A "large" firm in New York terms is one with over 100 attorneys. Partners in these firms sit on the boards of the nation's leading corporations and foundations (Hudson, 1973; Smigel, 1969). They fill high appointive posts in Washington, and they play key roles in the highest professional activities of the bar (Carlin, 1966:36; Ruesche-meyer, 1973:61).

Lawyers in medium-sized firms together with those lawyers in smaller firms with a quality practice constitute an intermediate level in terms of clientele, kind of work, income, prestige, compliance with professional norms, and various background characteristics. The most prestigious small and medium-sized satellite firms are those of attorneys who started their careers in large firms and moved out to set up their own practices (Rueschemeyer, 1973:52-53).

The bottom of the stratification system of the New York Bar, numerically large, is occupied by the majority of individual practitioners and small firm lawyers (Carlin, 1966:18; Reuschemeyer, 1973:49). Approximately 85% of New York City's lawyers are engaged in private practice. Slightly over one-half of New York lawyers were found to be members of firms: 17% were in small firms, 15% in medium-sized firms, and 21%, in large firms (Carlin, 1966:11). Carlin's data is twenty years old. We estimate that the number of lawyers in private practice has declined, but the percentages for those in private practice have remained the same.

The legal profession is highly specialized as to kinds of legal problems handled. There is a division by social class and by prestige as well. The differentiation of institutional arrangements for expert services relates to the position of the attorney in the stratification system. There is also a connection between the class division of clients; the legal character of their problems, which aligns various legal specialities with clients in different socioeconomic categories; and the class situation of the attor-neys representing the client (Rueschemeyer, 1973:23-24). Carlin (1966) found that 70% of all lawyers specialized in a single area of practice. Income differentiation, along the lines of firm size, type of work, and kind of status of client, is parallel to similar differences in prestige and professional regard (Rueschemeyer, 1973:50).

The stratification of the American bar is associated with legal needs of large corporations and financial institutions which are served by the lawyers who are best trained and who also come from families with higher average status than the rest of the bar. Lower-level political and judicial roles are open to the lower strata of the legal profession (Reuschemeyer, 1973:108)

Lawyers find their way into firms of different sizes and into different positions in the legal stratification system through a complex process of self-selection and recruitment. Religion, social class origin, choice of college and law school, and grades in law school all play important roles (Carlin, 1966:37).

Carlin (1966:29) found that lawyers at the top of the legal profession, i.e., those in large firms, came from higher social class backgrounds. Their fathers had more education or were in higher status occupations and made more money than the fathers of small-firm and individual practitioners. The large-firm lawyer was more likely to have earned a four-year college degree, to have attended one of the prestige colleges outside of New York City, and to have been a graduate of full-time university law schools such as Columbia, Harvard, or Yale. Ultimately, one's class rank in law school, the law school's prestige, and the previously mentioned factors determined the size of firm to which one is recruited.

For all lawyers in New York City, Carlin (1966:18-19) found that over 50% had fathers who were from the business classes (no doubt because of the large percentage of Jewish lawyers in New York City) and about 21% came from professional occupations. We will compare the social origins of ADAs in our sample with the profile described by Carlin for the New York bar as a whole.[2]

A Portrait of
the New York City Assistant District Attorney

Age, sex, and race. As is true in many American jurisdictions, most of the New York ADAs were quite young. Overall, 56% were under thirty years of age at the date of interviewing.[3] With regard to sex, the DA's office and the criminal justice system as a whole are overwhelmingly a male preserve. Kings County was 88.5% male; the Bronx, 93.8% male. These percentages are better than in the legal profession as a whole, where in 1971 women constituted only 2.8% of all lawyers (Knauss,

1976). But, it should be noted that the female ADAs in New York came from a higher socioeconomic status than the males and went to better schools. If they had been men, some would have been in higher status positions in the legal profession than that of an ADA.

There were few blacks and Puerto Ricans in the office. Our Kings County sample was all white; the Bronx sample had one black. This finding mirrors the legal profession as a whole, where blacks and other minorities have been underrepresented and excluded (Auerbach, 1976).

The New York DA's offices had long hired a few black attorneys, but that was because educated blacks had entered the political process. It was not part of any affirmative action type of effort. By the late 1960s it was extremely difficult politically and socially for a black or Puerto Rican attorney to work as a prosecutor, a fact reported in both offices.

Religious Affiliation. In recent years religious and racial discrimination in New York Bar has eased greatly (Smigel, 1969:370-371). Even the most blue-blooded corporate law firms usually have at least one Jewish partner, and many Jewish associates. Carlin (1966:18-19) found that slightly over 60% of the New York Bar was Jewish, 18% Catholic, and 18% Protestant. Seventy percent of Jewish lawyers were of Eastern European origin. Fifty-three percent of the Catholics were of Irish descent, and 56% of the Protestants were of British or Canadian origin. In the large Wall Street and Park Avenue firms, the percentage of white Anglo-Saxon Protestants was and remains quite high.

We found that ADAs are overwhelmingly Jewish and Catholic. In the two offices examined, 62.5% of the ADAs were Jewish, 31.9% were Catholic, and only 5.6% were Protestant.[4] Seventy-five percent of the Protestants were the sons of businessmen or professionals. Fifty-seven percent of Jewish ADAs were sons of professionals, 37.2 percent, sons of businessmen. Catholics came equally from all classes. Thirty-four percent of Jews and Catholics came from blue-collar backgrounds.

Seventy-five percent of the Protestants were born after 1942 compared with 54% of the office as a whole.[5] This indicates the broader recruitment efforts in both offices. Bureau chiefs were more likely to be Catholic, a reflection of their earlier entry.[6]

Church attendance was low. Thirty percent of the ADAs never attended church or synagogue. Fifteen percent, three-fourths of whom were Catholics, attended once each week. Only 22% attended once or more each week. Age was not a factor in frequency of church attendance.

National Origin. ADAs were largely second- and third-generation Americans. Their national origins paralleled those Carlin (1966) found for small and individual practitioners a generation ago. Thirty-five percent of the ADAs had foreign born fathers (surprising since only 21% of all New York staters have foreign parents; U.S. Bureau of the Census, 1976:12, 36).

If an ADA's parent was American born, the ADA was more likely to be from the business or professional classes. If the parent was foreign born, the ADA was more likely to be from a blue-collar background. (This is a common immigration pattern.)

Only 56.8% of Jewish ADAs' fathers were American born compared with 75% of Protestant ADAs' parents and 73.9% of Catholic ADAs' parents. Of the fathers of Jewish ADAs who were foreign born, 37% came from Germany or Austria, and 47% from Russia or Eastern Europe. Of the fathers of Catholic ADAs who were foreign born, 50% came from Italy and 33% from Ireland. Only 72.7% of Jewish ADAs' mothers were born in the United States, but 82.6% of Catholic ADAs' mothers were and 100 percent of Protestant ADAs' mothers were.

Most of the ADAs who were not second-generation Americans were third-generation. Only 19% of all of the grandparents were born in the United States. Thirty three percent of the ADAs had at least one grandparent born in the United States. Forty-two percent of the grandparents came from Russian and Eastern Europe, 12% came from Ireland, 11.1% from Germany and Austria, and 11.1% came from Italy. Only 7.1% of the Jewish ADAs had grandparents born in the United States compared with 75% of the Protestants and 31% of the Catholics.

In summary, New York ADAs were to a surprising extent the children of foreign-born parents. It is difficult to fully account for this. No doubt the fact that the offices surveyed were in New York City was a factor (although the New York City Bar is more native-descended than are these prosecutors). We suggest that many of these ADAs were bright children of intelligent parents who found themselves in reduced economic circumstances because of their recent immigrant status. The socioeconomic barriers resulting from that status precluded ADAs from attending the necessary schools for them to reach a higher level within the bar. That the prosecutor's office has remained a mobility channel for the children of the foreign born at a time when migration has long been rigidly fixed may reflect more the educational and class barriers to the legal profession than a conscious policy on the part of these offices.

The ADA and The Local Community. Eighty-five percent of the ADAs were New York City born and bred. Nearly 75% graduated from New York City high schools. The great percentage of New York City ADAs reflects the local nature of the office and its base in the community, at least in the white community. This high concentration of native sons in the prosecutor's office contrasts sharply with the geographically diverse origins of the legal elite that populate the offices of the larger law firms (Smigel, 1969:372).

All of the bureau chiefs in both offices were born and raised in New York City. There was no difference between those born before 1942 or after 1942 as to their New York City residence.

Broader recruitment efforts by both offices at the better law schools should increase the number of non-New York City ADAs. One should also expect a broadening of the geographical base from merit recruitment itself. A more important factor would be recruitment from underrepresented portions of the New York City population: black and Hispanic.

ADAs and Community Activity. There was a low level of community participation. Only 31% of the ADAs actively belonged to even one civic, religious, or other organization. We defined *active* as attending meetings more or less regularly or as offering professional services. Religious organizations affiliated with church or synagogue were the most frequently mentioned (10.24%) followed by local civic groups such as hospitals (7.3 percent). There was no correlation between age and increased community activity and no correlation between one's being a bureau chief and increased community activity.

There was, however, a correlation between when an ADA joined the office and his level of community activity. Forty-five percent of those who joined before 1968 were active in civic associations compared with only 24% of the new era ADAs. Kings County ADAs participated in more community activities than Bronx ADAs, regardless of when they joined the office.

The low participation of ADAs in community organizations is probably due to the fact that many of the ADAs were young, had just commenced their careers, and had not developed local community ties. The separation of the District Attorney's office from politics, the prohibition of outside practice, and the commencement of merit recruitment all decreased the incentive to join. The new ADA is more of a civil servant without the need to develop community bridges.

The ADA and Politics. After 1968 political activity clearly declined in both offices. Requirements that ADAs become members of the local political organization no longer existed. Political influences still existed in recruitment and appointment, but were minimal. This was the result of several factors: the policies of the district attorney, the younger age of the office, and the development of a "quasi-civil service" type of bureaucracy divorced from the political spoils system.

The divorce of the ADA from the political organization may be desirable in some respects, but it also means that one important link between the ADA and the political community in which the ADA enforces the law has been cut. The new "civil service" ADA's divorcement from his community in terms of political allegiances, community involvement, and demographic characteristics is a marked contrast to the past. It may have detrimental effects to the legal authority used in law enforcement systems.

The ADA and Professional Associations

Bar associations serve a variety of functions for the legal profession. They set the standards of the profession, establish norms, discipline those who violate professional rules, and pass on fellow lawyers who will ascend to the bench. The organized bar is also a trade association. Bar associations speak for the attorney on professional and public issues. They offer continuing legal education, legal research, libraries, and professional participation for members. They also reinforce the stratification of the profession (Auerbach, 1976).

Bar associations appeal to differing strata of the bar (Rueschemeyer, 1973:151; Carlin, 1966:34-35). There are several specialized bar associations in New York City composed of attorneys who have a common specialty, who practice before a particular bench or administrative agency, who have specialized interests, or who have a common ethnic, religious, or racial heritage. Each borough has its own association. The cleavages in the status structure of the bar are reflected in membership in local bar associations. Different associations serve essentially different strata of the bar.

Bar association participation by ADAs was relatively low and parochial. Nearly 28% of all assistants belonged to no bar association at all. Over one-quarter belonged to a specialty bar association, or state or national district attorneys association. Ten percent belonged to the New York State Bar Association, and 8.4% belonged to the American Bar Association. Only 1.5% of respondents were members of the Association of the Bar, the city's most prestigious association. Most of the ADAs who belonged to the latter three organizations were older attorneys. A total of 7% belonged to local bar associations, the Kings County, Brooklyn Bar, or the Bronx Bar Association. The minimal level of membership in "general" bar associations reflects the youth of the office and the prosecutor's professional isolation.

Educational Background

Education is often considered a most important variable in achieving upward social mobility. Blau and Duncan (1967) present evidence that education is the critical intervening variable in the intergenerational transmission of status. They found that education mediated and diminished the effects of one's background although socioeconomic origins clearly facilitated educational attainment. In the legal profession, educational attainment, however, is constant.

The more important variables are the status of the particular law school attended and one's academic achievement. Socioeconomic background has an important impact on which school one attends. Those attending private secondary schools have an advantage when applying to the better colleges. One's college can affect one's law school. Law school clearly affects one's job opportunities (ABA Journal, 1975:99). The educational background of ADAs offers an important variable in determining their place in the legal stratification system.

Secondary Education. Most ADAs attended New York City public or parochial schools. Forty-eight percent graduated from New York City public high schools, 19% from New York City Catholic high schools, and 4 percent from New York City Jewish schools. Four percent, all from Kings County, attended private, nonparochial schools.

Only 25.3% attended high schools outside of New York City, and almost all of those respondents attended New York metropolitan area suburban schools. Overall, 22.67% attended Catholic parochial schools, a lower percentage than those who attended Catholic colleges and universities. These figures indicate that both offices were overwhelmingly composed of "locals," raised and educated in the community.

Higher Education. The most important educational factor in determining status in the legal profession is the law school from which the attorney has graduated. While entry into law school is based on standardized testing, it is greatly eased by the nature of one's college or university. Carlin (1966:29) found that a lawyer's chance of reaching a high status position in the profession is fixed at a relatively early stage—in effect, when the prospective attorney enters college. He concluded that social class determined the kind of preparatory school one attends. Religion and social class determined one's college. And religion, social class, and college were the important variables deciding the quality of law school to which the prospective attorney would be admitted.[7]

The 468 lawyers listed in 1957 in the Wall Street firms studied by Smigel (1969:372) attended only 79 different colleges and universities. Sixty-four percent attended 19 colleges which would be judged "socially acceptable." Forty percent went to Harvard, Yale, or Princeton.

Similarly, the ADAs in the present study attended relatively few schools but not the elite schools attended by the Wall Street lawyers. Only 10% of all ADAs attended Ivy League or Seven Sister schools; 71.8% attended private colleges, and 28.2% attended public universities. Overall, 28.2% attended public schools, 28.2% attended private Catholic schools, and 43.6% attended private non-Catholic colleges or universities. Twenty of the 23 Catholic ADAs attended Catholic colleges.

ADAs of higher social classes were more likely to have attended a private non-Catholic university. The lower the social class the more likely the ADA had attended a public or a Catholic college. Sixty percent of the bureau chiefs went to public universities, a substantially higher percentage than the office as a whole. (This is probably a result of the generally lower SES of the chiefs.) Over 87% of the bureau chiefs who went to private colleges attended Catholic schools, compared with 39.2% of the office as a whole.

ADAs who were not bureau chiefs were less likely to have attended a Catholic college or a public university than bureau chiefs. This was both a function of social class and the fact that other ADAs were younger than most of the bureau chiefs.

Legal Education. The most important factors governing one's status in the legal profession are the quality of one's law school and one's class standing (Smigel, 1969:120-125). The importance of law school prestige cannot be overestimated. A survey (ABA Journal, 1975:61) of law firms of 50 or more attorneys in 29 cities found that Harvard Law School contributed more than 25% of all partners, and Yale, 8%.

Carlin (1966:19-20) found that 36% of the New York Bar had graduated from national, top quality law schools with full-time programs. Of those, 29% had attended just three: Harvard, Yale, and Columbia. Twenty-seven percent of the New York Bar had attended high quality mixed law schools. Thirty-six percent attended lower quality mixed law schools.

We updated Carlin's categories and ranked on the basis of national law schools, regional law schools, and local law schools. Twenty-two percent of the ADAs graduated from national law schools, but only 8% attended Columbia, Yale, or Harvard. In addition, 66.1% attended local law schools, 43% went to just two, Fordham and Brooklyn; 10.6% attended regional law schools, and 1% clerked for admission to the bar. Fewer ADAs (17%) attended lower quality law schools than the proportion of the New York attorneys reported by Carlin, namely 36%.

In Kings County, 43% of the office attended Brooklyn Law School. Twenty-two percent went to national schools. In the Bronx, 59% attended three local law schools: Brooklyn, St. John's, and Fordham. Considering New York University as a national school (although for New York City it is a local school), 23.2 percent attended national schools. Seventy-nine percent attended full-time day sessions; only 14% attended evening law school and 7% attended both.

In summary, ADAs attended local colleges and law schools. Two thirds of the ADAs responded that they were in the top third of the class. Only 16% made law review. They differed markedly in educational experience and achievement from attorneys in larger law firms. They are most analogous to the small partnership or individual practitioner. We predict that as the legal job market tightens and the merit bureaucracy becomes a tradition ADAs will be recruited from more national schools and will have attended more prestigious institutions.

The Social Origins of Assistant District Attorneys

In determining the ADA's social class origins, we asked father's occupation, income, and education. We then divided all responses about parents' occupations into five categories: lower blue collar, upper blue collar, lower white collar, business, and professional. Most of the occupations mentioned were easily categorized.

ADAs came from lower socioeconomic origins than most other members of the legal profession. The largest occupational groups to which the fathers of ADAs belonged was that of businessmen, 31%; next, 25% were professionals; 19% were lower blue-collar workers; 14% were upper blue-collar workers, and 11% were lower white-collar workers. These figures contrast with Carlin's (1966:18) findings that 50% of the New York Bar had fathers who were businessmen, 25% were children of professionals, and less than 25% came from blue-collar and lower white-collar backgrounds.

Those who entered the DA's office before 1968 came from lower socioeconomic origins than those who entered after. This suggests that the function of the DA's office as a mobility channel for immigrants and the lower class has declined and may continue to decline as the office continues to become professionalized. The new recruitment policies netted younger ADAs from higher socioeconomic origins. Of ADAs who were older than thirty, 43.3% came from blue-collar backgrounds compared with 23.6% of the younger ADAs. Fifty-six percent of ADAs who entered the DA's office before 1968 came from blue-collar backgrounds compared with 22% of those who entered later. Bureau chiefs came from a lower socioeconomic origin than other ADAs.

Father's Income. Only 12% of ADAs' parents earned under $5,000 at the time the ADA entered law school.[8] Twenty-four percent of the parents earned between $9,000 and $12,000 and 22.2% earned over $25,000. Almost 49% of the parents earned under $13,000.

Fathers's Educational Level. Despite the relatively low socioeconomic origins, parents' gross income, and the recent immigration of many

ADAs' parents, the educational level of ADAs' fathers was high. This may be the key to why so many of these ADAs became attorneys even though they came from more modest backgrounds than the New York Bar and the legal profession as a whole. Of the fathers 32.5% were high school graduates, 40.7% graduated from college, 20.3% graduated from professional schools. An additional 14.9% attended some college.

Income. ADAs were quite distressed over their low incomes and limits to salary increases. At the time of our surveys, the starting salary for an ADA was $12,500. In contrast, the starting salary for a Wall Street associate was between $22,000 and $24,000. In 1971 slightly over 54% of the ADAs earned between $13,000 and $15,000. Only 19% earned $19,000 or more.

Only 36% of the bureau chiefs earned over $25,000, an income attained by Wall Street associates two or three years out of law school. Normally it would take an ADA eight years to reach the $25,000 level.

By any standard when compared with lawyers in private practice, ADAs are underpaid. The median salary for the bar nationally is $30,000. By 1976 the starting salary of associates in large New York firms had risen to $25,000. A partner in a Wall Street firm with 100 lawyers, of which there are nearly 30, earns at least $100,000 a year by the age of forty (Goldstein, 1977:35).

In 1974 the American Bar Association studied 724 attorneys in Chicago in private practice. Only 8.4% earned less than $15,000; only 25% earned less than $20,000 (Goldstein, 1977:35). Over one-half of the attorneys surveyed in Chicago, where average salaries are less than in New York, earned over $30,000. ADAs were generally stymied in the $13,000 to $18,999 range until they became bureau chiefs or left for more lucrative places.

Working wives and other assets helped bring up the average family gross income. Fifty-three percent of the ADAs had gross family incomes over $19,000 and 30% had incomes over $25,000. Fifty percent of the bureau chiefs had gross family incomes over $25,000 compared with 26% of other ADAs. The average gross family income for ADAs was $18,000. The city's fiscal crisis has had a restraining influence on ADA salary increases.

The Placement of the ADA
Within the Legal Stratification System

In addition to the stratification of the New York Bar, the mobility of all but a few lawyers who begin in the largest law firms is quite limited. Moreover, the mobility chances of the attorney are closely tied to his educational and social background (Rueschemeyer, 1973:45). Lawyers tend to remain in the same stratum of the bar in which they began their professional careers, and movement is generally limited to no more than one step up or down (Carlin, 1966:32).

In New York, less than 2% of those who did not start out in large law firms ended up working there. The association between firm size, type of client, kind of work, and amount of income is such that the chances of lawyers in small firms to acquire a high status practice appears severely limited (Rueschemeyer, 1973:51). The choice of first employment has already limited the ADA's mobility chances and ultimate status in the profession as well as future career line. The first job choice, despite the reasons offered by the ADA, is to a great extent determined by education, origins, and, primarily, law school rank. Career patterns which have already been closely related to socioeconomic background and ethnic origin and to quality of college and law school are further affected by the first job choice. In terms of his educational and social background, the ADA compares most closely with the small and medium firm practitioners.

Another factor affecting his mobility chances is the training he receives on his first job. For the ADA who has entered the DA's office for training in litigation, his future career line is affected by the kind of training applicable to a particular client set. Unfortunately, a prosecutor's litigation experience does not prepare him adequately for the kinds of litigation engaged in by most private practitioners. The trial experience, caseload, and the nature of most litigation in the criminal justice system is not particularly transferable to representing corporate clients where counseling is more frequent than trial work. Nor is the prosecutor's experience particularly useful in complex civil litigation, where research on issues is specialized and exhaustive. Thus, even in the litigation area, the ADA is limited in his experience in servicing the upper reaches of the bar's clientele.

Most litigation involving major corporate clients occurs in federal court. Experience in the state court system, where the ADA usually practices, may not be an advantage. The ADA's special training and experience is in the area of representation of criminal defendants. But, the status of such work is at the bottom of the legal profession.

> Some fields are unattractive to many lawyers, and this may constitute the basis of specialization for a minority, often reached by default. In the American metropolitan bar: criminal law, negligence work, matrimonial matters, and work that involves local political institutions are often examples of this. These fields sometimes have a reputation for unethical and illegal practices.

Arthur L. Wood in his study of *The Criminal Lawyer* (1964:54) found that less than 14% of those who had more than 10% of their practice in the criminal area were in that particular work by preference. New York City lawyers working in the criminal area had a high rate of substantial violations of legal ethics. Rueschemeyer (1973:51) found that the criminal lawyer is at the bottom of the legal status hierarchy, and is accorded not just less prestige but is even viewed in distinctly negative terms.

To paraphrase Calvin Coolidge, the business of American law is business. Carlin found (1966;8) that

> 60 percent of the lawyers . . . assist business clients in obtaining financing; an equal proportion are on the lookout for investment opportunities for these clients; close to half are either officers or board members of client corporations (generally taking an active part in corporate affairs); approximately a third hold stock or have financial interest in such corporations.

ADAs receive little if any experience in the business-related aspects of the law: commercial transactions, corporate law, taxation, real estate, and securities. This further serves to hinder career mobility. Because of their training, they are most suited to become criminal lawyers and take their place at the bottom rung of the legal profession.

Career Goals and Realities

Most of the ADAs expected that they would remain with their office until their commitment was fulfilled and they had picked up sufficient training but could no longer afford financially to remain in the office, or until an attractive legal position (preferably in private practice) appeared. Others expected that they would leave for emotional and psychological reasons: when they felt their personal selves affected by the nature of their work. One ADA's views were typical. "You're not supposed to stay too long. Sixty percent leave after three years. The longer you stay the less career value is the ADA experience."

Forty-two percent of the ADAs said that in five years they hoped to be in the practice of law; 20.2% hoped to be a judge or the district attorney (60% of Bureau Chiefs in each office gave this last response). Only 11.5% expected to be in the same job, another law enforcement position, or government service of any sort. The low interest in continuing in the DA's office was not due to dissatisfaction with the work but with a feeling that circumstances—usually financial—would force a move elsewhere. Our follow-up study found that reality did not meet their expectations. Six years later, 35% of all of the ADAs were still prosecutors and 46 percent of all ADAs who could be located and in the job market were still in a district attorney's office. Only 23.7% of all ADAs were in private practice; 9% were in other law enforcement positions, and 7% were in judicial or political positions. Many of the former ADAs in private practice were solo practitioners or criminal lawyers, or they were in small partnerships. Only a very few had made the jump to respected medium-sized law firms. In short, as the studies of the stratification of the legal profession had led us to expect, there was little upward occupational mobility among ADAs, and, for that matter, little mobility of any kind.

CONCLUSION

The legal profession is highly stratified with limited mobility. One's final position in the status hierarchy of the profession is heavily determined by the status position of one's first job as a lawyer. That, in turn, is influenced by the prestige of one's law school which, in turn, is influenced by the prestige of one's college, which, in turn, is influenced by one's family socioeconomic background. Being an assistant prosecutor as the first job in one's legal career does little to enchance one's occupational mobility.

Assistant prosecutors in Kings and Bronx Counties, New York, are generally young, white males of Catholic or Jewish background. They are second- or third-generation Americans and New York City born and educated. They have attended local colleges and law schools, usually not the ones with "Ivy League" or national reputations. They came from lower socioeconomic origins more than is typical of the legal profession. In educational, economic, and social background characteristics, and within the legal profession, ADAs are similar to lawyers who are solo practitioners or members of small firms.

The training in criminal law these ADAs receive does not assist upward mobility. The skills developed prepare them primarily for the practice of criminal law, which many ADAs eventually enter. This type of practice, however, is at the bottom of the legal profession's stratification system.

There appear to be three career lines for prosecutors. One—which has recently declined—is the political career line. Here the office was a stepping-stone to higher political appointments or the job of assistant prosecutor was itself a final political reward. This career line declined when two new district attorneys began recruiting on the basis of objective qualifications.

The second is the merit career line. ADAs were appointed on the basis of merit. Many lawyers were attracted to the job because of their perception of what the career line would mean. They expected that they would receive excellent training and be given a great deal of discretion and have more responsibility than their peers in private practice. They expected they would eventually be in private practice in a much higher status position. The reality of this career line, however, is quite different. These attorneys did not leave the office as soon as they expected; and when they did, they almost always became criminal lawyers (which if anything in terms of status is a step down).

A third career line is beginning to emerge, the criminal justice/civil service career line. It involves a lateral movement into a growing criminal justice and judicial administration hierarchy. While ADAs do not consider their tenure as prosecutor as the start of a criminal justice career, they tend to get locked into it. This particular career line has become more attractive for a variety of reasons, particularly the availability of federal funds for numerous criminal justice projects. We speculate that prosecutors in the future will remain at their positions longer and more will become criminal justice civil servants.

Recruitment on the basis of merit and the emergence of a civil service of prosecutors may be regarded by some as an unqualified advance in the development of the American office of the public prosecutor. It may be possible in such offices to reach new levels of efficiency and evenhandedness in the administration of justice. But, there are trade-offs. The tendency is for the new breed of assistant prosecutors to have fewer ties to the community and to be drawn from the more prestigious law schools. This may mean that the price of professionalization will be social isolation of the prosecutor from the community whose values he is supposed to reflect and protect. The system of criminal justice may become even more an instrument of social control in the hands of one stratum in society for the rule of others. In an open, heterogeneous society, this development is at best a mixed blessing.

NOTES

1. Formerly, the Bronx and Brooklyn DA's offices were important parts of the local political structure. The position of prosecutor served as a mobility channel for lawyers of lower socioeconomic and ethnic origins. It became a capstone of a long political career, or a stepping-stone in the career line to higher politics. ADAs and district attorneys became judges or congressmen, or they moved into higher positions in government service. In 1968 a merit recruitment policy and a policy prohibiting ADAs from the ouside practice of law severed the office's old linkage to the political structure.

2. New York State is divided into four judicial departments. Carlin studied lawyers of the First Judicial Department, which comprises the Bronx and Manhattan but not Brooklyn, which is in the Second Department. The department in which a lawyer is admitted is based on his residence at the time of admission. Thus, many if not most of the lawyers admitted to the Second Department may practice in Manhattan which is in the First Department. One would expect that there is a great proportion of small firms and

individual practitioners in Brooklyn.

3. In the Bronx 69.2% of the office, including all of the females, were under thirty. All of the Bronx chiefs were over thirty. In Brooklyn 50% of the office but only two bureau chiefs were under thirty. In Brooklyn more ADAs recruited before 1968 remained in the office.

4. The Bronx was more Catholic than Kings County (36% to 29.8%). Kings was more Jewish (66% to 56%). The Bronx DA's office was a more Catholic borough traditionally, and Irish control of the political process lasted longer.

5. The year 1942 was used as a breakoff point since those born before 1942 were over thirty at the time of interviewing. Date entering the office was divided into pre- and post-1968, that year being the watershed when new recruitment policies were installed.

6. Seventy-one percent of the Bronx bureau chiefs were Catholic compared with 36% of the whole office. In Brooklyn, 28% of the bureau chiefs were Jewish compared with 56% of the office as a whole and 68.8% of ADAs other than bureau chiefs.

7. Carlin concluded that ultimately law school achievement, the reputation of the school, and religious background determined the size of firm one entered. We believe that religion, race, and sex have greatly diminished as negative variables in career mobility in the New York bar.

8. These figures are "soft" since incomes have increased dramatically in recent years because of inflation. Several ADAs' parents who earned less than $5,000 were in the job market in an earlier period. Thus, the parents of bureau chiefs earned less than others in the office. Nearly all of the bureau chiefs were older.

REFERENCES

ABA Journal (1975). "Harvard is heavy at the partnership level." January:61.

AUERBACH, J. S. (1976). Unequal Justice: Lawyers and Social Change in Modern America. New York: Oxford University Press.

BLAU, P. and O. DUNCAN (1967). The American Occupational Structure. New York: John Wiley.

CARLIN, J. (1966). Lawyer's Ethics. New York: Russell Sage.

GOLDSTEIN, T. (1977). "Law Fastest-Growing Profession, May Find Prosperity Precarious." New York Times, May 16:1.

HUDSON, W. J. (1973). Outside Counsel: Inside Director: Lawyers on the Boards of American Industry. New York: Law Journal Press.

KNAUSS, R. L. (1976). "Developing a representative legal profession." ABA Journal 62:591-592.

LYNN, K. S. (1963). The Professions in America. Boston: Beacon.

RUESCHEMEYER, D. (1973). Lawyers and Their Society. Cambridge: Harvard University Press.

SMIGEL, E. O. (1969). The Wall Street Lawyer. Bloomington: Indiana University Press.

SPILERMAN. (1977). "Careers, labor market structure and socioeconomic achievement." American Journal of Sociology 83:551-593.

U.S. Department of Commerce, Bureau of The Census (1976). Statistical Abstract of the United States 1976. Washington, D.C.: U.S. Government Printing Office.

VANNEMAN, R. (1977). "The occupational composition of American classes." American Journal of Sociology 82:783.

WOOD, A. L. (1964). The Criminal Lawyer. New Haven: College and University Press.

Chapter 10

PROSECUTORIAL DISCRETION IN GERMANY

KLAUS SESSAR

The institution of the German prosecutor (*Staatsanwalt*) has recently attracted attention among American legal commentators (see, e.g., Davis, 1976; Langbein, 1974, 1977; Goldstein and Marcus, 1977). The special attraction is the German requirement of compulsory prosecution of offenders. This requirement contrasts sharply with the situation in America, where prosecutors have almost absolute discretion in choosing whether to prosecute or not. Concern over how that discretion is being exercised has led American reformers to look for ways it might be controlled without interfering with the effective administration of justice. The German system seems to represent a model of how that might be done. This chapter will provide a closer look at the extent of prosecutorial discretion in Germany and at other factors which contribute to the effectiveness of the German system for the administration of justice.

The concept of compulsory prosecution dominates all aspects of the German prosecutorial system. The German prosecutor's attitude toward crime and punishment is far from pragmatic. The decision to prosecute is not predicated on consideration of costs (Schellhoss, 1974; Steffen, 1976:75). The German prosecutor does not ask, "How many offenses should be permitted and how many offenders should go unpunished?" (Becker, 1974:2). Rather, his decision making is dominated by the "principle of legality"[1] with discretion being left only to a narrow range of petty offenses (see Jescheck, 1970:509; Weigend, 1978). "[German] prosecutors regard compulsory prosecution and restraint of discretion as overriding principles." (Herrmann 1976:35).

This description of the rigid rule of law in German prosecutions evokes disbelief among foreign experts, especially Americans. In the United

States discretion is considered essential both for reasons of justice and practicality. The American prosecutor uses screening and plea bargaining processes as indispensable methods to reduce caseloads and achieve justice in individual cases (Miller, 1970:193; Cole, 1976:218). Americans are reluctant to believe that compulsory prosecution is feasible for them and are suspicious that it really does not work in Germany. They presume that somewhere in the German system of prosecution discretion must operate because no system of justice in a modern nation can possibly prosecute all crimes that come to its attention.

American cynics are correct in their assumption about the need for discretion, but they reveal the heavy influence of the American experience when they assume that the only way to have discretion and to achieve efficiency in the administration of criminal justice is through plea bargaining and initial screening. The German jurist would agree that not all deviant behavior which falls under penal law has to be punished, but would argue that necessary screening should be accomplished legislatively (e.g., by transforming an offense into a petty, noncriminal infraction to be handled by administrative authorities, or by making prosecution dependent on the victim's formal motion).

The German system of compulsory prosecution cannot be understood apart from this legislative context. Certain features of German substantive and procedural law make it feasible to keep prosecutorial discretion to a minimum. We will discuss in particular the fact that it is possible to have prosecutions without the participation of the public prosecutor, the fact that prosecution can be made contingent upon the prior approval of the victim, and also the availability of summary prosecution through the use of a "penal order" (*Strafbefehl*). We will show that as the crime problem increased in Germany the system of prosecution was not expected to mediate between the higher volume of cases and the available court resources (as happened in America). Instead, the legislature downgraded or decriminalized certain offenses and provided ways for dealing with criminality through administrative means. Finally, we will present the results of an empirical analysis of the German prosecutor's role and conduct with respect to his discretionary power within the context of the investigation of offenses and the decision whether or not to prosecute.[2]

LEGISLATIVE RESPONSE TO INCREASING CRIME

A proper understanding of the German legislature's effort to cope with the increase of crime requires that the reforms within the criminal justice system between 1968 and today be briefly examined. In 1968, almost all punishable acts were either felonies (*Verbrechen*), misdemeanors (*Vergehen*), or petty misdemeanors (*Ubertretungen*). The differentiation among the three types of offenses reflected different degrees of seriousness. Different minimum and maximum penalties were required by the law for each category. A further consequence of this tripartition was the distinct use of legally provided discretionary power. The prosecutor, for example, could dismiss a misdemeanor case with the consent of the judge if the guilt of the suspect were insignificant *and* the public interest did not require prosecution. For petty misdemeanors the judge's consent was not needed.[3] However, dismissal of felony cases was (and is) not permitted by law. In 1968 there were 742,650 people charged with felonies or misdemeanors under this system (see Table 1; statistics for petty misdemeanors do not exist.)[4]

In 1969, the "Petty Infractions Code" (Gesetz über Ordnungswidrigkeiten) was introduced, relieving the criminal justice system considerably, both qualitatively and quantitiatively. Numerous offenses, especially traffic offenses and those in the economic field, were changed into petty (noncriminal) infractions. As a result, administrative authorities, including the police, with a wide range of discretionary power (Langbein, 1977:592-96) prosecute such offenses by way of "penance money."[5] As a consequence of this law, the number of persons brought to trial generally decreased between 1968 and 1969 by about 4.4%, from 742,650 to 710,044; in the following year it did not reach the level of the year 1968 (see Table 1).

In the following years a chain of modifications brought further relief to the judiciary system. Many misdemeanors were abolished; abortion was liberalized; and some felonies, especially thefts under aggravating circumstances (in 1970), were changed into misdemeanors. This enabled these offenses to be disposed of by penal order or even, under the conditions set forth above (i.e., minor guilt and no public interest), to go unprosecuted. Thus, for example, the number of persons accused because of burglary (the most important type of a theft under aggravating circumstances) decreased between 1969 and 1970 by 9%.

In 1975, petty misdemeanors were abolished with most of them being turned into petty infractions. Perhaps the most incisive reform measure was the introduction of the victim's motion as a prerequisite for the prosecution of property crimes such as theft, fraud, embezzlement, receiving stolen goods. If damage is minor, neither police nor prosecuting attorney can investigate such acts or file a charge if the victim does not require it.

A further reform concerned the penalties themselves. There has been for many years a strong tendency to replace imprisonment by fines. Most misdemeanors can be penalized by fines (98% of all acts falling under the

Table 1: Development of the Number of Suspects, Accused, and Prosecuting Attorneys, Between 1965 and 1976

YEAR	SUSPECTS[a]	ACCUSED	PROSECUTING ATTORNEYS
1965	860,264	643,948	2,392
1966	917,695	683,526	
1967	968,121	713,383	
1968	980,133	742,650	
1969	988,914	710,044	
1970	1,026,863	738,141	
1971	1,000,841	769,047	
1972	1,039,078	791,382	
1973	1,023,129	807,936	
1974	1,062,199	813,632	
1975	1,112,996	779,219	
1976	1,189,453	839,679	3,233

a. excluding traffic offenses.

penal code are misdemeanors); prison sentences of up to six months can be given only under exceptional circumstances. The result of such reforming efforts has been a constant increase in fines in lieu of prison terms (from 64% in 1965 up to 84% in 1974, considering all convictions). The consequences for the prosecutor are considerable. If he makes a decision to charge and if he feels a fine is a sufficient sanction, he can move for a written penal order (Langbein, 1977:96-98). When the motion is approved by the judge, which is normally done on a routine basis, it becomes a final judgment sentencing the accused to a fine. If the accused objects to this procedure, the case is automatically diverted into normal judicial proceedings.

On the average, half of all punishable cases are prosecuted by penal orders.[6] Thus, the increasing significance of fines has meant a de facto transfer of sanctioning power from the court to the prosecuting attorney. However, this has not entailed a substantial administrative burden for the prosecutor, because these cases are easily disposed of. The defendant is prosecuted only in writing. Herein lies one reason for the superfluousness of discretionary power for reasons of caseload alone.

At first sight, the penal order seems similar to a plea bargaining process. According to the Uniform Rules of Criminal Procedure,[7] the prosecutor is to move for a penal order only if a confession is submitted in order to avoid possible objection and subsequent formal trial. This summary procedure saves considerable time. Hence, the prosecutor might be tempted to offer a defendant a penal order in exchange for a guilty plea (Jescheck, 1970:515-516). Such a deal is possible and must surely happen occasionally, but it has no general significance. Indeed, in our study we failed to find a single case. It is, of course, possible that this deal is completed verbally. However, this would presuppose some sort of personal interaction between the prosecutor and the defendant, which is seldom the case. Defense counsel who might interpose themselves between both parties participated in only 3% of all cases studied during the preliminary proceedings. Langbein (1977:97) is correct when he states that the accused is not represented and does not participate in this process; the sentence involved is offered to him on a "take-it-or-leave-it" basis (see also Goldstein and Marcus, 1977:269-270).[8]

Reforms of the Code of Criminal Procedure changed the extent of the discretionary power of the prosecutor. Since the 1975 abolition of petty misdemeanors, he has been allowed to dismiss a property offense without the judge's approval, provided that the damage involved is minor and that the public interest does not require prosecution. In all other cases, as before, the consent of the judge is needed (dismissal in felony cases is not possible).

The most contested of the recent reforms is the prosecutor's power to drop charges in certain cases in exchange for the suspect's agreement to repair the damage or to pay a certain amount of money to the state or to a nonprofit organization. This "pre-trial intervention" procedure was enacted in order to enable the prosecutor to devote more of his resources to serious criminality. Accordingly, this "diversion" is supposed to be used even if other cases concerning the same suspect have been dismissed before or if a more serious misdemeanor has since been committed. The practical significance of this measure, however, is not very great, since there are general restraints to the use of this discretion. Prosecutors whom we interviewed were afraid that this procedure might result in the introduction of some sort of plea bargaining with a higher chance of success for those who can afford a defense counsel or who have the means to pay any required sum.[9] Meanwhile this procedure is used to a limited extent only, because prosecutors are pressed by urgent pleas from the Minister of Justice, at least in the state of Baden-Wurttemberg.

Given that a large part of German criminality is petty criminality, the extent of discretion for German prosecutors seems to be considerable. According to the Criminal Statistics of the Police of 1976, one-third of all property offenses have caused damage of less than 100 German marks.[10] In addition, it can be assumed that the prosecutor when defining "minor guilt" will not only be guided by a fixed maximum value of damage (e.g., 50 or 100 marks), but will also take into consideration the average value of stolen or embezzled property. For example, since cars in general are more expensive than bicycles, theft of a Volkswagen worth 200 dollars might be seen as less serious than theft of a brand new bicycle worth 100 dollars. On the other hand, any such tendency to individualize the evaluation of guilt can be (and is) constrained by an extensive interpretation of the public need for law enforcement. Therefore, it is doubtful whether discretion has and will become a powerful element in criminal prosecution.

All the reforms of the last few years combined resulted in a 4.3% decrease in the number of accused persons between 1974 and 1975 (see Table 1). But like the introduction of the "Petty Infractions Code" in 1968, the reforms relieved the criminal justice system only for a short period; in 1976 the number of individuals brought to trial increased enormously.

ORGANIZATION OF THE OFFICE
OF THE GERMAN PROSECUTOR

The Federal Republic of Germany has 92 prosecutors' offices. The smallest employs 5 deputy prosecutors, and the largest, 150. The district of each office covers that of the district court (*Landgericht*) and of all magistrate courts (*Amtsgerichte*) which belong to the district court. A prosecuting attorney is a civil servant who, like judges and other lawyers, has passed two comprehensive state examinations after approximately 7 or 8 years of theoretical and practical training.[11] He is subordinate to the head of the local office, who is responsible to the state attorney general. The minister of justice of the state (*Land*) is at the top of the hierarchy. Prosecution is thus primarily the responsibility of the state rather than of the federal government. One of the significant differences between the American and German prosecutors is that the latter are not elected but appointed. They are controlled by the hierarchical organization in which they are employed rather than by the public—at least to the extent that their personal career is involved (see Cole, 1976:221-223). Consequently, the German prosecutor is for all intents and purposes immune from public opinion.

This fact is considered to be an important prerequisite for the legally required objectivity of the prosecutor. He is not a party in an adversarial system; he is required to act not only against but also in favor of the suspect at any stage of the proceedings. For example, we discovered that one-third of all fraud cases studies were dismissed because of lack of sufficient evidence even though the suspect had made a confession in the course of police investigation. Another consequence of the rule of objectivity is that while the prosecutor can never be sure that his case will win, he need not concern himself about this. In up to 20% of all cases we studied, the accused was acquitted by the trial judge, usually at the request of the prosecutor.

Each office has its own particular organization and surely its own strategies to organize daily work economically. It should not be over-looked that the use of such strategies constitutes a form of discretion. Problems of investigation and of decision making are sometimes solved according to administrative rather than strictly legal requirements. The best example of this is the treatment of cases with unknown offenders. According to the law, the search for the offender is a matter of evidence. Cases in which the offender has not been identified are not supposed to be treated differently than ones in which there are known offenders (but see Weigend, 1978:60-61). This means, in theory, that the police and the prosecutor should make every effort to find the offender. In practice, however, not much happens. Such cases are generally terminated by the use of a rubber stamp stating "dismissal because of unknown offender." Only in criminal homicide cases will the prosecutor not acquiesce in such results but will continue investigation (usually, however, with little success). Many attempts can be observed "to get rid" of such cases in this manner. This reflects the fact of limited case capacity and consequently of the practical need to restrict prosecution to cases with a named suspect.[12]

Other organizational strategies focus special attention on specific types of crime. This reflects new developments in criminal policy. In 28 German prosecutors' offices, special departments were established during the last few years to combat white-collar criminality. The prosecutors involved have participated in special training and are supported by bookkeepers, accountants, and experts on economics (Berckhauer, 1977:89-90). These additional resources constitute a discretionary decision since they are intended to increase the efficiency of law enforcement in some areas of criminality while neglecting others. Many other specializations by type of offense (in most offices criminal homicide cases are handled by special prosecutors) or by special crime situation typical in a district (e.g., organized crimes or gang crimes in big cities) exist.

Of particular interest to Americans where plea bargaining is often regarded as the solution for increased caseloads, the problem of caseload in Germany is solved by increases in the prosecutorial staff. The size of the staff is based on a complicated formula which takes into account the number and seriousness of the cases and the patterns of case disposition. On the basis of this formula, the number of German prosecutors has increased since 1965 by 35%, from 2,392 to 3,233. As a result of this increased staff together with the legislative reforms mentioned above, the number of suspects per prosecutor has not changed significantly. In 1965 the ratio was 1 prosecutor to 360 suspects, in 1976 it was 1 to 368 (see Table 1; figures exclude traffic offenses).

GERMAN PROSECUTORIAL DISCRETION IN ACTION

Our empirical study of the German prosecutor tried to disclose latent structures in his actions by constrasting the amount of discretion he has been given by law with the amount he actually exercises in practice. Generally we found a discrepancy between the two. The German prosecutor exercises more discretion than is authorized by law.

The first indications of discrepancies between law and practice come from the yearly statistics of the various prosecution offices. Among the 93 offices the ratio of charges to dismissals varied up to 30% in 1970. The smaller the office (hence, the smaller the district), the higher the number of charges per case. Our attention was therefore at first focused upon differences by office size. Accordingly, 8 offices were chosen on the basis of the combined criteria of size of office (i.e., number of prosecuting attorneys) and rate of charges. (The largest was Hamburg—145 attorneys, charging rate 19%; and the smallest was Hechigen—8 attorneys, charging rate 33%). Our analysis showed that differences by office size did exist, but they become less important when one controls for the nature of the local crime problem. The larger urban areas have a higher rate of theft. Most (up to 80%) of these offenders are never identified or apprehended. Therefore, these cases are almost always automatically dismissed (although in theory they are not supposed to be). This, then, accounts for the higher overall rate of dismissal in these offices.

Encouraged by our findings of an astonishingly high homogeneity in the distribution of charges and dismissals, we decided to analyze *common* patterns of decision making. About 5,500 randomly selected 1970 dossiers from these 8 prosecutor's offices were analyzed. The sample contained both cases in which the offender had been identified and ones where he was unknown. The following crimes were included: theft without aggravating circumstances (e.g., shoplifting, theft of unlocked cars) and under aggravating circumstances (mostly burglary and theft of locked cars); fraud; embezzlement; robbery; rape; and (petty) economic offenses.[13] The following analyses relate to the two main tasks of the prosecutor: investigation and the decision to dismiss or charge.

THE PROSECUTOR'S OFFICE
AS AN INVESTIGATING AGENCY

The prosecutor's legal task is to control the police investigations of each reported criminal case. Therefore, he is often called "head of the preliminary proceedings." However, except in a few sensational cases such as murder, big commercial crimes, and, recently, terrorism, he is seldom truly in a supervisory role (Steffen, 1976:50-56). Thus, a typical investigatory situation can be described as follows. An offense will usually be reported to the police who will then open and register a file. The police lack any discretionary power in deciding whether or not to file a case. They must follow up every suspicion and present all registered offenses—however vague the evidence may be—to the prosecutor who alone makes the final decision.[14] The police carry out all necessary investigations. The prosecutor will usually be informed only if it becomes legally necessary as, for example, when a warrant for pretrial detention is needed (Goldstein and Marcus, 1977:260).[15] (However, the prosecutor is usually informed immediately of murder cases.) If the police feel a case has been thoroughly investigated, they will forward it to the prosecutor who then must decide whether further investigation is necessary.[16] He can take over the investigation, for instance, in order to interrogate the suspect or witnesses personally (this rarely occurs); or he can return the case to the police for further inquiries. The law requires him to do everything to solve the case—regardless of its seriousness. It does not permit him to "filter" out cases, as American prosecutors are authorized to do.

We hypothesized that legal theory notwithstanding the German prosecutor did filter cases, and we attempted to discover this mechanism at work in his investigatory practices. Whenever parts of the case are missing, the prosecutor may demand them from the police, procure them himself, or decide he is satisfied with what he has. Furthermore, we suspected he is able to manage investigations in such a way that they are more likely to result in a dismissal than a charge.

In order to check this assumption, we divided our sample into two groups: those cases which the police described as completely cleared up and those described as having remaining evidence problems. We then compared the level of the investigative effort of the prosecutor in these two types of cases.[17]

Legal theory would lead one to expect that the prosecutor's level of investigative effort would be higher in those cases which the police indicated needed further investigation. But just the opposite was in fact the case. The prosecutor devoted more of his effort to those cases which the police had indicated were solved than to those in which further investigation was needed. This was true regardless of the seriousness of the offense.[18] Thus, in effect the prosecutor is admitting that he is unable to improve those weak cases. However, it might also be that he is taking the opportunity to get rid of a considerable percentage of his caseload without violating the rules of compulsory prosecution.

We also found a remarkable discrepancy between the police opinion that a case was "solved" (i.e., did not need further investigation) and the prosecutor's opinion whether it should be charged and go to trial, or be dismissed because of "insufficient evidence." As indicated in Table 2, the prosecutor dismissed because of insufficient evidence a substantial proportion of the cases which the police had indicated did not need further investigation (because theoretically the evidence was sufficient). Also noteworthy is that this discrepancy differs by type of crime. Eighty-seven percent of the embezzlement cases which the police said needed no further investigation were dismissed by the prosecutor because of insufficient evidence, but only 66% of the robbery cases were.

This discrepancy may be due in part to the fact that the prosecutor knows better than the police what the court will accept and refuse. But it is also possible that the prosecutor was implementing his own penal policy which was based not on factors of evidence alone but also on seriousness of offense. In order to test this latter hypothesis, we compared the prosecutor's charging decisions in misdemeanor cases with those in felonies. The reverse relationship between charge and investigation proved very significant: a decrease in the rate of charges within the range of misdemeanors by 8% corresponds to the conspicuous increase within the range of felonies by 23% when the prosecutor displayed investigative activities (Figure 1). The significance of these opposing tendencies, which are statistically significant, increases when one realizes that in our sample the misdemeanors accounted for 42% and felonies for 13% of all the officially registered suspects in 1970 (omitting traffic offenses).[19]

In short, our data suggest that the German prosecutor does exercise discretion. He tends to neglect cases with present evidence problems. Among the cases without such problems (as indicated by the police report) he tends to select for prosecution those cases involving more serious crimes.

THE PROSECUTOR'S OFFICE
AS A CHARGING AGENCY

Calling the prosecutor's office a "charging agency" is something of a misnomer because on the average three out of four cases are dropped (primarily cases with unknown offenders). The label refers to the main

Table 2: The Charging Decision of the Prosecutor by Police Opinion of Evidentiary Problems and by Type of Offense

		THEFT		FRAUD		EMBEZZLEMENT		ROBBERY		RAPE	
		The Police Report Stated the Case (Did or Did Not) Need Further Investigation									
Decision		Did	Did Not	Did	Did Not	Did	Did Not	Did	Did Not	Did	Did Not
Dismissed because of insufficient evidence		25	79	30	76	45	87	17	66	27	75
Charged		75	21	70	24	55	13	83	34	73	25
Total	%	100	100	100	100	100	100	100	100	100	100
	N	272	99	324	123	174	94	60	79	71	117

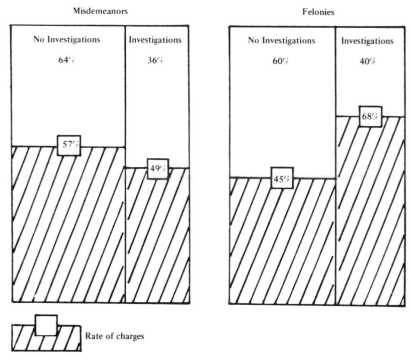

Figure 1: Percentage of Decisions to Charge by Investigative Efforts of the Prosecutor and Type of Offense

task of the prosecutor as it is his decision whether to charge or not. The charging decision involves two distinct considerations: evaluation of evidence and evaluation of guilt.

When the prosecutor is *evaluating evidence,* he is more or less free in his decisions. Some control is possible since the victim can file a formal complaint against the dismissal of "his" case. If it is rejected by the attorney general (chief prosecutor of the state), the victim can file a motion for a judicial decision, which would, if successful, force the prosecutor to file a charge. Although this procedure is very seldom used, it is nonetheless feared by the prosecutor. As a result, the status of the victim may influence his decision. When the prosecutor is *evaluating guilt,* significant possibilities of hierarchical control over his decision exist. According to Administrative Rules issued by some of the ministries of justice of the states (*Länder*) a deputy attorney must present each case which he wants to dismiss because of minor guilt to his superior for approval. It is also possible that "in-house" instructions attempt to standardize the criteria (for example, by fixing the maximum limit of property damage) by which "minor guilt" is defined. The strength of such controls differs from office to office depending upon size, organization, and the personal criminal policy of the head of the office. The victim can only file an administrative complaint for neglect of duty when the case is dismissed for "minor guilt." A motion for a judicial review is excluded. The varied possibilities for termination of proceedings were described extensively by Herrmann (1976). Consequently, only those instances for nonprosecution which are of special importance to this topic will be considered: dismissals due to insufficient evidence and because of insignificant guilt.

The Decision Not to Charge
Because of Insufficient Evidence

The main task of the prosecutor is to determine whether the evidence in the case is sufficient for conviction. As a result, he has a large *practical* discretionary power when he describes whether "probable cause" exists in any given case. We examined the factors which influenced his "evaluation of evidence" in two types of cases: petty and serious crimes. We found that if the damage (monetary value or physical injuries) was considerable or if the suspect had previously been convicted, the prosecutor was less inclined to drop the charge even if the evidence was weak. This might be explained by the possibility that the more serious the crime the more likely the accused is to retain defense counsel, which may hinder police investigation (see e.g., Mulkey, 1975:123).

Another criterion which markedly affects the prosecutor's evaluation of the evidence is the relationship between the suspect and the victim. Cases involving acquaintances, friends, or relatives of the victim are more likely than stranger-to-stranger crimes to be dismissed if they involve the crimes of theft, robbery, or rape. However, the opposite is true if the crime is fraud or embezzlement. The relationship between the perpetrator and his victim is usually considered to be a mitigating circumstance but is not regarded as such in the case of fraud or embezzlement because of the special breach of trust which is connected with these types of acts.

In summary, then, it seems the prosecutor uses *stricter* evidentiary rules in *minor* offenses than in *serious* offenses. It may be that even though the evidence might not support a conviction in the more serious cases, the prosecutor still charges the case in order to use the charge itself as a sanction (see also Bernstein et al., 1977:751). The latter assumption is supported by the fact that the prosecutor tends to regard prior criminal record as an element of proof and therefore to charge recidivists more readily than first offenders. This tendency is in part counterbalanced by the judge who, stressing the problem of proof more than the prosecutor, acquits more recidivists than first offenders.

The Decision Not To Charge
Because Of Minor Guilt

Even when there is probable cause to believe that the defendant is guilty, the prosecutor can dismiss the charge provided that the guilt is not significant and that the public interest does not require prosecution.[20] We analyzed how he interprets these two criteria. We hypothesized that the evaluation of guilt is linked to amount of damage involved. In order to verify this, we first established a rank order of categories of offenses according to the average amount of damage involved. For this purpose, we asked for the frequency of cases involving high damage (i.e., 500 marks or more). The rank order was as follows: (1) only 9% of the thefts without aggravating circumstances involved 500 marks or more so it ranked first; (2) then theft under aggravating circumstances (24% of these involved 500 marks or more); (3) then fraud (with 28%); then (4) embezzlement (with 34%). According to our hypothesis, the higher the anticipated damage is, the higher the actual damage can be and yet leave the case susceptible to dismissal. Therefore, the same rank-order of offense categories should be found when the average amount of damage associated with each offense is examined in those cases dismissed due to "minor guilt." This hypothesis was verified. The average amount of damage in cases which were dismissed because of minor guilt was: (1) theft without aggravating circumstances (62 marks); (2) theft under aggravating circumstances (252 marks); (3) fraud (466 marks); and (4) embezzlement (1,264 marks). This clearly shows that the prosecutor is relatively free in determining whether guilt is minor or not. Accordingly, this criterion does not prevent him from exercising wide discretionary power.

We turn, then, to the second criterion that the prosecutor must meet before a case can be dismissed for "minor guilt," namely, the requirement that no public interest is involved. It can be shown that while this criterion provides the prosecutor with some discretion, (i.e., the option to dismiss a case because it lacks a public interest), it is not used in practice as an efficiency measure to reduce caseloads. Quite the contrary, as indicated in Table 3, as the crime rate for a particular offense increases, the prosecutor is more likely to charge (rather than dismiss) those crimes. Apparently a high rate of occurrence for a particular offense is interpreted by the prosecutor to mean that there is a public interest at stake even if the crime is otherwise not an objectively serious one and could have been dismissed for "minor guilt."

Table 3: Percentage of Decisions not to Charge Because of Minor Guilt of All Cases Without Evidence Problems (Suspects over 18 Years Old) and the Statistical Rank-Order of the Offenses

OFFENSE	RATE OF DISMISSALS	RATE OF OFFENSES PER 100,000 POPULATION[a]
Theft under aggravating circumstances	6% (12%)[b]	1,051
Theft without aggravating circumstances	10% (10%)	1,469
Fraud	20% (27%)	277
Embezzlement	21% (28%)	59
Violation of subsidiary laws in the economic field	26%	0.1

a. SOURCE: Criminal Statistics of the Police 1970
b. Percentages in parentheses refer to all cases of that type of offense with a damage less than 100 marks

Thus, it is not the concrete criterion of minor harm done but the more abstract criterion of a lack of nonexisting public interest that operates as a check on prosecutorial discretion in these cases. Legally authorized prosecutorial discretion allows the prosecutor to individualize justice in specific cases, but it is not used to relieve the caseload problem in the system. It is not used as an efficiency measure. This fact has not changed since the reform of 1975.

A third criterion for the evaluation of minor guilt is prior conviction. In all cases in our sample, regardless of type of offense, the probability that a case would be dismissed was significantly lower if the defendant had a prior criminal record (cf. Mulkey, 1975:123).

The Criminal Policy of the Prosecutor

The decision of the prosecutor not to charge either because of insufficient evidence or because of insignificant guilt contains some constant features regardless of the rationale used. If the damage is high or the suspect previously convicted, dismissals decrease; factors which have to do with the seriousness of crime shape equally the definition of "probable cause" and of "minor guilt." The practice, in fact, does not always differentiate so clearly between the two ways of terminating a case as we had theoretically assumed. If, for example, the prosecutor has problems of proof in an insignificant case, he may choose the shorter way and drop it because of minor guilt. By doing this, he simultaneously avoids the victim's possible motion for a judicial review of his decision. It is also possible that a petty offense which probably would lead to the conviction of the suspect is occasionally dropped because of insufficient evidence in order to avoid the superior's control. The separation of the evaluation of evidence from the evaluation of guilt is often fictitious. Rather, in certain circumstances the prosecutor has his own conception of which cases should be brought to trial and which lack prosecutive merit.[21] He does this in circumstances where he is dealing with a misdemeanor case, where the evidence is still somewhat ambiguous, or where the public interest does not require prosecution.

The remaining possibilities for prosecutorial discretion are clearly shown (see Figure 2). We established two polar categories and related them to the charging decision of the prosecutor. One category is where there is minor damage (up to 500 marks) and no previous conviction of the suspect. The other is where there is serious damage (more than 500 marks) and a prior conviction. This part of our analysis is based on all cases which were dismissed either because of lack of evidence or because of insignificant guilt or which were brought to trial. The sample included juvenile cases and the following crimes: theft with and without aggravating circumstances, fraud, embezzlement, and robbery.

We can now show that both reasons for nonprosecution are used *together* to differentiate between petty and serious offenses within each type of offense. The rate of dismissals for each type of crime differ between these two extreme categories. They differ by 16% for theft, by 19% for fraud, by 22% for embezzlement, and by 32% for robbery. Of special interest is the handling of robbery cases. The prosecutor is not legally permitted to dismiss them on the basis of "minor guilt." So this restriction is obviously being compensated for by increased dismissals on the basis of insufficient evidence.

CONCLUSIONS

"The [American] literature on pretrial screening is dominated by one theme—procedures for reaching charging decisions and the effectiveness of pretrial screening for reducing court loads" (Jacoby, 1977:4). Accordingly, Americans have become intrigued by reports of the German system of prosecution. They wonder how a system with compulsory prosecution can be compatible with the efficient administration of justice in modern societies with substantial crime problems (see Weigend, 1978:45-46).

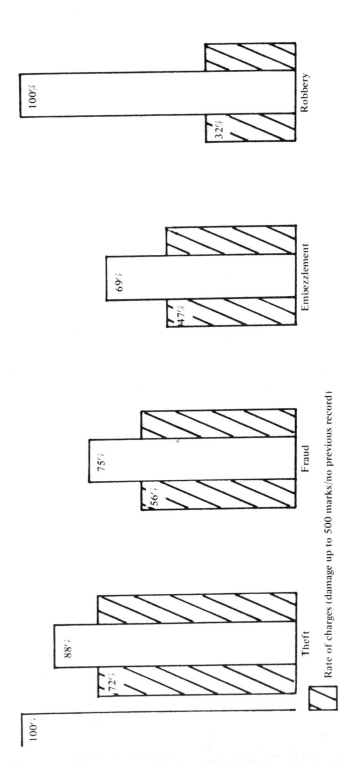

Figure 2: The Charging Decision of the Prosecutor, by Seriousness of the Offense

Rate of charges (damage up to 500 marks/no previous record)

Rate of charges (damage more than 500 marks/previous record)

They have come to believe that there is only one solution to the problem of overburdened criminal justice systems, namely that the prosecutor should serve as conservator of the system's resources through the practical use of plea bargaining and the discretion to discontinue prosecution. We have shown that in Germany the *entire* criminal justice system, including the legislative component, makes efforts to relieve the glut of cases and preserve the operation of the system. This is done through decriminalization, by making prosecution contingent upon the victim's formal motion, by turning felonies into misdemeanors, by extending the discretionary power of the prosecutor, and finally by simply increasing the staff of prosecutorial offices. This wide range of measures attempts to accomplish a balance between the requirements of and the possibilities of effective law enforcement. However, Table 1 reveals that regardless of all of these efforts the number of accused persons continues to increase—30% between 1965 and 1976. Much more could be done to reduce caseload (for example, by making the prosecutor more prone to use the recently extended diversionary procedures).

We studied prosecutorial discretion before the reforms of 1975 and noticed that while the prosecutor had a certain discretionary power to define "minor guilt," public interest in law enforcement was a barrier to the extensive use of this discretion. The amount of damage did not necessarily hinder the classification of guilt as insignificant. However, the frequency of occurrence of an offense constituted the public interest in prosecution, regardless of the amount of damage involved. This outcome is in contradiction to any cost/benefit analysis. Thus reforms of 1975 have not changed this outcome very much, since public interest continues as the most important criterion. The narrow range of prosecutorial discretion is hierarchically controlled but is also an integral part of the prosecutor's professional principles.

Statistical analysis helped to disclose latent structures of differential politics of prosecution. The prosecutor uses the problems of proof to create discretion. This first became evident by analysis of his investigative activities. Not only does he neglect weak cases, but his investigations increase dismissals rather than charges if misdemeanors are concerned (Figure 1). In cases where the evidence is weak, regardless of the type of offense, the seriousness of the criminal event (i.e., the extent of damage or the existence of previous convictions) is the most discriminating factor in determining whether the prosecutor will charge the case.

The ability of a prosecutor to choose not to charge on the ground that guilt is minor or that evidence is not sufficient is flexible enough to individualize prosecution even when the law seems to be very rigid (as in the case of felonies). At the same time, it enables prosecutors to concentrate upon serious criminality.

Within this prosecutorial ability might be found some of the humanitarian aspects which are pointed out in American contributions to the problem of prosecutorial discretion (see Cole, 1972:144-145; Weigend, 1978:87). Although legal variables such as damage or previous convictions were primarily analyzed, it could be shown that the prosecutor is also sensitive to other aspects of the crime, including, for example, the relationship between the suspect and victim. It can be concluded that, regardless of his resoluteness to fully enforce the law, the specific features of a case are taken into account—but only within the boundaries that have repeatedly been mentioned above. It must be emphasized that no discretion, formal or informal, is possible when there are no problems of proof and the crime is of a serious nature.

NOTES

1. "§ 152 StPO [Code of Criminal Procedure]:

I. To prefer the public charge is the function of the prosecution.
II. Except as otherwise provided by law, it is obliged to take action in case of all acts which are punishable by a court and capable of prosecution, so far as there is sufficient factual basis."

The translation is from The German Code of Criminal Procedure (1965), in 10 American Series of Foreign Penal Codes [H. Niebler, trans.] (South Hackensack, N.J.: Rothman).

2. This empirical analysis is based on a study of the decision-making processes of the German prosecutor conducted by members of the Criminological Department of the Max-Planck-Institute for Foreign and International Criminal Law, Freiburg/Germany, from 1973 to 1976 (Blankenburg, Sessar, and Steffen, 1978).

3. "§ 153 StPO [Code of Criminal Procedure]:

I. Petty offenses are not prosecuted if the guilt of the actor is minor, unless there is a public interest in obtaining a judicial decision.
II. If in case of a minor crime the guilt of the actor is insignificant and if the public interest does not require enforcement, the prosecution may terminate the proceedings, with consent of the court competent for the decision on opening the main proceeding."

For the translation, see note 1. "Petty offenses" are more precisely, or at least more understandably, translated as "petty misdemeanors" and "minor crimes" as "misdemeanors"; see also Herrmann (1976:33).

4. All official crime figures refer either to the yearly published Rechtspflegestatistik (Criminal Statistics of the Courts) with information about the accused and the convicted, or to the Polizeiliche Kriminalstatistik (Criminal Statistics of the Police) with information about the offenses which have an estimate rate of 50% of all registered offenses.

5. It is remarkable that the German Constitutional Court based its decision sustaining the constitutionality of petty infractions (among others) on an otherwise expected "overcriminalization."

6. Unpublished Criminal Statistics of the Prosecutor's Offices (1970).

7. The Uniform Rules of Criminal Procedure are guidelines for all prosecution offices (see Herrmann, 1976:29, n. 57); they serve to establish homogeneity in many parts of the decision-making process, including the question of how to use discretionary power.

8. Plea bargaining as a reduction of charge in return to the defendant's plea guilty (Alschuler, 1968) may happen in single cases but is unknown as a common phenomenon of the criminal justice system (Schumann, 1977:201). The "principle of legality" requires not only the prosecution of a crime in the case of sufficient evidence but also its prosecution under its full legal definition. Of course, an offense may sometimes be downgraded. However, this does not occur in return for a confession; rather, it occurs in order to adjust the rule to the realities of life in a single case. For example, in order to avoid lifelong imprisonment, murder may be changed into manslaughter, should there be a close relationship between the suspect and the victim (see Sessar, 1975:40, with respect to court decisions), attempted manslaughter into assault and battery if the victim precipitated the act, and so on.

9. Diversionary means of this kind are well known and, it seems, widely used in the United States (see National Advisory Commission on Criminal Justice Standards and Goals, 1973:95).

10. In 1970 (year of our investigation) the exchange rate for 100 German marks was about 36 dollars.

11. The so-called *Amtsanwalt* exists in some Federal States. He has the same rights and duties as the Staatsanwalt, but is not an academician and is responsible for petty offenses only.

12. The rates of unknown offenders are enormously high and are steadily growing—from 35.2% in 1961 to 55.2% in 1976 (except traffic offenses). The Criminal Statistics of the Police of 1976 show the following rates (selected offenses):

- fraudulent conversion, receiving stolen good, offenses in violation of subsidiary laws in the economic field 0-2%
- criminal homicide, fraud, drug offenses, forgery of documents 4-7%
- embezzlement, dangerous assault and battery 14-16%
- rape 27%
- robbery 46%
- theft without aggravating circumstances 59%
- theft under aggravating circumstances 80%

13. For the methods used, see the English summary in Blankenburg, Sessar, and Steffen (1978).

14. Little research as dealt with the question of the extent to which the police fail to register offenses reported to them. One study in a medium-sized city found that the police refused to register 14% of all complaints. These concerned mostly petty offenses in which the suspect and the victim had a close personal relationship (Kürzinger, 1978:206-207).

15. The American situation seems to be similar in this respect, to include the efforts on the part of the prosecutor to recover control over the whole investigative process (see Silbert, 1977), obviously with little success in the United States (as well as in Germany; see Sessar, 1976).

16. The ritual of "shopping around," described by Cole (1976:216-217), i.e., the search for a prosecutor who is sympathetic to the police's view on a case, is not possible,

since the initials of the suspect's name (in case of an unknown offender the initials of the victim) or the area in which the crime occurred establish the competence of the prosecuting attorney.

17. In this context, investigation is intended to include any action taken by the prosecutor to return the file to the police for further investigations or any investigatory action taken by the prosecutor himself.

18. Thus, our results are similar to those of Forst and Brosi (1976:17). They report that the strength of a case is directly related to the level of effort the American prosecutor invests in a case. He spends more time on the stronger cases. However, the similarity here cannot be pushed too far, because Forst and Brosi's definition of strength of the case is substantially different from ours.

19. On April 1, 1970, theft under aggravating circumstances, a felony, was turned into a misdemeanor. Obviously the prosecutor's attitude did not change as quickly since this type of theft was treated much more like rape or robbery than theft without aggravating circumstances, fraud, or embezzlement.

20. Theoretically, this rule also is valid for juveniles (see § 42 [2] JGG [Juvenile Court Act], but different procedure is customary; the prosecutor asks the judge to admonish the juvenile or presents him with an imposition. Afterwards the case is dismissed (§ 45 (1) JGG). This procedure is also used with misdemeanors only. In the following analyses this way of settlement of cases is excluded.

21. For similar but explicitly acknowledged strategies used by American prosecutors, see Miller, 1970:154-155.

REFERENCES

ALSCHULER, A. W. (1968). "The prosecutor's role in plea bargaining." University of Chicago Law Review 36:50-112.

BECKER, G. S. (1974). "Crime and punishment: An economic approach," pp. 1-54 in G. S. Becker and W. M. Landes (eds.), Essays in the Economics of Crime and Punishment. New York: National Bureau of Economic Research.

BERCKHAUER, F. H. (1977). "Wirtschaftskriminalität und Staatsanwaltschaft. Eine Untersuchung materiellrechtlicher und organisationsspezifischer Bedingungen für die Strafverfolgung von Wirtschaftsdelikten." Law dissertation, Universtität Freiburg/Br.

BERNSTEIN, J. N., W. R. KELLY, and P. A. DOYLE (1977). "Societal reaction to deviants: The case of criminal defendants." American Sociological Review 42:743-755.

BLANKENBURG, E., K. SESSAR, and W. STEFFEN (1978). Die Staatsanwaltschaft im Prozess strafrechtlicher Sozialkontrolle. Berlin: Duncker & Humblot.

COLE, G. F. (1976). Criminal Justice: Law and Politics. North Scituate, Mass.: Duxbury Press.

DAVIS, K. C. (1969). Discretionary Justice: A Preliminary Inquiry. Baton Rouge: Louisiana State University Press.

_____(1976). "American comments on American and German prosecutors," pp. 60-74 in K. C. Davis (ed.), Discretionary Justice in Europe and America. Urbana: University of Illinois Press.

FORST, B. E. and B. K. BROSI (1976). "A theoretical and empirical analysis of the prosecutor." Unpublished manuscript.

GOLDSTEIN, A. S. and MARCUS, M. (1977). "The myth of judicial supervision in three "inquisitorial" systems: France, Italy, and Germany." The Yale Law Journal 87:240-283.

HERRMANN, J. (1976). "The German prosecutor." Pp. 16-59 in K. C. Davis (ed.), Discretionary justice in Europe and America. Urbana: University of Illinois Press.

JACOBY, J. E. (1977). The prosecutor's charging decision: A policy perspective. Washington, D.C.: National Institute of Law Enforcement Assistance Administration. U.S. Department of Justice.

JESCHECK, H. -H. (1970). "The discretionary powers of the prosecuting attorney in West Germany." The American Journal of Comparative Law, 18:508-517.

KÜRZINGER, J. (1978). Private Strafanzeige und polizeiliche Reaktion. Berlin: Duncker & Humblot.

LANGBEIN, J. H. (1974). "Controlling prosecutorial discretion in Germany." The University of Chicago Law Review, 41:439-467.

_____(1977). Comparative criminal procedure: Germany. St. Paul, Minn.: West Publishing.

MILLER, F. W. (1970). Prosecution: The Decision to Charge a Suspect with a Crime. Boston: Little, Brown.

MULKEY, A. M. (1975). "Adjudication as the administrative procedures of charging and plea bargaining: The roles of prosecution and defense," pp. 121-130 in J. A. Gardiner and M. A. Mulkey (eds.), Crime and Criminal Justice: Issues in Public Policy Analysis. Lexington, Mass.: Lexington Books.

National Advisory Commission on Criminal Justice Standards and Goals (1973). A national strategy to reduce crime. Washington, D.C.: National Advisory Commission on Criminal Justice Standards and Goals.

SCHELLHOSS, H. (1974). "Kosten des Verbrechens," pp. 157-161 in G. Kaiser, F. Sack, and H. Schellhoss (eds.), Kleines Kriminologisches Wörterbuch. Freiburg/Br.: Herder.

SCHUMANN, K. F. (1977). Der Handel mit Gerechtigkeit. Funktionsprobleme der Strafjustiz und ihre Lösungen am Beispiel der amerikanischen plea bargaining. Frankfurt/Main: Suhrkamp.

SESSAR, K. (1975). "The familiar character of criminal homicide," pp. 29-42 in I. Drapkin and E. C. Viano (eds.), Victimology: A New Focus. Vol. 4: Violence and its Victims. Lexington, Mass.: Lexington Books.

_____(1976). "Zu einem neuen Verhältnis zwischen Polizei und Staatsanwaltschaft. Ein Beitrag aus empirischer Sicht." Kriminalistik 30:534-538.

SILBERT, E. J. (1977). "The role of the prosecutor in the process of criminal justice." American Bar Association Journal 63:1717-1720.

STEFFEN, W. (1976). Analyse polizeilicher Tätigkeit aus der Sicht des späteren Strafverfahrens. Wiesbaden: BKA-Forschungsreihe.

WEIGEND, T. (1978). Anklagepflicht und Ermessen. Die Stellung des Staatsanwalts Zwischen Legalitätsund opportunitätsprinzip nach deutschem und amerikanischem Recht. Baden-Baden: Nomos.

ABOUT THE AUTHORS

JAMES A. CRAMER is currently Assistant Director, Project on Plea Bargaining in the United States at the Institute of Criminal Law and Procedure, Georgetown University Law Center. He received his Ph.D. from the University of Tennessee, Knoxville. He has taught at the University of Tennessee, Virginia Commonwealth University, the University of Maryland, European Division, and the Institute of Criminal Justice and Criminology, University of Maryland.

JAMES J. FISHMAN is Associate Dean and Associate Professor of Law, Pace University School of Law. Formerly, he was the Assistant Director of the Institute of Judicial Administration, Inc. He coauthored *Limits of Justice: Court's Roles in Desegregation of Education Integration* (with Kalodner) and coedited *Practicing Law in New York City* (with Kaufman). He received an A.B. and an A.M. from the University of Pennsylvania and a J.D. from New York University.

WILLIAM A. HAMILTON is President of the Institute for Law and Social Research. He was a corecipient of one of the 1978 Rockefeller Public Service Awards. For the last several years he has directed the effort to develop, implement, and transfer the PROMIS computer system. He received a B.A. from the University of Notre Dame.

FREDERICK A. HUSSEY holds an M.S.W. and a Ph.D. in Social Welfare from the Heller School of Brandeis University, as well as a master's degree in experimental psychology. He is currently Assistant Professor in the Administration of Justice Program at Pennsylvania State University. He is the codirector of a project examining the implementation of determinate sentencing in Maine and has done research in the areas of the police, parole, and manpower policy. He has coauthored

277

(with David Duffee and John Kramer) *Criminal Justice: Organization Structure and Analysis* and is presently writing a text on probation and parole with David Duffee. He has published in psychological and criminal justice journals, including *Criminology* and *Crime and Delinquency*.

JOAN E. JACOBY is Research Associate at the Bureau of Social Science Research, where she is currently directing research on prosecutorial discretion. She was the founder and Executive Director of the National Center of Prosecutorial Management of the National District Attorneys Association and the Director of the Office of Crime Analysis of the District of Columbia. She received a B.A. from Boston University and an M.A. from American University. She is the author of *The Prosecutor's Charging Decision: A Policy Perspective* and several other articles dealing with the prosecutor.

JOHN H. KRAMER is Assistant Professor of Criminal Justice at Pennsylvania State University. His research interests have focused on the effect of legal sanctions on self-concept and neutralizations, and recent developments in criminal sentencing. Besides three texts in the area of Criminal Justice, he has published in *Criminal Law Bulletin, International Journal of Sociology,* and other journals.

STEPHEN P. LAGOY is Assistant Professor of Criminal Justice at Pennsylvania State University. He received his B.S.F.S., M.S., and J.D. from Georgetown University, Northeastern University, and the University of Maine School of Law respectively. His primary research interests have been prosecutorial discretion and recent developments in sentencing, and he has recently published in the *American Criminal Law Review, Criminal Law Bulletin* and *Crime and Delinquency*. He is also a member of the Massachusetts, Pennsylvania, and Maine bars.

WILLIAM F. McDONALD is Deputy Director of the Institute of Criminal Law and Procedure and Associate Professor of Sociology at Georgetown University. He is currently directing a national study of police-prosecutor relations and was a staff member of the Institute's national study of plea bargaining. He has written on several aspects of the criminal justice system, particularly the victim's role in the administration of justice. He is editor of *Criminal Justice and the Victim*. He received a B.A. from the University of Notre Dame, an M.Ed. from Boston University and a D. Crim. from the University of California at Berkeley.

HENRY H. ROSSMAN is Senior Research Associate with the Institute of Criminal Law and Procedure, Georgetown University Law Center. He is currently involved in the national study of police-prosecutor relations. He has participated in research on plea bargaining and the evaluation of pretrial release. He received a B.A. from the University of Miami and is completing a Ph.D. in sociology from Temple University.

KLAUS SESSAR is a research criminologist in the Criminological Department of the Max-Planck-Institute for Foreign and International Penal Law, Freiburg/Breisgau (Germany). He received his Dr. jur. from the University of Freiburg/Breisgau in 1971 and a Master of Arts in Sociology from Boston University in 1973.

JAY A. SIGLER is Professor of Political Science at Rutgers University, Camden, New Jersey, and is Acting Director of the Graduate Program in Public Policy. Professor Sigler has written eight books and contributed to several others. His comparative criminal justice research is based in part on his field work in Europe in 1974-1975 during which time he interviewed various prosecuting officers.

PAMELA J. UTZ has been associated with the Center for Study of Law and Society, University of California, Berkeley, since 1972. She graduated from Antioch College in 1969, and in 1977 earned the Ph.D. in Sociology from the University of California, Berkeley, where she has also lectured.

WILLIAM F. WESSEL was the First Assistant District Attorney in New Orleans, Louisiana, from 1974 to 1977. He is presently in private practice in New Orleans. He graduated magna cum laude with a B.B.A. from Loyola University in New Orleans and received an L.L.B. from Tulane University. He formerly lectured in business and business law at Loyola and Xavier Universities.